International Relations

International Relations
A Handbook of Current Theory
Edited by

Margot Light
and
A.J.R. Groom

Frances Pinter (Publishers), London

First published in Great Britain in 1985 by
Frances Pinter (Publishers) Limited
25 Floral Street, London WC2E 9DS

British Library Cataloguing in Publication Data

International relations: a handbook of current
    theory.
    1. International relations
    I. Light, Margot.   II. Groom, A.J.R.
    327.1'01   JX1395
    ISBN 0-86187-527-3

Typeset by Folio Photosetting, Bristol
Printed by SRP Ltd, Exeter

Contents

Introduction

Almost a decade ago a group of scholars based in Britain and loosely associated with the Centre for the Analysis of Conflict (CAC) decided to undertake an evaluative survey of the theoretical literature in International Relations (IR). They found their task intellectually stimulating because it forced them not only to draw an intellectual map of the field as it was portrayed in the literature, but also to indicate developing areas and unexplored territories which required urgent investigation. Since the publication of that survey the literature has continued to expand and intellectual developments have not stood still. It is time, therefore, for another assessment of the IR theory literature.

The group of scholars who agreed to undertake this task quickly discovered that a mere 'update' of the literature was insufficient. Besides the changed composition of the team, which is now less closely associated with CAC, there have been substantive changes. A decade ago, for example, systems theory, particularly General Systems Theory (GST), was considered to be a particularly promising approach to social science as a whole. While systems analysis as a mental construct for bringing order to transactional data retains its vigour and centrality in the pluralist or world society approach to IR, as well as taking on new guises such as regimes, GST has not advanced significantly since the situation described in 1978. On the other hand, realism has staged a 'come-back' in the form of neo-realism; there has been a long-overdue assimilation of various forms of structuralism into mainstream IR; there is a greater awareness of the implications of paradigms and a continued and profitable exploration of the political sociology of world society, particularly in the context of conflict studies, ethnic politics, universal needs, secession, and the like. The study of IR is changing and the literature is changing with it. This volume reflects the changes.

The *Handbook* is an evaluative study. It surveys those aspects of the

1

subject which are evolving and the attendant literature that the authors deem to be important. The contributors provide insights about the current state and future outlook of those aspects of the field in which they are expert. It aims not only to guide, but also to stimulate, even to provoke the reader. But it is also, perforce, a selective guide, rather than an encyclopaedia or compendium. Choice implies that criteria have been used, and these need to be specified to the reader.

This book is confined to the theoretical and conceptual aspects of IR. While it is concerned with both the paradigmatical and epistemological aspects of the subject, case studies, history, reference works, data books and the like are, for the most part, eschewed. The limitations are draconian in a further respect: although some 'classics' have been included, our primary concern is to survey the literature of the last decade. Much attention has been given to books and monographs published in Britain and North America, despite the frequency with which innovative ideas first come to attention in article form. Indeed, readers can always rummage with profit through the index of key journals such as *World Politics*, *Review of International Studies*, *International Studies Quarterly*, *Journal of Peace Research*, *International Organisation* and *Millennium*. But of greater moment than these quasi-technical criteria for selection is the intellectual filter employed by the contributors.

The authors of the *Handbook* have at least one fundamental trait in common: a penchant for conceptual thinking and a firm commitment to theory building in IR. However, this does not imply that they share a conceptual framework. Nevertheless, Banks, Burton, de Reuck, Hoffman, Little, Mitchell, Oppenheim and the editors are members of CAC and, in their own research, work primarily within the parameters of the world society (or pluralist) framework. This approach has no generally accepted definition, although there is a measure of agreement that both the level of analysis and the unit of analysis are a function of the research problem. But it is not merely the question of an interdisciplinary approach. Rather the focus is upon the adisciplinary treatment of universal phenomena such as conflict, decision-making, development, integration or identity seen in the context of world society (and social science) as a whole. Systems of transactions, their structures no less than their processes, are the focus of attention, as is the degree to which such structures and processes are legitimized. This points to decision-making as an important concern. But beyond the decision-making process and structures, the needs theorists have pointed to the individual, with his unchanging needs and implacable search for their fulfilment, as the irreducible unit of analysis, thus ensuring that the old debate between 'nature' and 'nurture' lives on in the world society approach. The question is ultimately an empirical one and a utilitarian one: does it help us to know and accomplish better what we want as individuals in society?

Such considerations are likely to engender a conceptual debate not only among contributors to this volume, but also among its readers. The controversy in the literature has suggested a two-fold division of the book: the debate between and within paradigms constitutes the first part, *The Paradigmatic Debate*. The second part of the book, *Partial Theories*, includes surveys of the evolution of the 'islands' of theory within the field of IR. Banks sets out the principal divisions in the contemporary inter-paradigm debate (realist, pluralist and structuralist), with their antecedents. Each of the three paradigms noted by Banks is then analysed in an evaluative and selective manner. Hoffman analyses the normative manifestations of the realist paradigm, as well as classical normative theories. Burton sets out the pluralist approach and Brown examines the contribution made by dependency theorists and neo-Marxists to the study of IR. In the last few years a new controversy has riven the field, transcending the traditionally accepted boundaries between paradigms: this new debate is analysed by Little in 'Structuralism and Neo-Realism'. The debate between paradigms was initially articulated in terms of the epistemological bases of social science, and the extent to which social science could be studied in the same way as natural science. It is a debate which still sometimes arouses both passion and ire and is described in Nicholson's essay on methodology. The first section ends with a brief personal synthesis by de Reuck of the contrasting and complementary trends in the literatures. In the second section of the book, the evolution of various 'islands' of IR theory, some confined to one paradigm, others roving between paradigms, is examined: power, conflict, strategy, foreign policy analysis, integration and disintegration, the relevance of anthropology and psychology are all examined, as is the place that they find in IR textbooks.

Our friends who have contributed to this volume have provided us with invaluable insight and information. Moreover, they have remained our friends, tolerating our cajoling with good-natured patience, encouraging us and persisting themselves in what must sometimes have seemed a thankless and burdensome task. We offer our thanks to them in the belief that the reader will benefit from their labours. Even more painstaking has been the bibliographic research of Vivienne Jabri on whom we have been particularly dependent. Finally, we have tried the goodwill of Elizabeth Dorling and Georgina Strutt far beyond the bounds of duty in their secretarial assistance at the University of Kent. Our thanks to them all, to Linda Dobbs who had no duty, but helped anyway, to the University of Kent for facilitating our work by appointing Margot Light as a Visiting Scholar for the Autumn of 1984 and to the University of Surrey for granting her sabbatical leave for the academic year.

Margot Light
A.J.R. Groom
Guildford and Canterbury, March 1985.

Part One:
The Paradigmatic Debate

1 The Inter-Paradigm Debate

Michael Banks

London School of Economics and Political Science and CAC

Everyone who studies international relations (IR) must confront the problem of trying to understand the world society as a whole. To do this is to theorize. All discussion of world affairs rests upon assumptions about which things are the ones that really matter. This applies to everything in IR: from the causes of war to human rights; from Paraguayan foreign policy to nuclear weapon deployment in Europe; from economic sanctions to the reform of the UN. The importance of prior assumptions is self-evident if the topic itself is theoretical, like conflict resolution or decision-making. But it is not so obvious in the case of statements that seem at first to be explicitly factual, such as a reference to terrorism in Ireland or to the rise of a market economy in China. Upon reflection, it becomes clear that terrorism is extremely hard to define, and that a market economy depends on a whole series of conditions including mobility of labour, freedom of information, an entrepreneurial class and so on. Terrorism, therefore, can only be properly identified in the context of a theory of social stability and change; and a market economy only within a theory that deals with politics and culture, not just economics.

It follows that it is wrong to think of 'theory' as something that is opposed to 'reality'. The two cannot be separated. Every statement that is intended to describe or explain anything that happens in the world society is a theoretical statement. It is naive and superficial to try to discuss IR solely on the basis of 'the facts'. This is because whatever facts are selected – any at all – are literally abstract. They are chosen from a much bigger menu of available facts, because they are important. The question is: why are they important? And the answer to that is: because they fit a concept, the concept fits a theory and the theory fits an underlying view of the world. In the same way, each 'island' of theory in the literature of IR (about deterrence, say, or political integration) is itself part of a more general mental map

7

which shows how the world society is structured and which aspects of it are the most significant. This chapter is concerned with these general schemes of thought.

Of course, everyone who begins the study of IR is already equipped with an image of the world's geography, climate, politics, economy and culture. But this impression is rarely as coherent and rigorous as social science requires, which means that the serious student of IR needs to consider afresh the problem of how to picture world society as a whole. To do this is not easy. There are more than four billion people, living in more than 170 states, and spread across five continents. Fortunately for the IR theorist, modest generalization is immediately possible in that everyone shares a single ecosystem, has similar needs and hopes, and is subject to the interdependent effects of global industry and trade. But in other ways they are very different: in nationality, ethnicity, language, culture, social system, ideology, and especially levels of wealth and forms of political organization. Together, all these similarities and contrasts make for a highly complex world society. The problem for the theorist is to simplify the complexity without distorting it. That task, in turn, requires attention to the procedures of theory-building.

Theory-building

Theory consists of both analysis and synthesis. To analyse is to unravel, to separate the strands, or to take to pieces. To synthesize is to reassemble, to piece together the parts in such a way as to compose a whole that makes sense. General theory in IR, then, consists of dividing the human race into sections, noting the significant properties of each, examining the relationships between them, and describing the patterns formed by the relationships. Interesting problems arise at every stage. Some of these are methodological. How should we set about observing things, defining them, measuring them and comparing them? Others are theoretical, because theory consists of forming ideas or concepts to describe aspects of the world, classifying them, and considering the various ways in which they interact. How many sections of world society are there? How should they be subdivided? What properties of each section are we interested in? Which relationships matter, and for what purposes? In short, what are the appropriate units of analysis, what are the significant links between them, and what are the right levels on which to conduct the analysis? And there are further theoretical questions even beyond these, because all theories of society are, at root, ideological. Theories simultaneously express the political values of the theorist, and also help to shape the world which is being analysed. Human beings, as Bernstein [12] points out, need to be acutely critical of their own assumptions.

The State of the Discipline

None of these questions has ever had definite answers in the study of IR – and that is just as it should be. If any discipline is to remain alive and well, then its general theory must be constantly undergoing challenge and modification. This is because progress in knowledge consists of asking new questions, hopefully getting better answers, and checking the answers (again, a matter of method) for accuracy, simplicity, consistency and normative implications. The field cannot offer unquestioned 'truths' about the structure and processes of the world society. But it can offer a reasonably coherent general explanation, however tentative, which shows how the specific research areas (such as arms control or economic development) fit together into an overall scheme.

Today, the field contains not one but three such general explanations: realism, pluralism and structuralism. Strictly, they should be called 'paradigms', but they are also more casually termed perspectives, approaches, world views, frameworks or general theories. The debate about their respective merits occupies centre stage in the discipline, although much of the literature about it tends to be very confused. There are two main reasons for the confusion. First, there are more analysts than synthesizers. Most scholars do not conduct research on general theory at all, but instead on smaller-scale problems which produce 'islands' of theory, as described in subsequent chapters of this *Handbook*, and in an excellent paper by Holsti [41]. Second, old and new approaches are intermingled. The current literature has inevitably grown out of the past, and much of it either describes old debates or mixes contemporary issues with the earlier ones.

The History of Thought

In historical terms, there are two main groups of writings about IR theory: works published before, and after, the First World War. The earlier group forms the classical heritage of IR. It contains studies of political theory, law, history and diplomacy produced over several centuries before the shock of the Great War created a professional discipline for the study of world politics. Much of this literature is of superb quality and continuing relevance, as Parkinson [78] and Wolfers [106] have argued. It has also inspired a body of more recent scholarship which seeks to draw upon the classical insights. Valuable contributions include Wight on comparative state systems [103], Beitz on justice [11], Nardin on law [73], Donelan on reason of state [29], Walzer on the morality of war [101], and Mayall on international community [65]. This neo-classical school is described further in Chapter 2 of this *Handbook*.

The second historical category is that created by teaching and research as IR became established in universities after 1918. During its growth, first in the West and later worldwide, the academic discipline has developed through three stages. These are usually known as the traditional, behavioural and post-behavioural periods. The full sequence is described by Banks [6, 7, 8] and in [5] and [9]. It has formed the theme of McClelland's 'fourth wave' paper [60] and of an edited book by Maghroori & Ramberg [62].

Within each of the periods since 1918, there has been a 'great debate' about general theory, which means that the inter-paradigm debate of the 1980s is the third in the succession. Realism–idealism came first, running right through the traditional period from 1918 to 1950 and reaching an intellectual peak with Carr's masterly critique of idealism in 1939 [23]. Before Carr, idealist or liberal views dominated the field, fuelled by the horrors of the Great War. After Carr (and after appeasement had failed to prevent the Second World War), the realist school not only took charge but produced an all-pervasive general theory of power politics, elegantly censured by Hoffmann [40].

Then, in the 1950s, the first debate was pushed aside. Behaviouralism erupted, and its crusade for empiricism and scientific procedures provoked a confrontation with traditionalists which lasted through the 1960s. At its onset in 1955, the state of the discipline was majestically surveyed by Wright [107]. The sharp exchanges, sometimes called 'revolutionary', were fully analysed in Knorr &

Rosenau [50], and the eventual successes and failures were vividly narrated in the autobiographical essays commissioned by Rosenau [85]. Like idealism before it, behaviouralism never challenged the underlying realist paradigm; it focussed on research methods, as idealism had focussed on values and policy prescriptions. Both left the crucial state-centric assumptions of realism in command.

From about 1970 onward, the post-behavioural phase developed into a triangular 'inter-paradigm' debate which did focus on the assumption of a state-centric world. By 1980 realism was pitted against structuralism and pluralism. Awareness of just how deep were the new divisions came hesitantly at first, beginning with discussion of the importance of Kuhn's 'paradigm' philosophy [56] for the field, and then accelerating. The pattern is well recorded in a series of articles on 'how many paradigms are there?' A representative sample would begin with Phillips [81] and Lijphart [59] in 1974, and follow via Inkeles [42] in 1975, Sullivan [92] and Banks [8] in 1978, Rosenau [83] in 1979, and Pettman [79] in 1981, to the most searching piece to date: Alker & Biersteker [1] in 1984. Their survey analyses IR syllabuses in leading US universities, deplores the extreme parochialism thus revealed, and identifies a wider global discipline which is split between traditional–realist, liberal–behavioural and radical–dialectical approaches.

General Theory: Texts, Surveys and Commentaries

Against a background of such variety in approaches, it is not surprising that introductions to IR tend to be selective in their coverage. Many textbook authors feel obliged to concentrate on the 'real world', which means that their analytic framework is swamped in facts about current events. Of the introductory works which do concentrate exclusively on theories, the best available is by Dougherty & Pfaltzgraff [30]. It is far from ideal, because its 1980 revision achieved only a partial updating; coverage of structuralism is especially weak. But it does have the widest range. Taylor's edited collection [94] makes a good companion for it, being simpler and less compressed. Garnett's contribution [35] is helpful but old-fashioned, and there are several constructive sections in the book on the teaching of IR by Kent & Nielsson [46]. The full breadth of the competing paradigms debate is well represented in the articles selected for the Open University reader by Smith, Little & Shackleton

[91], and also in the impressive study of the causes of war by two historians, Nelson & Olin [74].

The behavioural movement and its aftermath produced a series of fine commentaries on theory, among which the lively, easily read account by Morgan [70] is notable. The major compendium by Rosenau [86] is dated but still of relevance, and Sullivan's text [93] contains useful summaries of research. The outstanding treatment, however, is the devastating critique of realism by Vasquez [99]. It illustrates the strengths of behaviouralism better than any other study, and its discussions of epistemology, of anomalies and their relation to general theory, and of the importance of the inter-paradigm debate, together make it one of the most significant works published in IR since 1945. Vasquez demonstrates two things conclusively: that the behavioural movement, like postwar traditionalism before it, was dominated by realist assumptions; and that realist general theory cannot properly explain world politics.

The Paradigms Compared

Not even Vasquez, however, gives a systematic comparison of the issues at stake in the inter-paradigm debate, although several efforts to produce such a study were reported to be under way by 1985. So the reader must turn to the specialized literature within each paradigm. Each of the three starts with a wholly different basic image. For realists, the world society is a system of 'billiard-ball' states in intermittent collision. For pluralists, it is a 'cobweb', a network of numerous criss-crossing relationships. For structuralists, it is a 'multi-headed octopus', with powerful tentacles constantly sucking wealth from the weakened peripheries towards the powerful centres.

Upon these contrasting foundations, the proponents of each paradigm have erected a structure of theory. Each of the three is coherent in its own terms, but each also contradicts the others. The contradictions are most distinctive in relation to the major theoretical categories of actors, dynamics and dependent variables. On actors, realists see only states; pluralists see states in combination with a great variety of others; and structuralists see classes. On dynamics, realists see force as primary; pluralists see complex social movements; structuralists see economics. On dependent variables, realists see the task of IR as simply to explain what states do;

pluralists see it more grandly as an effort to explain all major world events; and structuralists see its function as showing why the world contains such appalling contrasts between rich and poor.

From these fundamental differences, many others flow. The three paradigms each have fairly obvious strengths and weaknesses. They also lead to contrasting judgments of how wide a scope the study of IR should have. Realists define the boundaries of their subject in a narrow, state-centric fashion, often preferring the term 'international politics' to describe it. Pluralists widen the boundaries by including multinational companies, markets, ethnic groups and nationalism as well as state behaviour, and call their subject IR or world society. Structuralists have the widest boundaries of all, stressing the unity of the whole world system at all levels, focussing on modes of production and treating inter-state politics as merely a surface phenomenon.

The most confusing usages occur at the level of specific concepts – the building-blocks of any theory. Some concepts are found only in one paradigm, because they are of crucial importance to it: deterrence and alliances in realism, ethnicity and interdependence in pluralism, exploitation and dependency in structuralism. Others, however, are used with broadly similar meanings in all three: power, sovereignty, and law, for example. Yet others, like imperialism, the state, and hegemony, are used in all three but with sharply different interpretations. In consequence, the task of reading the IR literature is partly a matter of disentangling the various usages. Many writers borrow concepts from other paradigms, which helps to explain the confusing nature of much writing in IR. Pluralists are the worst offenders in this respect, often following such paths as the logic of regime formation, the role of misperception in foreign policy or the domestic sources of international conflict – and then retreating to a respectably 'realist' conclusion which fails to follow from the argument.

Writings on Realism

As the oldest and still the most widely accepted of the three paradigms, realism has acquired the best-developed literature. Its classical ancestry reaches back to Thucydides, Machiavelli, Hobbes and Clausewitz, all of whom stressed the compelling insecurity of the sovereign state and, in consequence, the characteristic features of power politics in relations between states: the primacy of foreign policy, the central role of war and the essentially political and amoral character of IR. In the twentieth century, these ideas have been continually recast to fit contemporary circumstances. Writings from the traditional period are now mostly out of print, but Thompson [97] gives a first-rate assessment of Aron, Carr, Niebuhr, Herz, Lippmann and others, while Bull [18], Morgenthau [71], and Wight [102] can sometimes still be purchased; all tend to crowd the IR shelves of libraries. This group provides the background reading for any study of contemporary theory in IR. The majority of introductory texts continue to draw heavily upon it; the subfield of strategic studies (see Chapter 10) has grown directly from it, and its theories form the unstated paradigm for many accounts of the foreign policies of individual states.

When behaviouralism began in the 1950s, it was seen as a wholesale rejection of realism. But it turned out to be only an attack on its research methods, offering no effective substitute for its general theory. The behavioural efforts in quantification, simulation and even theory-building mainly proceeded from realist assumptions throughout the 1950s and 1960s. Only in the 1970s did realism begin to falter under the impact of genuinely competing paradigms, most prominently in the form of dependency theory (structuralism) and interdependence theory (pluralism). But a realist fight-back quickly appeared, with Cohen [26] asserting a political (not economic) analysis of imperialism, Tucker [98] rejecting claims for distributive justice, Bull [19] reasserting the importance of forcible intervention, Krasner [52] writing political economy with a neo-mercantilist tinge, and Gilpin [36] reasserting the role of war as an agency of change. With others, these scholars have tacitly formed a 'neo-realist' school, leading *International Organization* [43] to convene a lively symposium on the new trend, with papers by Ashley, Gilpin, Kratochwil and Andrews. But the single most widely read contribution to neo-realism has been the advanced text by Waltz [100], establishing him not only as the paradigmatic successor to Carr and Morgenthau but also as the source of the newly fashionable term 'structural realism'. This label reflects Waltz's tendency to borrow concepts from other paradigms, and especially his misappropriation of the term 'structural', to give scientific weight to the ancient power-politics ideas of hierarchy and the balance of power. Ruggie's critique [87] of this is excellent.

Realists share the state-centric paradigm with the idealists, their opposite numbers in the realist–idealist debate. Idealism is also found, of course, among advocates of each of the competing paradigms. But it is most easily recognizable among those who agree with the realists about the nature of the problems posed by world politics while disagreeing with them about what should be done in response. Whereas realists deploy conservative doctrines, arguing for example that powerful states should take direct responsibility for world order and that reform is not just impracticable but positively dangerous, idealists proceed to liberal doctrines; for them, power can be tamed. They advocate progressive reform, via such devices as disarmament, collective security, strengthened law, sanctions against aggressors, and even – potentially – world government. All this is based upon the same primary ingredients of theory as those found on the realist theoretical menu: sovereignty, power and diplomacy.

In the real world, traditional idealism of the sort advocated by John Hobson and Woodrow Wilson has been responsible for major changes in the practice of IR, especially in the first half of this century, as Clark [24] points out. But its influence has waned since the 1940s, under the combined pressure of the cold war–detente–cold war seesaw in great power relations and the hegemony of conservative/realist thought in IR. The literature, however, is certainly there. Thompson [97] indicates its high quality in the traditional period, through his biographies of Wright, de Visscher, Toynbee and others, while the doctrines have been sustained more recently by such spirited publicists as Falk [31], Claude [25], Beitz [11], Johansen [45], Wilson [105], and – wearing their idealist, rather than their structuralist, hats – Galtung [33] and Thompson [96]. Also in this category are the many normative writers on disarmament, the laws of war, human rights, neutralism, global ecology, peacekeeping and various aspects of UN reform. Their efforts have been reinforced in the past decade by the emergence of intellectual pressure groups: specialized team efforts by scholars, politicians and activists who have mapped out pathways to a better world without necessarily breaking new theoretical ground in the process. Especially noteworthy in this respect are the two Brandt Reports [13, 14], together with the Palme Report [77], the work of the World Order Models Project, led by Mendlovitz [66], and the series of Club of Rome projects in combination with other efforts at normative global modelling, surveyed by Nicholson [75] and Brucan [17].

The Pluralist Paradigm

Pluralist thinking, also known as world society theory, is the newest of the three approaches, having emerged as a distinct paradigm only in the 1970s. Many scholars have assisted in its development, although some insist that while they prefer international 'relations' to international 'politics', they remain realists by conviction. Keohane's treatment of political economy is a typical instance [47, p. 14]. Pluralism is unassertive, because its main premise is that the world is highly complex. This assumption induces modesty in its exponents, in contrast to the confident stridency of some realist and structuralist writings. As Rosenau observes in Maghroori & Ramberg [62, p. 3], it presents the world as a multi-centric, rather than state-centric or global-centric, system of relationships. Its origins lie in a series of discoveries and developments in different subfields of IR, all of which have converged, like a river formed by many streams, to produce a single paradigm.

Crucial among these, for mainstream theory, was the recognition in the 1970s that realism contains numerous anomalies: events and relationships which can be explained only by shifting to radically different assumptions. Integration was among the first, forecast with remarkable insight by Mitrany [69] in the traditional period, and examined by Deutsch and others in the behavioural period. Lijphart [59] spells out the implications (and see Chapter 12). Other anomalies followed, including the role of misperceptions, as shown by Jervis [44]; the ambiguities of 'power' (see Chapter 8); and the complexities of policy-making generally (see Chapter 11). All this is assessed by Vasquez (99) and Rosenau [84]. Burton, who is by far the most important contributor to the new paradigm, has argued in his 1984 book [20] that all foreign policy can be explained by domestic factors – an ultimate contradiction of realism. Peace research has also identified anomalies which undermine realism, particularly the multiplicity of parties involved in conflict, as Mitchell shows [68], and its demonstration of the importance of ethnicity, group identity and the self-determination of non-state actors generally as prime movers of events (see Chapter 3).

Non-state actors have also inspired international political economy, on which a wave of 1970s literature gave powerful impetus to the new pluralism. Multinational companies and interdependence in trade, monetary and other relationships have been highlighted by Keohane & Nye [48, 49], Morse [72] and many others; the whole group is thoroughly examined in Barry Jones & Willetts [10]. Writers in this subfield, split between neo-mercantilist, liberal, and radical views, mirror the wider inter-paradigm debate in IR. The majority favour a 'modified realist' view; the illogicality of their unwillingness to face the fundamental implications of their work is nicely demonstrated by O'Meara [76] in his trenchant analysis of the fashion among political economists for 'regime' theory, as exemplified in the work assembled by Krasner [53].

What pluralism has lacked, so far, is a powerful synthesis of its basic precepts and policy implications which would compare with the work of Carr, Morgenthau and Waltz among the realists, and sway opinion more generally in IR. But a series of partially successful efforts have been undertaken, including Banks [9], which is the only wide-ranging and critical study; Mansbach [63], which contains excellent introductory material; Burton's successful text of 1972 [21]; and Mansbach & Vasquez's attempt to blend pluralism with foreign policy analysis in an 'issue-area' paradigm [64]. But pluralism still relies heavily on its most persuasive specialized studies, such as Axelrod on the logic of co-operation, derived from game theory [4], Azar and others [5] on the structure of conflict, and Willetts [104] on transnational pressure groups.

The Literature of Structuralism

Unlike realism and pluralism, structuralist general theory is not a product of academic IR. But in common with both the conservative and idealist strands of state-centric realism, it does draw upon a heritage of classical theory. This includes the early Christian and humanist concerns with justice and the fate of the individual, the Kantian philosophy of morality, the dialectics of Hegel and above all the historical materialism of Marx, Engels and subsequently Lenin. Together, these strands create a problem today in selecting the best term to use in referring to the whole approach: 'dialectics', 'Marxism', 'social class theory', 'historical materialism' and others are found in the literature. 'Structuralism' is used here merely to distinguish the paradigm from realism and pluralism.

Structuralism's distinguished classical background has rarely been given full credit in academic IR during the twentieth century. Once the study of IR became institutionalized in universities, most of its professoriate regarded structuralist ideas as false, or unduly normative, or politically subversive. And so it has flourished only on the fringes of the field, rather than within the conservative mainstream. As Alker & Biersteker observe [1, p. 137], this has been especially true of the United States, where the discipline has been noticeably weakened by this shortcoming despite its great strength in other respects.

The importance of the paradigm, however, is unquestionable. This is not just because Marxist–Leninist thought has been established as official orthodoxy in the many states which call themselves socialist, or 'of socialist orientation'. Nor is it only because so many world events have been brought about in the name of Marxism: violent political events such as revolutions or horrifying acts of terrorism, and radical diplomatic events including demands for distributive justice and for 'new orders' in the fields of political economy and information flow. Instead, the importance of structuralism is dependent far more upon its intellectual quality. Social scientists, in all countries and in all fields, owe a major debt, whether acknowledged or not, to the basic Marxist insights: the bridge between economics and politics, the latent solidarity of groups whose objective interests are linked by common circumstance, and the progressive unfolding of historical changes in response to technological development and its expression in laws, ideologies and governmental institutions.

Within IR, there is a widespread impression that structuralism has made significant contributions only to the study of imperialism and dependency. It is, however, a misleading impression, brought about by the way that IR has evolved and not by the relative importance of those topics within structuralism. The theory of imperialism loomed in the shadows of IR throughout the half-century of traditionalism and behaviouralism, until it was brought into the light by Galtung [32]. The theory of dependent relationships, developed first in Latin America, was also forced into the centre of attention by important writers working outside the major centres of Western scholarship (see Chapter 4). If the academic mainstream of IR had found a way to incorporate the major concerns of structuralism in addition to these two significant but partial topics, it seems likely that mutual enrichment would have occurred. The strongest areas of structuralist inquiry – the nature of the state, ideology, conflict, and the process of change – are all problems for the other paradigms, just as Kuhnian theory would predict.

Given the great size and range of the structuralist paradigm, reference must be made to synoptic works which deal with the entire general theory: its method, its views of class formation and class struggle, its treatment of ideology and social theory, and its analysis of history. This body of ideas is alive and under continuous development and reformulation. To grasp its depth, it is necessary to read some of the major contributions which start with interpretation of the great classics, apply them to present conditions and contribute to the many fierce debates within neo-Marxism. Examples are Gramsci [37], Poulantzas [82], Althusser [2] and Laclau [57], all substantial figures in the extension and refinement of the paradigm. An excellent introduction to the Marxist interpretation of politics is given by Miliband [67], and a comprehensive – though somewhat hostile – survey of the currents of thought in the whole approach is given in the three volumes by Kolakowski [51]. Larrain's discussion of ideology [58] is helpful, and the school of critical theorists is clearly introduced by Held [39].

Specific applications of the general theory to the nature and problems of IR, while not plentiful in English, do exist in other languages. Several attempts at application have been made from outside the paradigm, by authors who are interested in the structuralist perspective but do not themselves share it. Of these, Pettman [80] is interesting but unduly complicated; Kubalkova & Cruickshank [55] is helpful, although laboured; and a useful introduction is in Thorndike [in 94]. However, it is much more persuasive to read authors who display the convictions of the paradigm while addressing IR problems. Among these, the two books by the Romanian scholar Brucan [15, 16] are outstanding, along with Skocpol on revolution [90] and the short discussions by Cox [27, 28] which are among the best in the field. Shaw's collection of papers on war and society [89] is a welcome publication, as are the articles by MacLean [61, and in 22]. The reissue of Deutscher's essays on IR topics is a reminder of the intellectual force of the 1930s generation of Marxist thinkers so woefully ignored by traditional IR. Galtung's major treatise [34] combines peace research, idealism and incisive social science in a characteristically impressive manner. Militarism in all its aspects has been explored in many publications, for example by Thompson and others on cold war doctrine [95, 96], by Sen [88] on the links between militarism and industrial growth, by Ashley [3] on long-term trends and by Halliday [38] in the context of East–West relations. Poverty and distributive justice, topics almost inaccessible to other paradigms, are probed in Galtung [34].

Although these structuralist-inspired excursions into the mainstream of academic IR are scattered and uneven in their scale and quality, they hold out the prospect of substantial improvement in the discipline. As the inter-paradigm debate develops and flourishes, scholarship in IR is at last emerging from the intellectual cage in which it was imprisoned by postwar traditional realism. Instead of an endless and fruitless effort to find meaningful patterns in the jumbled succession of inter-state clashes and compromises, the inter-paradigm debate makes it possible to explore the linkages up and down the levels of analysis. For the first time, we may be able to identify and measure the factors which cause particular societies to be aggressive or peaceable in their external relations; or to see means of removing the causes of terrorism rather than treating the symptoms; or to understand how to build institutions which can promote justice in the world society by methods other than disruption and struggle.

Seen from this perspective, the inter-paradigm 'debate' should be seen as a discourse about choice of analytic frameworks, rather than as a militant confrontation between mutually incompatible world views. In so far as the pluralist paradigm really is addressing itself to new questions about hitherto unemphasized relationships, then it is not disproving the realist paradigm. It is passing by, to engage in a separate conversation with the subject-matter. Similarly, there is no necessary contradiction between a realist model of destabilizing changes in military hardware, and a structuralist model of conflict dynamics produced by peace researchers; the first approach deals with surface manifestations, the second with underlying causes. Students of the field, from undergraduates to presidential advisers, can choose and compare. The inter-paradigm debate provides stimulus, hope and even excitement in the demanding business of analysing international relations.

Bibliography to Chapter 1

1. Alker, H.R. Jr. & Biersteker, T.J. 'The Dialectics of World Order: Notes for a Future Archeologist of International Savoir Faire'. *International Studies Quarterly*, vol. 28, no. 2, 1984, pp. 121–42.
2. Althusser, L. *Essays on Ideology*. London, Verso, 1984.
3. Ashley, R.K. *The Political Economy of War and Peace: The Sino-Soviet-American Triangle and the Modern Security Problematique*. London, Frances Pinter and New York, Nichols, 1980.

4. Axelrod, R. *The Evolution of Cooperation.* New York, Basic Books, 1984. (Distributed in UK by Harper & Row, London).
5. Azar, E. (ed.) *The Theory and Practice of Conflict Resolution.* Brighton, Wheatsheaf and College Park, MD, Center for International Development, University of Maryland, 1985.
6. Banks, M. 'General Theory in International Relations: New Directions'. *Millennium: Journal of International Studies,* vol. 8, no. 3, 1979, pp. 252–66.
7. _____ 'Where we are now'. *Review of International Studies,* vol. 11, no. 3, 1985, pp. 220-37.
8. _____ Ways of Analyzing the World Society. In *International Relations Theory: A Bibliography,* ed. A.J.R. Groom & C.R. Mitchell. London, Frances Pinter and New York, Nichols, 1978, pp. 195–215.
9. _____ (ed.) *Conflict in World Society: A New Perspective on International Relations.* Brighton, Wheatsheaf and New York, St. Martin's Press, 1984.
10. Barry Jones, R.J. & Willetts, P. (eds), *Interdependence on Trial: Studies in the Theory and Reality of Contemporary Interdependence.* London, Frances Pinter and New York, St. Martin's, 1984.
11. Beitz, C.R. *Political Theory and International Relations.* Princeton, NJ & Guildford, Princeton University Press, 1979.
12. Bernstein, R.J. *The Restructuring of Social and Political Theory.* London, Methuen, 1979 and Philadelphia, PA, University of Pennsylvania Press, 1978.
13. The 'Brandt Commission' I. Report of the Independent Commission on International Development Issues. *North-South: A Programme for Survival.* London, Pan and Cambridge, MA, MIT Press, 1980.
14. The 'Brandt Commission' II. Report of the Independent Commission on International Development Issues. *Common Crisis.* London, Pan and Cambridge, MA, MIT Press, 1983.
15. Brucan, S. *The Dialectic of World Politics.* New York, Free Press and London, Collier-Macmillan, 1978.
16. _____ *The Dissolution of Power: A Sociology of International Relations and Politics.* New York, Alfred A. Knopf, 1971.
17. _____ 'The Global Crisis'. *International Studies Quarterly,* vol. 28, no. 1, 1984, pp. 97–109.
18. Bull, H.N. *The Anarchical Society: A Study of World Order.* London, Macmillan and New York, Columbia University Press, 1977.
19. _____ (ed.) *Intervention in World Politics.* Oxford and New York, Oxford University Press, 1984.
20. Burton, J.W. *Global Conflict: The Domestic Sources of International Crisis.* Brighton, Wheatsheaf and College Park, MD, Center for International Development, University of Maryland, 1984.
21. _____ *World Society.* London & New York, Cambridge University Press, 1972.

22. Buzan, B. & Barry Jones, R.J. (eds), *Change and the Study of International Relations*. London, Frances Pinter and New York, St. Martin's, 1981.

23. Carr, E.H. *The Twenty Years Crisis, 1919–1939*. London, Macmillan, 1981 and New York, Harper & Row, 1964.

24. Clark, I. *Reform and Resistance in the International Order*. London & New York, Cambridge University Press, 1980.

25. Claude, I.L. *Power and International Relations*. New York, Random House, 1962.

26. Cohen, B.J. *The Question of Imperialism: The Political Economy of Dominance and Dependence*. London, Macmillan, 1974 and New York, Basic Books, 1973.

27. Cox, R.W. 'Gramsci, Hegemony and International Relations: An Essay in Method'. *Millennium: Journal of International Studies*, vol. 12, no. 2, 1983, pp. 162–75.

28. _____ 'Social Forces, States and World Orders: Beyond International Relations Theory'. *Millennium: Journal of International Studies*, vol. 10, no. 2, 1981, pp. 126–55.

29. Donelan, M.D. (ed.) *The Reason of States: A Study in International Political Theory*. London & Winchester, MA, Allen & Unwin, 1978.

30. Dougherty, J.E. & Pfaltzgraff, R.L. Jr. *Contending Theories of International Relations: A Comprehensive Survey*. New York & London, Harper & Row, 1981.

31. Falk, R.A. *A Study of Future Worlds*. New York, Free Press and London, Collier-Macmillan, 1975.

32. Galtung, J. 'A Structural Theory of Imperialism'. *Journal of Peace Research*, vol. 8, no. 1, 1971, pp. 81–117.

33. _____ *There Are Alternatives! Four Roads to Peace and Security*. Nottingham, Spokesman Books and Chester Springs, PA, Dufour Editions, 1984.

34. _____ *The True Worlds: A Transnational Perspective*. New York, Free Press and London, Collier-Macmillan International, 1980.

35. Garnett, J.C. *Commonsense and the Theory of International Politics*. London, Macmillan and New York, State University of New York Press, 1984.

36. Gilpin, R. *War and Change in World Politics*. Cambridge & New York, Cambridge University Press, 1984.

37. Gramsci, A. *Selections from the Prison Notebooks*. (Edited and translated by Q. Hoare and G. Nowell Smith.) New York, International Publishers and London, Lawrence & Wishart, 1973.

38. Halliday, F. *The Making of the Second World War*. London, Verso Editions and NLB, 1983. (Published in the USA as *The Origins of the Second Cold War*, New York, Schocken, 1983.)

39. Held, D. *Introduction to Critical Theory: Horkheimer to Habermas*. London, Hutchinson and Berkeley, CA, University of California

Press, 1980.

40. Hoffmann, S. 'An American Social Science: International Relations'. *Daedalus*, vol. 106, no. 3, 1977, pp. 41–60.

41. Holsti, K.J. 'Along the Road to International Theory'. *International Journal*, vol. 34, no. 2, 1984, pp. 337–65.

42. Inkeles, A. 'The Emerging Social Structure of the World'. *World Politics*, vol. XXVII, no. 4, 1975, pp. 467–95.

43. *International Organization*. Symposium on the New Realism. vol. 38, no. 2, 1984, pp. 225–328.

44. Jervis, R. *Perception and Misperception in International Politics*. Princeton, NJ, & Guildford, Princeton University Press, 1976.

45. Johansen, R.C. *The National Interest and the Human Interest: An Analysis of U.S. Foreign Policy*. Princeton, NJ & Guildford, Princeton University Press, 1980.

46. Kent, R.C. & Nielsson, G.P. (eds), *The Study and Teaching of International Relations: A Perspective on Mid-Career Education*. London, Frances Pinter and New York, Nichols, 1980.

47. Keohane, R.O. *After Hegemony: Cooperation and Discord in the World Political Economy*. Princeton, NJ & Guildford, Princeton University Press, 1984.

48. Keohane, R.O. & Nye, J.S. *Power and Interdependence: World Politics in Transition*. Boston, Little Brown, 1977.

49. _____ (eds), *Transnational Relations and World Politics*. Cambridge, MA & London, Harvard University Press, 1973.

50. Knorr, K. & Rosenau, J.N. (eds), *Contending Approaches to International Politics*. Princeton, NJ & Guildford, Princeton University Press, 1969.

51. Kolakowski, L. *Main Currents of Marxism. Its Origins, Growth and Dissolution* (3 volumes). Oxford & New York, Oxford University Press, 1981.

52. Krasner, S.D. *Defending the National Interest: Raw Materials Investments and US Foreign Policy*. Princeton, NJ & Guildford, Princeton University Press, 1978.

53. _____ (ed.) *International Regimes*. Ithaca, NY & London, Cornell University Press, 1983.

54. Krippendorff, E. *International Relations as a Social Science*. Brighton, Harvester Press, 1982 and Atlantic Highlands, NJ, Humanities Press, 1981.

55. Kubalkova, V. & Cruickshank, A.A. *Marxism-Leninism and the Theory of International Relations*. London & Boston, MA, Routledge & Kegan Paul, 1980.

56. Kuhn, T.S. *The Structure of Scientific Revolutions*. (International Encyclopaedia of Unified Science), Chicago & London, University of Chicago Press, 1970.

57. Laclau, E. *Politics and Ideology in Marxist Theory: Capitalism, Fascism,*

Populism. London, Verso Editions and New York, Schocken, 1979.

58.   Larrain, J. *Marxism and Ideology*. London, Macmillan and Atlantic Highlands, NJ, Humanities Press, 1983.

59.   Lijphart, A. Karl. W. Deutsch and the New Paradigm in International Relations. In *From National Development to Global Community*, ed. R.L. Merritt & B.M. Russett. London & Boston, Allen & Unwin, 1981, pp. 233–51.

60.   McClelland, C.A. On the Fourth Wave: Past and Future in the Study of International Systems. In *The Analysis of International Politics*, ed. J. Rosenau *et al.* New York, Free Press and London, Collier-Macmillan International, 1972, pp. 15–40.

61.   MacLean, J. 'Political Theory, International Theory and Problems of Ideology'. *Millennium: Journal of International Studies*, vol. 10, no. 2, 1981, pp. 102–25.

62.   Maghroori, R. & Ramberg, B. (eds), *Globalism Versus Realism: International Relations' Third Debate*. Boulder, CO, Westview, 1982.

63.   Mansbach, R.W. *et al.*, *The Web of World Politics: Non State Actors in the Global System*. Englewood Cliffs, NJ, Prentice-Hall & London, Prentice-Hall International, 1976.

64.   Mansbach, R.W. & Vasquez, J.A. *In Search of Theory: A New Paradigm for Global Politics*. New York & Guildford, Columbia University Press, 1981.

65.   Mayall, J. (ed.) *The Community of States: A Study in International Political Theory*. London & Winchester, MA, Allen & Unwin, 1983.

66.   Mendlovitz, S. (ed.) *On the Creation of a Just World Order: Preferred Worlds for the 1990s*. New York, Free Press and London, Collier-Macmillan, 1977.

67.   Miliband, R. *Marxism and Politics*. Oxford & New York, Oxford University Press, 1977.

68.   Mitchell, C.R. *The Structure of International Conflict*. London, Macmillan and New York, St. Martin's, 1981.

69.   Mitrany, D. *A Working Peace System*. Chicago, Quadrangle Books, 1966.

70.   Morgan, P.M. *Theories and Approaches to International Politics: What Are We To Think?* New Brunswick, NJ & London, Transaction Books, 1981.

71.   Morgenthau, H.J. *Politics Among Nations: The Struggle for Power and Peace*. New York, Alfred Knopf, 1985.

72.   Morse, E.L. *Modernization and the Transformation of International Relations*. New York, Free Press and London, Collier-Macmillan, 1976.

73.   Nardin, T. *Law, Morality and the Relations of States*. Princeton, NJ & Guildford, Princeton University Press, 1983.

74. Nelson, K.L. & Olin, S.C. *Why War? Ideology, Theory and History.* Berkeley, CA & London, University of California Press, 1980.
75. Nicholson, M.B. 'Progress and Problems in World Modelling'. *Review of International Studies*, vol. 10, no. 3, 1984, pp. 239–46.
76. O'Meara, R.L. 'Regimes and Their Implications for International Theory'. *Millennium: Journal of International Studies*, vol. 13, no. 3, 1984, pp. 245–64.
77. Palme Commission, *Common Security: A Programme for Disarmament.* London, Pan, 1982.
78. Parkinson, F. *The Philosophy of International Relations: A Study in the History of Thought.* Beverly Hills, CA & London, Sage, 1977.
79. Pettman, R. 'Competing Paradigms in International Politics'. *Review of International Studies*, vol. 7, no. 1, 1981, pp. 39–50.
80. _____ *State and Class: A Sociology of International Affairs.* London, Croom Helm and New York, St. Martin's, 1979.
81. Phillips, W.R. 'Where Have All the Theories Gone?' *World Politics*, vol. XXVI, no. 2, 1974, pp. 155–88.
82. Poulantzas, N. *Classes in Contemporary Capitalism.* London, Verso and New York, Schocken, 1978.
83. Rosenau, J.N. 'Muddling, Meddling and Modelling: Alternative Approaches to the Study of World Politics in an Era of Rapid Change'. *Millennium: Journal of International Studies*, vol. 8, no. 2, 1979, pp. 130–44.
84. _____ 'A Pre-Theory Revisited: World Politics in an Era of Cascading Interdependence'. *International Studies Quarterly*, vol. 28, no. 3, 1984, pp. 245–306.
85. _____ (ed.) *In Search of Global Patterns.* London, Collier-Macmillan International and New York, Free Press, 1976.
86. _____ (ed.) *International Politics and Foreign Policy: A Reader in Research and Theory.* New York, Free Press, 1969.
87. Ruggie, J.G. 'Continuity and Transformation in the World Polity: Toward a Neorealist Synthesis'. *World Politics*, vol. XXXV, no. 2, 1983, pp. 261–85.
88. Sen, G. *The Military Origins of Industrialisation and International Trade Rivalry.* London, Frances Pinter, 1984. (Published in the USA as *The Military Roots of Industrialization and Trade Disputes*, New York, St. Martin's, 1983.)
89. Shaw, M. (ed.) *War, State and Society.* London, Macmillan and New York, St. Martin's, 1984.
90. Skocpol, T. *States and Social Revolutions.* Cambridge & New York, Cambridge University Press, 1979.
91. Smith, M. *et al.*, (eds), *Perspectives on World Politics.* London, Croom Helm for the Open University Press, 1981.
92. Sullivan, M.P. 'Competing Frameworks and the Study of Contemporary International Politics'. *Millennium: Journal of International*

Studies, vol. 7, no. 2, 1978, pp. 93–110.

93. _____ *International Relations: Theories and Evidence.* Hemel Hempstead & Englewood Cliffs, NJ, Prentice Hall, 1976.

94. Taylor, T. (ed.) *Approaches and Theory in International Relations.* London & New York, Longmans, 1978.

95. Thompson, E.P. *The Poverty of Theory and Other Essays.* London, Merlin Press, 1978 and New York, Monthly Review Press, 1980.

96. Thompson, E.P. *et al., Exterminism and Cold War.* London, Verso Editions and NLP and New York, Schocken, 1982.

97. Thompson, K.W. *Masters of International Thought.* Baton Rouge, LA & London, Louisiana State University Press, 1980.

98. Tucker, R.W. *The Inequality of Nations.* New York, Basic Books and Oxford, Martin Robertson, 1977.

99. Vasquez, J.A. *The Power of Power Politics: A Critique.* London, Frances Pinter and New Brunswick, NJ, Rutgers University Press, 1983.

100. Waltz, K.N. *Theory of International Politics.* Reading, MA & London, Addison-Wesley, 1979.

101. Walzer, M. *Just and Unjust Wars: A Moral Argument with Historical Illustrations.* New York, Basic Books, 1977 and Harmondsworth, Middx., Penguin, 1980.

102. Wight, M. *Power Politics.* Leicester, Leicester University Press and New York, Holmes and Meier, 1978.

103. _____ (ed. H.N. Bull), *Systems of States.* Leicester, Leicester University Press and Atlantic Highlands, NJ, Humanities Press, 1978.

104. Willetts, P. (ed.) *Pressure Groups in the Global System: The Transnational Relations of Issue-Orientated Non-Governmental Organizations.* London, Frances Pinter and New York, St. Martin's, 1982.

105. Wilson, A. *The Disarmer's Handbook: Of Military Technology and Organization.* Harmondsworth, Middlesex and New York, Penguin Books, 1983.

106. Wolfers, A. *Discord and Collaboration: Essays in International Politics.* Baltimore, Johns Hopkins University Press, 1966.

107. Wright, Q. *The Study of International Relations.* New York, Irvington, 1984.

2 Normative Approaches

Mark J. Hoffman
University of Keele and CAC

Any new student of international relations (IR) has to cope with a wealth of historical detail which tends to be organized around and within a handful of concepts such as sovereignty, diplomacy, international law, the national interest, power and the balance of power. The main concern of the discipline tends to be with the 'real' world. While interesting theoretical questions are recognized, they are generally considered to interfere with an understanding of what states and statesmen really do. This relegation of theoretical concerns to the backwaters of IR is especially apparent in the somewhat neglected area of normative political theory. International morality and the normative aspects of IR may, at best, be the subject of one or two lectures in an introductory course and, while Wight [in 28], Goodwin [in 133] and Savigear [in 133] emphasize their importance in international theory, any consideration of morality is absent from most commonly recommended general textbooks. Notable exceptions are Carr [29], Morgenthau [103], Aron [2], Bull [20] and Holsti [64]. However, normative aspects of IR have not been completely ignored and there is a large body of normative theory available. The purpose of this chapter is to set out the four dominant normative approaches – the legal, realist, classical and cosmopolitan.

The Roots of Normative Theory

The roots of normative theory can be found in the classics of political philosophy: from Plato and Aristotle to Aquinas and Augustine, and from Grotius, Vattel, Wolff and Pufendorf to Hobbes, Locke, Rousseau, Kant, Hume, Burke and Mill. There are many edited anthologies and texts on individual authors which serve as an introduction to this literature, although nothing can substitute for reading the original texts.

Many of the normative questions that concern IR are similar to those to be found in the works of these classical philosophers. Normative approaches in IR seek to deal with the perennial questions of justice, rights, duties and obligations. However, normative approaches do not form a cohesive whole, although there is a cohesiveness in the kinds of questions considered and the *way* in which they are dealt with, a manner which is free of the 'scientific' methodology of behaviouralism and which is classical and philosophical in orientation, attitude, approach and argument. But the normative approach in IR cannot simply be equated with 'classicism'.

The Legal Approach*

The first overt concern with normative questions coincides with the birth of IR as a discipline. IR originated as an essentially normative, reformist search for a remedy to the problem of war in an international system that lacked an overarching political authority. There was a desire to build a 'commonwealth of nations' based on international law and international organizations. This uncomplicated view of international relations made it virtually synonymous with international law. The ideas and ideals of the inter-war period can best be summed up in the phrases 'peace through law' and 'peace through institutions' which form the central kernel of the legal approach. As Suganami has so clearly pointed out [in 133], this approach did not just materialize with the discipline of IR, but had a long tradition in thought and practice with its roots in the writings of Saint-Simon, Kant and Grotius. What was new about the inter-war period was the number of people who adhered to the idea and the enthusiasm with which it was pursued, as seen in the League and the Kellogg–Briand Pact.

Although this view constituted the focal point of the discipline for over 20 years, much of the literature now seems dated. The exemplar of the approach is to be found in Lauterpacht [83, 84], the most thoroughly constructed work within this framework. Indeed, Carr cites Lauterpacht as a prime example of the 'idealism' he objected to in his devastating critique of the utopian thinkers of the period [29]. Lauterpacht's reply to Carr remained unpublished until after his death [84]. Useful discussions of the utopian tradition criticized by Carr can be found in Clark [30, 31], Goodwin & Taylor [55], Manual

& Manual [95], the debate between Nicholson [108] and Savigear [123] and in Taylor [132].

Lauterpacht argued that all disputes, including those in the sphere of international politics, can be reduced to contests of a legal nature. There are no inherently 'political' conflicts. He believed that international law was morally superior to international politics. Perfection of the legal system would bring about changes in politics. Law and lawyers could thus be a progressive force in building an international judicial system that would command respect and the ideal of peace. Brierly [12, 13, 14] is another example of this approach, although he differed from Lauterpacht in that he saw international law as underpinning the political order, not preceding it.

With the failure of the League and the attempts to outlaw aggression, a deep disillusionment set in with the legalist approach, a disillusionment from which it would never fully recover despite its resurgence in later years. International law itself moved away from its normative basis and took on a decidedly positivistic, sociological outlook. The high point of this trend is to be found in the works of Kelsen [75, 76], but it can also be seen in the works of Corbett [33], Friedmann [50] and Schwarzenberger [125].

While the normative aspects of international law resurfaced in the works of Jessup [70, 71] and Jenks [69], it was not until the mid-1960s and the concern about US involvement in Vietnam that the legalist approach became revitalized. This revitalization can be found in the work of Falk [41, 42, 43, 46], particularly in the massive four volume work on international law and the war in Vietnam [45]. Another important example of this revitalization is McDougall [91, 92], who saw law as an instrument for facilitating the pursuit of shared values. For McDougall, the essence of law is not in the rule of conduct, but in the conduct itself. Law is thus co-extensive with politics. The resurgence in the approach was maintained throughout the 1970s and 1980s through articles such as those by Johnstone [73] and Falk [39] on the foundations of justice in international law. It is also to be found in a number of works on the legal restraints on warfare. Best [7] is a highly recommended example, but it can also be seen in Bailey [3], Brownlie [18], to a certain extent in Walzer [143], as well as in volumes by Roberts & Guelff [121], Ferenez [48] and Friedman [49] which seek to bring together various international documents and treaties relating to the laws of war.

A second area in which the legal approach has found new

relevance is that of human rights. Lauterpacht [85] is one of the earliest examples, while Brierly [12] argues for the need to develop international conventions, such as the UN Document on Basic Human Rights, which would clarify the duties states have towards their citizens. Brownlie [17] provides an excellent compendium of these international legal documents on human rights. Buergenthall & Hall [19] contain some useful essays on international law, human rights and the Helsinki process and the essays by Buergenthall, Hehir and Wicclair in Brown & Maclean [15] discuss the developing legal consensus on the legitimate concerns about human rights in the international community. The chapter on humanitarian law in Robertson [122] is recommended, and so is Falk [40], though here his populist hat is more to the fore. McDougall, Laswell & Chen [90] seek to expound the place of human rights within McDougall's concept of minimum world public order.

Despite this resurgence, the legal approach to normative questions in IR has never reclaimed the dominant position it had in the inter-war period. It was replaced by the realist and classical approaches to normative theory.

The Realist and Classical Approaches

Wolfers [150] has distinguished between two broad approaches to normative theory: the continental and the Anglo-Saxon. The former recognizes a deep conflict between morality and the *raison d'être* of the state which cannot be reconciled. State *raison d'être* must obviously have the upper hand. The Anglo-Saxon school is predominantly concerned with the application of accepted principles of morality and their codification so that they can inform the foreign policy process. It is assumed that states and statesmen enjoy considerable freedom of action and this allows and forces them to act on the basis of normative considerations. As a result of the disillusionment with the legal, 'peace through law' approach (which many would place within Wolfers' Anglo-Saxon tradition) and the rise of realism as the dominant approach within IR, these two approaches came to be the dominant normative frameworks of IR. The first represents what might be called the moral scepticism of realism, the second is the classical approach to normative questions.

As Wolfers [150] has pointed out, the continental version of realism left little room and no incentive for normative thinking. The discipline was now concerned with relations between states based on the principles of power and the national interest. This, in conjunction with the preference of the behaviouralists for 'scientific' method-ology, accounts for the lack of interest in the normative aspects of IR mentioned at the beginning of this chapter.

Yet this view of realism as being without moral content can be overstated. As Goodwin [in 133] argues, the realist approach is saturated with normative presuppositions that accord moral primacy to the state and its security interests. There are four general arguments, all of which derive from the Hobbesian tradition: the idea of a moral vacuum, moral relativism, the duality of morality and the primacy of the national interest. Useful extended discussions can be found in Wolfers [150], Stern [130], Thompson [134, 135, 136, 137, 138], Suganami [131], Beitz [5], Butterfield [27 and in 28], Williams [149], Hare & Joynt [58], the essays by Miller [in 114], Vincent [in 114], Smith [in 114] and Pettman [in 114].

The moral scepticism of realism derives from the view that international politics is amoral and that statesmen operate in a moral vacuum. Morality, as embodied in the ideals of justice and equality, can only be defined in the context of a well-ordered society, such as is found at the national level. States, unlike individuals, have not developed a set of generally agreed norms that constitute an 'international morality'. The absence of an overarching political authority in the international system prevents normative questions arising. It is, therefore, impossible to pass moral judgment on the actions of statesmen or to expect them to consider moral judgments in their decision-making. As a result, normative thinking has no place in international relations.

The second realist argument is based on moral relativism: international morality is possible only if there is a fair expectation that states will act in accordance with universally agreed principles and norms. But international anarchy prevents any such expecta-tion. Instead there is a plurality of norms and value systems and no real basis for choosing between them. Thus ethical or normative rules cannot be made the basis of political action as no one moral framework can dictate what is right to all the others. Oddly enough, implicit in this view is the universal principle of non-intervention in the affairs of others.

The third general argument is that of the duality of morality. This view argues that 'public' morality precludes the application of moral principles that may apply to the individual. The moral action which may be required of the individual or within the state is not applicable outside of the state. There, ethical considerations are of a different kind and must be related to the circumstances and epoch in which states find themselves. Norms are related to contexts and morality becomes consequentialist.

The fourth argument is compatible with and in some ways derivative of the above three. This view holds that statesmen have an overriding moral obligation to serve the national interest of their country. Given the nature of man, the state and the international system, statesmen cannot be expected to sacrifice the national interest for universal principles.

Each of these arguments can be found (often combined together) in the writings of such realists as Niebuhr [109, 110], Aron [2], Garnett [52], Good [54], Carr [29], Morgenthau [100–105], Lippman [87], Kennan [77, 78, 79], Osgood & Tucker [111], Herz [60, 61], Hoffmann [62, 63], Howard [65], Thompson [134–138], Schwarzenberger [126], Kissinger [80, 81] and Hare & Joynt [58]. They can also be found in the work of the neo-realists such as Waltz [141], the articles in the symposium on neo-realism in *International Organization* [66], that on Morgenthau in *International Studies Quarterly* [67] and in Spegele's efforts [129] at revitalizing the ethical and evaluative basis of realism.

In contrast to these views derived from the continental tradition, there is a view that derives from the Anglo-Saxon tradition. This approach might be termed, after Bull [21], the classical approach to normative thinking. It is a particular kind of universalistic approach which historically has appealed to the English-speaking world, particularly Britain. It has its roots in and still encompasses the two somewhat contradictory traditions of natural law and the idea of the social contract.

The natural law tradition evolved from the theological claim that it is right to do some particular act because God has commanded it. In the writings of Pufendorf, Vattel, Wolff and Grotius, natural law lost its theological basis. In its secularized version it starts from the rationalist premiss that the individual is endowed with the capacity for reason. The application of right reason cannot fail to conclude that it is self-evidently right to do or not to do a particular act. The intrinsic appeal of the tradition is the argument that the individual possesses inherent dignity, an intellectual ability to discern right from wrong and a capacity for just action. A fuller discussion of the natural law tradition is provided in Midgley [99], Sigmund [128], d'Entreves [35] and Gierke [53].

The idea of social contract originates in the writings of Hobbes, Locke and Rousseau. It starts from the view that man is inherently competitive. The best way to increase mutual well-being and security against the threats posed by this competitiveness is to channel it by entering into a 'social contract' that regulates behaviour through agreed norms, customs, principles and rules. Society will thus be united by common conceptions of the nature of rights, duties and obligations.

Both traditions can be found in the writings of the classical approach. Within the approach there is an almost self-conscious effort to recall the style and use the concepts and ideas found in classical political theory. However, while the classical approach, like classical political theory, is still concerned with the idea of the state, it does not seek to elevate the idea of the national interest or the necessity of state to the level of a supreme moral obligation. Instead it focuses on the idea of 'international society'. In many ways this is the defining characteristic of this approach. It has led Jones [74] to write of an 'English school' of IR.

The idea of international society refers to the conception of a system of states related to one another in terms of common practices, customs, norms, principles and rules, based either on the natural law tradition or on the idea of a social contract. In the absence of an overarching political authority, they provide the basis for determining what is just or unjust action in the context of international relations. International society is not merely an assemblage of actors whose actions affect one another. It is similar to any other society in that there are expectations regarding certain types of action and standards against which such action can be measured and judged. The moral basis of this society is embodied in an adherence to the principles of non-intervention, self-determination, *pacta sunt servanda*, the maintenance of a balance of power, the right to self-defence and the rules of *jus ad bellum* and *jus en bello*. The central point is that morality exists independently from national interest.

There is a substantial literature on the classical approach, of which the best examples are Wight [147, 148] on the system of states and power politics, Butterfield & Wight [28], the rather idiosyncratic work of Manning [94], James [68], Luard [88] and some of the essays in Porter [115]. Especially fine examples are in the writings of Bull [20, 21, 22, and in 28] and in the trilogy of collected essays by the BISA

International Theory Group and edited by Donelan [37], Mayall [96] and Navari [107]. An interesting recent addition is the book by Nardin [106] in which he sets out the argument in favour of the idea of international society, arguing that law and morality are the indispensable foundations for such a society. What is required, however, is not to define the ends of that society, but to set the limits of justifiable action within it. Law and morality should regulate relations among states with differing and even incompatible goals. Nardin then discusses the implications of this view for the laws of war and for international justice.

The classical approach has had its greatest impact on the complex theory of the just war. One of the best examples is Walzer's highly readable and remarkable theory of aggression [143]. In some ways his work can be included in the legal approach, but given its Lockean roots, it is best considered part of the classical approach. Unfortunately, his case against the utilitarian logic of 'military necessity' is undermined by his own arguments regarding the justification for pre-emptive strikes and his idea of 'supreme emergency'. Other useful discussions of the just war theory can be found in Johnson [72], Ramsey [116, 117, 118, 119], Wells [146], Wasserstrom [145], Melzer [97], Paskins & Dockrill [113] and the collection of essays in Held, Morgenbasser & Nagel [59], as well as those in Cohen, Nagel & Scanlon [32]. Donelan [36] provides an outline of the Grotian view of war, Greenwood [57] discusses the relationship between *jus ad bellum* and *jus en bello*, while Paskins [112] raises interesting questions regarding the ethical obligations of the scientific community in terms of the just war tradition.

One of the most interesting areas that has arisen out of the just war theory is the discussion of the ethical aspects of nuclear deterrence. An excellent modified Kantian position can be found in Paskins & Dockrill [113]. Differing views of the ethics of deterrence are presented in Ramsey [117] and Walzer [143] and the consequentialist view is detailed in Hare & Joynt [58]. McMahan [93] offers an interesting discussion of the ethical arguments for and against unilateral nuclear disarmament by Britain. The essays by moral philosphers in Blake & Pole [8, 9] are also highly recommended. Goodwin [56] has edited one of the best sets of essays capturing all sides of the debate and the chapters by Paskins and Hockaday are particularly valuable.

The Cosmopolitan Approach

The fourth general approach to normative thinking in IR can broadly be described as the cosmopolitan approach. This approach seeks to extend the framework of morality and just action beyond the borders of the state, trying to develop the idea of a non-state, international morality that can be applied globally and not just to the state or within the state. It is a direct reaction to the dominance of the realist and classical approaches in that it is trying to move beyond the idea of morality based on the principles of non-intervention and self-determination and the autonomy of states. Its purpose is to bring back into the realm of moral scrutiny whole areas of social interaction that have been removed from international relations by the moral scepticism of the realists and the moral principles implied in the idea of international society. There are two main orientations within the cosmopolitan approach: they might conveniently be termed the philosophical and the non-philosophical.

Within the philosophical category there have been several attempts to build upon Rawls' work on distributive justice [120]. Rawls' ideas and arguments are very comlex and cannot really be summarized briefly, but he attempts to present a more generalized conception of justice which moves the ideas of the social contract found in Locke, Rousseau and Kant to a higher level of abstraction. He proposes the ideas of the hypothetical contract, the original position and the 'veil of ignorance', in which each individual knows the state of society, but does not know his or her place within it and must decide in agreement with all other members of society what principles, norms and rules are to guide behaviour. The result, Rawls argues, would be distributive justice in society. Inequalities would be justifiable only if they produced benefits for the whole of society. Discussions of the applicability of Rawls' ideas to IR can be found in Barry [4], Brewin [in 37], Smith [in 114], Danielson [34], Scanlon [124] and Amdur [1], among others.

Beitz [5] has made one of the most ambitious attempts to apply Rawls' ideas to IR. He criticizes the views of moral scepticism and the 'morality of state' and goes on to argue that relations among nations ought to be constrained by a principle of distributive justice. There are multiple and extensive forms of international social activity which occur both in the context of the state and beyond it, and they produce costs and benefits that would not otherwise exist. As a result, he argues, it is irrational not to have a principle to guide the distribution of the benefits and burdens of social activity. It is equally irrational not to have a principle to guide the distribution of natural resources. Importantly, the global distributive principles that Beitz has in mind apply ultimately to the individual and not the state. These principles, Beitz argues, form a *prima facie* warrant for practical efforts at structural and distributive reforms.

A second ambitious example of the philosophical approach can be seen in Shue [127]. Shue maintains that there are a set of economic rights that are as basic as civil and political rights. He argues that the logic and structure of the argument which supports security as a basic right (i.e. no other rights can be enjoyed unless it is guaranteed) holds true for food, health, political participation and freedom of movement. Shue rejects the notion that there are positive rights and negative rights, and argues that the primary duty of the state is to act to secure the basic rights of all men? These basic rights also imply certain duties, such as avoiding depriving others, protecting others from deprivation and aiding the deprived. As a result, the recognition of subsistence rights at the international level implies significant duties for the developed world in regard to the less developed world and, as Beitz argues, requires structural reforms.

Another, rather different example of the philosophical approach can be found in Linklater [86] who, in many ways, represents a merger between the classical and cosmopolitan approaches. He develops an ethical theory of IR by highlighting the dichotomy between our identity and obligations as citizens and those as part of the community of mankind. He argues that our identity as citizens must always be subordinate to our identity as part of mankind.

The debate between the cosmopolitan approach and the realist and classical approaches represents one of the most significant in IR to date. The nature and flavour of this debate can be seen in Walzer [142, 144], Luban [89], Doppelt [38] and the other contributions in Brown & Shue [16], as well as by comparing Hoffmann [62], Hare & Joynt [58] or Tucker [140] with Beitz or Shue.

The non-philosophical orientation of the cosmopolitan approach can best be seen in the Brandt Reports [10, 11], the work of the World Order Models Project [6, 44, 46, 82, 98] and in the peace research work of authors such as Galtung [51]. It is also implied in the world society/human needs approach of Burton [23, 24, 25], though the world society paradigm has yet to examine and articulate clearly its normative presuppositions. The work of Rawls, Beitz and Shue may offer a sound philosophical basis from which to start.

Conclusions

As Banks has noted in Chapter 1, thinking about international relations necessarily entails some kind of theorizing (implicit or explicit) about world society. The same can be said with regard to normative theory: each kind of theory (realism, pluralism or structuralism) necessarily involves some conception (implicit or explicit) of the place and role of normative theory within it.

As this chapter has shown, it is possible to point to a progression of sorts in normative approaches to IR: from the legal, 'peace through law' approach of the inter-war period, to the realist and classical approaches of the post-war period, through to the cosmopolitan approach which started to develop in the late 1970s and early 1980s as the discipline became cogniscent of and concerned with issues such as human rights and the economic inequalities in world society. It is not simply a coincidence that this progression in normative approaches broadly coincides with the movement in IR theory outlined by Banks. Nor is it coincidence that the cosmopolitan approach has developed roughly at the same time a the rise of alternative perspectives to realism (see Chapter 5). In many ways the sources of both are the same – a questioning of the continued relevance of the dominant paradigm. It is clear that normative concerns have a continued relevance in the present global situation and therefore in the study of IR. Given the range of subjects dealt with by IR, it might be said that it is impossible to have a comprehensive theory of IR which does not incorporate and account for the normative aspects of world society.

Bibliography to Chapter 2

1. Amdur, R. 'Rawls' Theory of Justice: Domestic and International Perspectives'. *World Politics*, vol. XXIX, no. 3, pp. 438–61.
2. Aron, R. *Peace and War: A Theory of International Relations.* Melbourne, FL, Krieger, 1981 and London, Weidenfeld & Nicholson, 1967.
3. Bailey, S. *Prohibitions and Restraints in War.* London & New York, Oxford University Press, 1972.
4. Barry, B. *The Liberal Theory of Justice: A Critical Examination of the Principal Doctrines in 'A Theory of Justice' by John Rawls.* New York & Oxford, Clarendon Press, 1971.
5. Beitz, C.R. *Political Theory and International Relations.* Princeton, NJ & Guildford, Princeton University Press, 1979.

6. Beres, L.R. *People, States and World Order*. Itasca, IL, Peacock Press, 1981.
7. Best, G. *Humanity in Warfare*. London, Weidenfeld & Nicholson and New York, Columbia University Press, 1980.
8. Blake, N. & Pole, K. (eds), *Dangers of Deterrence: Philosophers on Nuclear Strategy*. London & Boston, Routledge & Kegan Paul, 1983.
9. _____ *Objections to Nuclear Defence: Philosophers on Nuclear Deterrence*. London & Boston, Routledge & Kegan Paul, 1984.
10. The 'Brandt Commission' I. Report of the Independent Commission on International Development Issues. *North-South: A Programme for Survival*. London, Pan and Cambridge, MA. MIT Press, 1980.
11. The 'Brandt Commission' II. Report of the Independent Commission on International Development Issues. *Common Crisis*. London, Pan and Cambridge, MA, MIT Press, 1983.
12. Brierly, J.L. *The Basis of Obligation in International Law*. Oxford & New York, Clarendon Press, 1959.
13. _____ *The Law of Nations*. Oxford & New York, Clarendon Press, 1963.
14. _____ *The Outlook for International Law*. Oxford & New York, Clarendon Press, 1944.
15. Brown, P.G. & Maclean, D. *Human Rights and US Foreign Policy*. Lexington, MA, Lexington Books, 1982 (distributed in the UK by Gower, Aldershot).
16. Brown, P.G. & Shue, H. (eds), *Boundaries: National Autonomy and its Limits*. Totowa, NJ, Rowman & Littlefield, 1982 (distributed in the UK by Costello, Tunbridge Wells).
17. Brownlie, I. *Basic Documents on Human Rights*. Oxford & New York, Clarendon Press, 1971.
18. _____ *International Law and the Use of Force by States*. Oxford & New York, Clarendon Press, 1963.
19. Buergenthall, T. & Hall, J.H. (eds), *Human Rights, International Law and the Helsinki Accords*. Monteclaire, NJ, Allanheld, Osman & Co., 1977 (distributed in the UK by Costello, Tunbridge Wells).
20. Bull, H.N. *The Anarchical Society: A Study of World Order*. London, Macmillan and New York, Columbia University Press, 1977.
21. _____ 'International theory: the case for the classical approach'. *World Politics*, vol. XVIII, no. 3, 1966 pp. 361–77.
22. _____ 'Order vs Justice in International Society'. *Political Studies*, vol. 19, no. 3, 1971, pp. 269–83.
23. Burton, J.W. *Dear Survivors*. London, Frances Pinter and Boulder, CO, Westview, 1983.
24. _____ *Deviance, Terrorism and War: The Process of Solving Unsolved Social and Political Problems*. Oxford, Martin Robertson and New York, St. Martin's, 1979.
25. _____ *World Society*. London & New York, Cambridge University

Press, 1972.
26. Butterfield, H. *Christianity, Diplomacy and War*. London, Epsworth Press, 1953.
27. _____ 'The Scientific vs the Moralistic Approach to International Affairs'. *International Affairs*, vol. 27, no. 4, pp. 411–22.
28. Butterfield, H. & Wight, M. (eds), *Diplomatic Investigations: Essays in the Theory of International Politics*. London, Allen & Unwin and Cambridge, MA, Harvard University Press, 1966.
29. Carr, E.H. *The Twenty Years Crisis, 1919–1939*. London, Macmillan, 1981 and New York, Harper & Row, 1964.
30. Clark, I. *Reform and Resistance in the International Order*. London & New York, Cambridge University Press, 1980.
31. _____ 'World Order Reform and Utopian Thought: A Contemporary Watershed'. *Review of Politics*, vol. 41, no. 1, 1979, pp. 96–120.
32. Cohen, M. *et al.* (eds), *War and Moral Responsibility*. Princeton, NJ & Guildford, Princeton University Press, 1974.
33. Corbett, P.E. *Law and Society in the Relations of States*. New York, Harcourt, Brace, 1951.
34. Danielson, P. 'Theories, Intuitions and the Problem of World-Wide Distributive Justice'. *Philosophy of the Social Sciences*, vol. 3, no. 4, 1973, pp. 331–40.
35. d'Entreves, A.P. *Natural Law*. London & Orleans, MA, Hutchinson, 1970.
36. Donelan, M.D. 'The Grotian Image of War'. *Millennium: Journal of International Studies*, vol. 12, no. 3, 1983, pp. 233–43.
37. _____ (ed.) *The Reason of States: A Study in International Political Theory*. London & Winchester, MA, Allen & Unwin, 1978.
38. Doppelt, G. 'Walzer's Theory of Morality in International Affairs'. *Philosophy and Public Affairs*, vol. 3, no. 1, pp. 1–26.
39. Falk, R.A. 'The domains of Law and Justice'. *International Journal*, vol. 31, no. 1, 1975–6, pp. 1–18.
40. _____ *Human Rights and State Sovereignty*. New York & London, Holmes & Meier, 1980.
41. _____ *The International Law of Civil War*. Princeton, NJ & Guildford, Princeton University Press, 1971.
42. _____ *Legal Order in a Violent World*. Princeton, NJ & Guildford, Princeton University Press, 1968.
43. _____ *The Status of Law in International Society*. Princeton, NJ & Guildford, Princeton University Press, 1970.
44. _____ *A Study of Future Worlds*. New York, Free Press and London, Collier-Macmillan, 1975.
45. _____ (ed.) *The Vietnam War and International Law* (4 volumes). Princeton, NJ & Guildford, Princeton University Press, 1965, 1968, 1969, 1972.
46. Falk, R.A. & Black, C. (eds), *The Future of the International Legal Order:*

Trends and Patterns. Princeton, NJ & Guildford, Princeton University Press, 1969.

47.   Falk, R.A. *et al.* (eds), *Studies on a Just World Order* (2 volumes). Boulder, CO, Westview Press, 1982, 1983 (distributed in the UK by Bowker, Epping).

48.   Ferenez, B. (ed.) *Defining International Aggression: The Search for Peace* (2 volumes). Dobbs Ferry, NY, Oceana Publications, 1976.

49.   Friedman, L. (ed.) *The Law of War* (2 volumes). New York, Random House, 1968.

50.   Friedmann, W. *The Changing Structure of International Law*. New York & Guildford, Columbia University Press, 1964.

51.   Galtung, J. *The True Worlds: A Transnational Perspective*. New York, Free Press and London, Collier-Macmillan International, 1980.

52.   Garnett, J.C. *Commonsense and the Theory of International Politics*. London, Macmillan and New York, State University of New York Press, 1984.

53.   Gierke, O. *Natural Law and the Theory of Society: 1500–1800* (translated by E. Baker). Boston, Beacon Press, 1957.

54.   Good, R.C. National Interest and Moral Theory: The 'Debate' Among Contemporary Political Theorists. In *Foreign Policy in the Sixties: The Issue and the Instruments*, ed. R. Hilsman & R.C. Good. Baltimore & London, Johns Hopkins University Press, 1965.

55.   Goodwin, G. & Taylor, K. *The Politics of Utopia: A Study in Theory and Practice*. London, Hutchinson and New York, St. Martin's, 1982.

56.   Goodwin, G. (ed.) *Ethics and Nuclear Deterrence*. London, Croom Helm and New York, St. Martin's, 1982.

57.   Greenwood, C. 'The Relationship between *ius ad bellum* and *ius en bello*'. *British Review of International Studies*, vol. 9, no. 3, 1983, pp. 221–34.

58.   Hare, J.E. & Joynt, C.B. *Ethics and International Affairs*. London, Macmillan and New York, St. Martin's, 1982.

59.   Held, V. *et al.* (eds), *Philosophy, Morality and International Affairs*. Oxford & New York, Oxford University Press, 1974.

60.   Herz, J.H. *International Politics in the Atomic Age*. New York, Columbia University Press, 1962.

61.   _____ *Political Realism and Political Idealism: A Study of Theories and Realities*. Chicago, Chicago University Press, 1951.

62.   Hoffmann, S. *Duties Beyond Borders: On the Limits and Possibilities of Ethical International Politics*. Syracuse, NY, Syracuse University Press, 1981.

63.   _____ *The State of War: Essays in the Theory and Practice of International Politics*. New York, Praeger, 1965 and London, Pall Mall, 1966.

64.   Holsti, K.J. *International Politics: A Framework for Analysis*. Englewood Cliffs, NJ & London, Prentice-Hall International, 1983.

65. Howard, M. Ethics and Power in International Politics. In *The Causes of War*, ed. M. Howard. London, Temple & Smith and Cambridge, MA, Harvard University Press, 1983.

66. *International Organization*. Symposium on the New Realism. Vol. 38, no. 2, 1984, pp. 225–328.

67. *International Studies Quarterly*. Symposium in Honour of Hans J. Morgenthau. Vol. 25, no. 2, 1981, pp. 182–241.

68. James, A. (ed.) *The Bases of International Order*. London & New York, Oxford University Press, 1973.

69. Jenks, C.W. *The Common Law of Mankind*. London, Stevens and New York, Praeger, 1958.

70. Jessup, P.C. *A Modern Law of Nations*. New York, Macmillan, 1948.

71. _____ *The Uses of International Law*. Ann Arbor, MI, University of Michigan Law School, 1959.

72. Johnson, J.T. *Just War Tradition and the Restraint of War*. Princeton, NJ & Guildford, Princeton University Press, 1981.

73. Johnstone, D.M. The Foundations of Justice in International Law. In *The International Law and Policy of Human Welfare*, ed. R.J. Macdonald *et al.* Rockville, MD & The Hague, Sijthoff & Noardhoff, 1978.

74. Jones, R.E. 'The English School of International Relations: A Case for Closure'. *British Review of International Studies*, vol. 7, no. 1, 1981, pp. 1–13.

75. Kelsen, H. *General Theory of Law and States*. Cambridge, MA, Harvard University Press and Oxford, Oxford University Press, 1945.

76. _____ *Principles of International Law* (revised and edited by R.W. Tucker). New York, Holt, Rinehart and Winston, 1976.

77. Kennan, G.F. Ethics and Foreign Policy: An Approach to the Problem. In *Foreign Policy and Morality: A Framework for a Moral Audit* ed. T.M. Hesburgh & L.J. Halle. New York, Council for International Relations, 1979.

78. _____ 'Foreign Policy and Christian Conscience'. *Atlantic Monthly*, vol. 203, no. 5, 1959, pp. 44–9.

79. _____ *Realities of American Foreign Policy*. Princeton, NJ & Guildford, Princeton University Press, 1954.

80. Kissinger, H.A. *The White House Years*. Boston, Little, Brown and London, Weidenfeld & Nicholson, 1979.

81. _____ *The Years of Upheaval*. London, Weidenfeld & Nicholson and Michael Joseph and Boston, Little, Brown, 1983.

82. Kothar, A. *Footsteps in the Future: Diagnosis of the Present World and a Design for the Future*. New York, Free Press and London, Collier-Macmillan, 1974.

83. Lauterpacht, H. *The Functions of Law in the International Community*. Oxford, Clarendon Press and Toronto, Carswell, 1933.

84. _____ *International Law: Being the Collected Papers of Hersch Lauterpacht* (Edited by E. Lauterpacht, 4 volumes). Cambridge & New

York, Cambridge University Press, 1977.

85. _____ *International Law and Human Rights*. London, Stevens and New York, Praeger, 1950.

86. Linklater, A. *Men and Citizens in the Theory of International Relations*. London, Macmillan and New York, St. Martin's, 1981.

87. Lippman, W. *The Public Philosophy*. London, Hamilton and Boston, Little, Brown, 1955.

88. Luard, E. *Types of International Society*. Oxford, Oxford University Press and New York, Free Press, 1976.

89. Luban, D. 'The Romance of the Nation-State'. *Philosophy and Public Affairs*, vol. 9, no. 3, 1980, pp. 392-7.

90. McDougall, M.S. *et al.*, *Human Rights and World Public Order: The Basic Policies of an International Law of Human Dignity*. New Haven & London, Yale University Press, 1961.

91. _____ *Studies in World Public Order*. New Haven & London, Yale University Press, 1960.

92. McDougall, M.S. & Feliciano, F. *Law and Minimum World Public Order: The Legal Regulation of International Coercion*. New Haven & London, Yale University Press, 1961.

93. McMahan, J. *British Nuclear Weapons: For and Against*. London, Junction Books, 1981.

94. Manning, C.A.W. *The Nature of International Society*. London, Macmillan, 1975.

95. Manual, F.E. & Manual, F.P. *Utopian Thought in the Western World*. Oxford, Blackwell and Cambridge, MA, Harvard University Press, 1979.

96. Mayall, J. (ed.) *The Community of States: A Study in International Political Theory*. London & Winchester, MA, Allen & Unwin, 1983.

97. Melzer, Y. *Concepts of Just War*. Leyden, Sijthoff, 1975.

98. Mendlovitz, S. (ed.) *On the Creation of a Just World Order: Preferred Worlds for the 1990s*. New York, Free Press and London, Collier-Macmillan, 1977.

99. Midgley, E.B.F. *The Natural Law Tradition and the Theory of International Relations*. London, Elek, 1975.

100. Morgenthau, H.J. *Dilemmas of Politics*. Chicago & London, Chicago University Press, 1958.

101. _____ *In Defence of the National Interest*. Lanham, MA, University Press of America, 1983.

102. _____ 'The Mainsprings of American Foreign Policy: The National Interest vs. Moral Abstractions'. *American Political Science Review*, vol. XXXXIV, no. 4, 1950, pp. 849-590.

103. _____ *Politics among Nations: The Struggle for Power and Peace*. New York, Alfred Knopf, 1985.

104. _____ *Scientific Man vs Power Politics*. Chicago & London, Chicago University Press, 1946.

105. _____ 'The Twilight of International Morality'. *Ethics*, vol. 56, no. 1, 1948, pp. 77–99.
106. Nardin, T. *Law, Morality and the Relations of States*. Princeton, NJ & Guildford, Princeton University Press, 1983.
107. Navari, C. *The Condition of States: A Study in International Political Theory*. London, forthcoming.
108. Nicholson, P.P. 'Philosophical Idealism and International Politics: A Reply to Dr. Savigear'. *British Journal of International Studies*, vol. 2, no. 1, 1976, pp. 76–83.
109. Niebuhr, R. *Christian Realism and Political Problems*. London, Faber, 1954 and New York, Kelley, 1969.
110. _____ *Moral Man and Immoral Society*. New York & London, Charles Scribner & Sons, 1932.
111. Osgood, R. & Tucker, R.W. *Force, Order and Justice*. Baltimore, Johns Hopkins University Press, 1967.
112. Paskins, B. Prohibitions, Restraints and Scientists. In *Explorations in Ethics and International Relations*, ed. N.A. Sims. London, Croom Helm and New York, St. Martin's, 1981.
113. Paskins, B. & Dockrill, M. *The Ethics of War*. London, Duckworth and Minneapolis, University of Minnesota Press, 1979.
114. Pettman, R. (ed.) *Moral Claims in World Affairs*. London, Croom Helm and New York, St. Martin's Press, 1979.
115. Porter, B. (ed.) *The Aberystwyth Papers: International Politics 1919–1969*. London & New York, Oxford University Press, 1972.
116. Ramsey, P. *Deeds and Rules in Christian Ethics*. Lanham, MA, University Press of America and Cambridge, Cambridge University Press, 1983.
117. _____ *The Just War: Force and Political Responsibility*. Lanham, MA, University Press of America and Cambridge, Cambridge University Press, 1983.
118. _____ A Political Ethics Context for Strategic Thinking. In *Strategic Thinking and Its Moral Implications*, ed. M.A. Kaplan. Chicago & London, Chicago University Press, 1973.
119. _____ *War and the Christian Conscience*. Cambridge, Cambridge University Press and Durham, NC, Duke University Press, 1961.
120. Rawls, J. *A Theory of Justice*. Oxford & New York, Clarendon Press, 1972.
121. Roberts, A. & Guelff, A. (eds), *Documents on the Laws of War*. Oxford & New York, Clarendon Press, 1982.
122. Robertson, A.H. *Human Rights in the World*. Manchester, Manchester University Press, 1972.
123. Savigear, P. 'Philosophical Idealism and International Politics: Bosanquet, Treischke and War'. *British Journal of International Studies*, vol. 1, no. 1, 1975, pp. 48–59.
124. Scanlon, T. 'Rawls' Theory of Justice'. *University of Pennsylvania Law*

44 *Mark J. Hoffman*

Review, vol. 121, no. 5, 1973, pp. 1020–69.

125. Schwarzenberger, G. *Frontiers of International Law*. London, Stevens, and Dobbs Ferry, NY, Oceana, 1962.

126. _____ *Power Politics: A Study of World Society*. London, Stevens, 1964.

127. Shue, H. *Basic Rights*. Princeton, NJ & Guildford, Princeton University Press, 1980.

128. Sigmund, P.E. *The Natural Law Tradition in Political Thought*. Lanham, MA, University Press of America, 1983.

129. Spegele, R.D. 'On Evaluative Political Realism'. *Millennium: Journal of International Studies*, vol. 14, no. 1, 1985, pp. 39–63.

130. Stern, G. Morality and International Order. In *Bases of International Order*, ed. A. James. Oxford & New York, Oxford University Press, 1973.

131. Suganami, H. 'A Normative Enquiry in International Relations: The Case of "pacta sunt servanda" '. *British Review of International Studies*, vol. 9, no. 1, 1983, pp. 35–54.

132. Taylor, T. Utopianism. In *International Relations: British and American Perspectives*, ed. S. Smith. London & New York, Blackwell, 1985.

133. _____ (ed.) *Approaches and Theory in International Relations*. London & New York, Longman, 1978.

134. Thompson, K.W. 'Beyond National Interests: A Critical Evaluation of Reinhold Niebuhr's Theory of International Politics'. *Review of Politics*, vol. 18, no. 2, 1955, pp. 167–88.

135. _____ *Christian Ethics and the Dilemmas of Foreign Policy*. Lanham, MA, University Press of America, 1983.

136. _____ *Morality and Foreign Policy*. Lanham, MA, University Press of America, 1983.

137. _____ *Political Realism and the Crisis in World Politics*. Lanham, MA, University Press of America, 1983.

138. _____ 'Power, Force and Diplomacy'. *Review of Politics*, vol. 44, no. 4, 1981, pp. 410–35.

139. _____ Theory and International Studies in the Cold War. In *Theory of International Relations: The Crisis of Relevance*, ed. A. Said. Englewood Cliffs, NJ & Hemel Hempstead, Prentice-Hall, 1968.

140. Tucker, R.W. *The Inequality of Nations*. New York, Basic Books and Oxford, Martin Robertson, 1977.

141. Waltz, K.N. *Theory of International Politics*. Reading, MA & London, Addison-Wesley, 1979.

142. Walzer, M. The Distribution of Membership. In *Boundaries: National Autonomy and Its Limits*, eds. P.G. Brown & H. Shue. Totowa, NJ, Rowman & Littlefield, 1981.

143. _____ *Just and Unjust Wars: A Moral Argument with Historical Illustrations*. New York, Basic Books, 1977 and Harmondsworth, Middx., Penguin, 1980.

144. _____ 'The Moral Standing of States: A Reply to Four Critics'. *Philosophy and Public Affairs*, vol. 9, no. 2, 1980, pp. 209–29.
145. Wasserstrom, R. (ed.) *War and Morality*. Belmont, CA, Wadsworth, 1970.
146. Wells, D.A. 'How Much Can the "Just War" Justify?' *Journal of Philosophy*, vol. 66, no. 4, 1969, pp. 819–29.
147. Wight, M. *Power Politics*. Leicester, Leicester University Press and New York, Holmes & Meier, 1978.
148. _____ (ed. H.N. Bull) *Systems of States*. Leicester, Leicester University Press and Atlantic Highlands, NJ, Humanities Press, 1978.
149. Williams, B. *Morality: An Introduction to Ethics*. New York, Harper & Row, 1972 and Harmondsworth, Middx, Penguin, 1973.
150. Wolfers, A. *Discord and Collaboration: Essays in International Politics*. Baltimore, Johns Hopkins University Press, 1966.

* I am indebted to Hidemi Suganami for clarifying my thoughts on this material.

3 World Society and Human Needs

J.W. Burton

Center for International Development, University of Maryland and CAC

Introduction

In the study and application of conflict resolution in international society we are currently facing a shift from one conceptual framework to another. A new science of international conflict resolution is evolving. While it is now well articulated in several texts, there is not yet a library of books that focus exclusively on the subject since the books are scattered over many disciplines, and sometimes touch upon some particular aspect of the subject. For example, in a world system of multi-ethnic societies, clearly ethnicity is an important topic for conflict resolution. References to it are in sociology and anthropology, but are not dealing with conflict resolution as such. This means that librarians are not in a position to group together relevant books. There is not, in this sense, a separate and self-contained discipline.

There is, nevertheless, a distinctive thought system which represents a paradigm shift of a fundamental kind. While its roots historically are in international relations (IR), the study of conflict resolution represents a distinctive departure from power balances and the defensive and deterrent strategies associated with traditional IR. The emphasis is on the analysis of the human needs and interests of those concerned in a particular conflict situation, and the means of satisfying them.

In discussions of the conceptual nature of IR generally, and the means of dealing with problems of conflict within the global society, there are those who plead for, and teach within, a liberal approach that includes all contending theories. This is a characteristic of a transition stage from one paradigm or thought system to another: until a consensus has developed there is a tendency to entertain contending approaches to a subject, dwelling on what are claimed to be the strengths and weaknesses of each.

However, the power or coercive approach to IR, articulated within a framework of law and order, cannot any longer be sustained as an adequate explanation of behaviour at this level, and does not provide a basis for conflict resolution, as Banks has recently argued [in 5]. An understanding of relations between states and the practice of conflict resolution require an analytical approach. The power theories of behaviour are simplistic in the extreme. They make possible only description, for they take no account of the hidden data of motivation and intent that give rise to the employment of power. They do not provide a basis for conflict resolution which requires a process which uncovers fundamental goals, in addition to perceived interests, so that there can be an exploration of options that meet the needs of all parties.

The discipline has now to unburden itself of past theories. 'Liberalism' in these conditions reflects a misunderstanding of what has been happening in the last twenty years in the interdisciplinary studies of IR and conflict resolution.

Some shift in thought in IR theory has occurred in recent years and this has been promoted to a large degree by recent experience with conflict resolution. It is the handling of particular cases that draws attention to hidden behavioural data that traditional IR theory has missed. Events data that have been tracked for a period of years have shown patterns of behaviour that cannot be explained in power terms, and have drawn attention to behavioural reasons why conflicts persist [Azar, in 5]. Reports on particular conflict situations that have been dealt with by conflict resolution processes point to similarities between conflicts, in particular the similarity of the behavioural motivations that drive nations to war [Azar, in 5]. This, in turn, has made possible a theory of conflict resolution [Burton, in 5]. In this way the findings on conflict have begun to feed back into IR theory, making possible a better understanding of situations such as Sri Lanka, Cyprus, the Middle East and East–West relations, and of international society generally.

It is argued in this chapter that the shift in thought that has taken place is characterized by a shift from the state and its power as the unit of analysis, to the identity group to which the individual owes allegiance. Nation-states may be identity groups, but in modern conditions of multi-ethnic states this is rarely the case. If the identity group is taken as the unit of explanation of relations between states, then it follows that the sources of conflict at the international level are likely to be within states. Situations such as exist in Cyprus and

Lebanon spill over into the international system. This has recently been argued by Burton in the context of Soviet–US relations [7].

In the consideration of a bibliography or a teaching syllabus, science should not give way to some desire for social harmony among scholars. The liberal approach would, clearly, enable us to present an extensive bibliography on conflict resolution, its origins and its points of departure from traditional thinking. Such an approach still prevails in the teaching of IR and conflict management. Unfortunately it leaves it to students to make up their own minds when teachers have not been able to come to grips with realities and to break away from classical and academically safe thinking. This does no service to thought, to students or to the practical tasks of resolving international and inter-communal conflicts. Where data and logic lead, we must follow, regardless of the response of those who are wedded to traditional thought and practice.

In this chapter previous thinking and processes regarding conflict resolution are termed 'settlement' approaches. They are dealt with only in so far as it is necessary to refer to them in an exposition of 'resolution' processes. We are not dealing with some overlapping notions, but with a new set of ideas and assumptions. This is the nature of the paradigm shift. It has a history, it relates to the past; but it produces an integrated theory which is self-contained and self-explanatory.

The Problem of Language

Any conceptual development necessarily creates problems of language. The sharp differences that are present and which need to be articulated, are not readily communicated because the same terms are often used in the two distinctive thought systems. For example, the term *conflict resolution* is still used even when conventional enforced settlement is being discussed. *Mediation* is used to mean both third-party interventions designed to impose a settlement, and those that seek to facilitate direct interactions between parties. *Negotiation* is used to cover not only bargaining, but also problem-solving outside any power framework. When a new paradigm emerges a new language is required to describe the new conceptual notions requiring a special jargon. It is more convenient to use existing terms, while giving them special meanings. This is why we make a distinction between 'settlement' and 'resolution', two terms that have mostly been used interchangeably.

The Nature of Conflict

The term 'conflict' itself needs clarification. Here we are concerned with conflict that has significant implications for world society and global peace. The term is used usually for the range of arguments, tensions and violent conflicts that occur both within and between societies. However, there are some important differences between ordinary social interactions and conflicts involving fundamental values. It would be convenient to have different terms to describe the ordinary tensions in life that are regarded as conflictual, and the kind of violent conflict which is our concern here. Otherwise we are led, as many have been, to make the trite observation that there is always conflict in all societies and that therefore the problem that concerns us is to find means of managing conflict generally. We totally reject this broad definition of conflict. At the international level and inter-state levels we are not dealing with conflicts that may be subject to law enforcement and legal determination. We are dealing with issues for which men and women are prepared to give their lives, and to use against others weapons of mass destruction. We do not have separate terms and, therefore, must always be aware of the meaning that is being given to 'conflict', taking care not to be led into the trap of treating all these different forms of conflict as being the same phenomenon.

The difference between ordinary day-to-day tensions in relationships at all levels, from the family to the state, and conflict is an important one to make. It is no less important to understand that there are high levels of conflict at all social levels, from the family to the state. In traditional theory there has been a distinction made between conflict at different social levels. International conflict is said to be different in kind from conflict at other social levels. We have now moved to the belief that high levels of conflict at all levels have some common features when they touch upon the needs and values that are an inherent part of the human and social organism. There is something in common between the behaviour of the individual who defies social norms because of his inherent needs that must be satisfied, and the behaviour of social groups that are prepared to defy the wider society, even at great cost, in the pursuit of their goals. In neither case can there be settlement imposed by courts or by the state. In both cases some other process is required if the conflict is to be resolved.

In short, we are making a clear distinction between, on the one hand, *forms* of conflict and *levels* of conflict. Traditional thinking in IR has focussed on levels of analysis, and has ignored the issues at stake. At all levels, including the international, there are conflicts of interests which can be negotiated, mediated, subjected to judicial determination and bargained over. At all levels there are also conflicts involving needs and values which cannot be compromised, traded or repressed.

The distinction between interests that can be negotiated or even denied, and needs that are ontological to the human species and which can neither be traded nor suppressed, differentiates two meanings of the term 'conflict'. Traditional means of settlement may be appropriate in conflicts of interest (subject to reservations), but they are unlikely to be relevant or effective in dealing with conflicts involving human needs.

Another distinction must be drawn in defining conflict. Conflicts involve interests and needs. They also involve tactics. War is a tactic to achieve interests or needs. Frequently conflicts are defined in terms of tactics and the underlying interests or needs remain beneath the surface. In industrial relations, wage demands sometimes disguise dissatisfaction with management. Wages are then negotiated instead of working conditions. In international relations, disputes over territory or boundaries sometimes relate to anxieties over security or values attached to ethnic identity, and are negotiated or give rise to wars without the underlying problems being addressed. The resolution of conflict requires processes that reveal hidden motivations and intentions so that underlying issues, which usually remain hidden in power-bargaining and adversary behaviour, become clear.

This distinction between tactics, interests and needs has important implications for resolution processes and for those researching and practising conflict settlement and resolution. Fisher, for example, adopting a legal approach, seeks to improve bargaining techniques, believing that settlement and resolution can be combined in processes by which parties amend draft agreements which are sometimes prepared by a third party or mediator [10]. Others, like Kelman, adopt a problem-solving approach which is analytical, in which the third party assists in analysis without putting proposals forward and in which options that satisfy both parties are explored [14]. These two approaches have been divergent. The distinction between conflicts of interest and conflicts over needs clarifies the separate roles of each approach. It must be emphasized, however, that conflicts of interests are likely to have underlying deeper issues that do not appear in a bargaining or negotiating situation.

The Unit of Explanation

Traditional IR scholars are suspicious of any reference to human needs and the psychological dimensions of behaviour. Their unit of explanation of events in world society is the state. For purposes of explanation they place particular emphasis on the power of the state. The addition of a psychological or an anthropological dimension threatens their model. Events such as the US defeats in Vietnam, Iran and Lebanon, and the Soviet stalemate in Afghanistan, are treated as anomalies rather than an indication that the power model has failed. However, the empirical evidence is building up: the power model makes it difficult to explain why great powers prove ultimately to be impotent giants creating problems for, and even destroying, smaller states, but without resolving conflicts.

The concept of human needs, and especially the need for identity, leads to a different explanation of events in world society. The notion of power as the controlling element in world society is not discarded, but its location is changed. Effective power does not reside in the state as such, but in identity groups. At some stage of history the city state may have been an identity group. However, in the modern world there are few nation-states and few mono-ethnic communities. The community groups in Lebanon, Cyprus or Sri Lanka, are more powerful than the state. It is these with which individuals identify and to which they give their loyalty.

It follows that it is necessary to adopt a global view, not an inter-state view of world society if we are to understand the nature of international conflict. Few conflicts can be described as inter-state. Lebanon, Cyprus, El Salvador, Kampuchea, North and South Korea, are all conflicts of international concern, but they all have domestic components. Moreover, the Soviet–USA conflict has its origins in domestic system failings [7]. The separation of domestic from international, which is a feature of traditional IR studies, has been misleading and has led to false notions of the nature of conflict.

There is probably no phenomenon that can accurately be labelled international conflict that is not a spillover of domestic system failings and domestic politics.

These systems failings and their political manifestations reflect failure to satisfy human needs such as identity, participation and distributive justice and reflect a lack of legitimization of government authority. The unit of explanation of conflict in world society and the locus of power is the identity group within states, sometimes extending across state boundaries.

Needs Theory

Two self-evident observations are relevant. The first is that the human individual has particular capabilities, certain limitations in response and, therefore, certain needs to be secured within the environment for there to be survival. Obvious needs are food and water. However, an important part of survival is growth and development. The new-born can survive only if it develops. The survival-growth mechanism requires an environment that is consistent: without consistent response there can be no learning. A sense of identity of self is required so that the individual can experience separation of self from the environment. It requires a measure of physical security for there to be consistency in response. It must have, therefore, some capability to control the environment for these purposes.

Thus we can deduce that the human organism and human societies have certain needs which must be fulfilled that are social in character and, in terms of species survival, that are at least as important as the so-called 'basic' needs of food and water [Wedge, in 5].

Our second self-evident observation is related. Conflicts of interest or of tactics in the pursuit of these needs can be negotiated, but the pursuit of such needs cannot be suppressed. It is these two self-evident observations that are at the base of the paradigm shift to which we have referred.

The scholar who has made the greatest contribution to needs theory is Sites in a book whose title aptly describes his thesis, *Control: The Basis of Social Order* [21]. He argues that psychologists and political scientists have placed too much stress on the socialization process. The individual cannot be socialized into behaviour that is inconsistent with human needs. These needs are essentially the needs associated with development, identity, recognition, security and all that is implied in these terms. The individual *will*, separately or in association with identity groups, use all possible means and all possible power to control the environment for the purpose of pursuing these needs. The only constraint on this seemingly anarchic behaviour is that the individual and group also have needs for valued relationships with others, for it is through these that security, identity and recognition ultimately are acquired. Social conformity or socialization is limited to that which contributes to valued relationships. Law and order imposed by coercive authorities can be maintained only to the extent that relationships with authorities are valued. Thus pursuit of valued relationships assures loyalty to the identity group – the nation, the community, the ethnic group, or, if circumstances require, a deviant society.

There is one implication of this theory that is of wider significance. Human behaviour cannot be isolated into compartments of life – family, communal, national and global. Needs theory has implications for all aspects of human behaviour, at all social levels. In the IR area it has implications for foreign policy generally, and for strategic policy in particular. Power approaches that locate power in the state are as outmoded as are settlement processes in conflict management.

The Interdisciplinary Literature

It will at once be clear that a bibliography on international conflict resolution must commence with studies traditionally regarded as being outside the scope of IR, such as sociology, anthropology, psychology and even biology [6].

The paradigm shift which has taken place in the study of IR and conflict resolution occurred even earlier in other disciplines and IR now has to catch up. Moreover, there are wide implications in this shift for policy generally.

There is a widespread erosion of authority in all societies, especially where ethnicity and class create divisions. The law and order, coercive and central power paradigm developed under conditions in which there were small communities, war lords who kept order in conditions of feudalism, and clear-cut roles and limited identities. These conditions still persist even in developed societies.

Industrial relations provide one example. However, they have been and are being modified by the persistent pursuit of human needs. They are under direct threat by organized violence wherever they do exist in their early feudal form, as in parts of Latin America. It is this persistent human struggle for control that is so frequently equated with 'communism' in Western societies, despite the fact that the same struggle threatens to disrupt socialist societies when they do not permit the participation necessary to satisfy the drive for achieving identity.

When Gurr writes a book entitled *Why Men Rebel* [13], he is pointing to the inadequacies of the old paradigm by suggesting that there are fundamental reasons for rebellion. Rebellion is not due merely to anti-lawful behaviour for some reason of personal interest or personal deviance from the accepted social norms: it is due to the perception of relative deprivations. But the link forged by observations of reality does not always lead to the kind of shift in basic assumptions which characterizes a paradigm shift. There is evidence of disquiet, but not a move to an alternative explanation of behaviour. There is a literature that reflects dissatisfaction with the old paradigm, without moving out of it. Gurr, for example, relies on distributive justice as the key variable in the explanation of conflict. Davies [8] relies on disappointment in expectations. Both theories would be enriched by being placed within a wider framework of human needs, which includes distributive justice as a component of identity and recognition, and the fulfilment of expectations as a function of consistency in response.

The Community in Politics

These considerations direct our attention to the role of the individual and of identity groups within states. This is an emerging field of interest, thanks to the work of Alger [1]. He stresses how members of any society, far removed from the location of central authorities, participate in international relations in their daily living, through their work in international corporations, their purchase of imported goods and the effect on them of international functional agreements such as the rules which govern aircraft flights. He appeals to ordinary people to explore their environments and ways in which they can influence international relations through greater participation in local government.

Future Developments

It will be seen that the shift in thinking is new and still incomplete. We are using a vocabulary that represents particular concepts within the state-power framework, and something quite different within an identity-power framework. Data have been gathered within the state-power framework. We have counted the number of states, the number of wars that have taken place between states, we have traced the growth of inter-governmental institutions, we have measured GNP and we have statistics on arms expenditures and on weapons. However, we have little data relevant to a needs or identity-group framework. This lack of hard data, reflecting an absence of operational definitions of concepts, inhibits much needed communication and further advances in the science of conflict resolution.

In a needs framework, for example, the notion of legitimacy is central. The degree to which authorities are valued by their electorates reflects the extent to which structures and policies facilitate the pursuit of human needs. We have definitions of legality – effective control and recognition by other states – but we have no definition of legitimacy and no data regarding the number of states that can be regarded as legitimate. If we had, we could predict conflict. The same is true of democracy. In a power framework it means majority government. But is it 'democratic' for a majority ethnic group to impose its values on a minority ethnic group? While we have measures of GNP, we have no measures of the quality of life. There can be high GNP in conditions of severe unemployment among particular age and race groups; there can be inadequate social services, except for those within the reach of the relatively well off; there can be gross inequalities that create a sense of injustice. Then there is the notion of development, which has been defined in narrow economic terms. However, there cannot be development without conditions of peaceful relationships, without political structures and institutions that make possible the development of the individual.

These are the areas in which research is required. As yet few attempts have been made to apply the techniques developed in the 1960s to the emerging paradigm. A start has been made by one US scholar, Azar [2], whose interest in the nature of 'protracted social conflict' has led him to gather data relevant to the ethnic and developmental aspects of conflict.

The Problems of Structure

Inevitably we are led to a consideration of political structures and political institutions, and the degree to which they make possible the fulfilment of human needs. When the USA endeavoured to impose a strong central government in Lebanon to achieve a stable regime, it was acting within a power or coercive framework that defined democracy and law and order in power terms. But it was confronting values that were attached to identity groups, and the need for the security and recognition of cultural differences. For this reason US policy could not succeed. In Cyprus the government of the majority, acting within the traditions of Western political philosophy, sought a political structure that made second class citizens of the Turkish minority and it was doomed to fail. In the Middle East, in Africa, and in the economically developed world, as migrations occur there will be increasing numbers of conflicts within states and across boundaries, as identity groups – which include class groups – seek means of pursuing their security and developmental needs.

Conclusions

Taking human needs as the unit of explanation can be denigrated as being value oriented or an ideological approach. This is not what lies behind a needs approach to world society. We are seeking to discover what the nature of conflict is and the means by which it can be avoided. Experience and theory suggest that conflict cannot be avoided by the exercise of power by authorities within states, or by great powers in the international system. Since domestic and international conflict are one and the same thing, we shall miss the explanation we seek if we have a conception of global politics that is inter-state. We must seek the origins of apparently international conflict in the failings of domestic systems to provide for the needs of peoples. The communist–capitalist conflict between the Soviet Union and its allies and the USA and its allies reflects failings and insecurities in both systems, each blaming the other for its own inadequacies. The legitimacy of authorities is the focus of attention in the new paradigm, not their powers of coercion or defence.

Curriculum and Bibliography

This is the theoretical framework. From this can be deduced a curriculum. The curriculum will determine the relevant bibliography.

We are dealing with a paradigm shift. We are involving students and readers in a new experience. We are asking them to examine their unrecognized assumptions, the hidden assumptions that are in the background when they are thinking about conceptual notions such as democracy, legality and legitimacy, majority government, a world society that is not state-centric, human needs in relation to the right of authorities to govern. A starting point must be about thinking. The works of Kuhn [15], who dealt with intellectual revolutions, and of Popper [19], who emphasized the need for testing by falsification, are relevant. Even more relevant, perhaps, is the work of Peirce [in 16] who argued, unlike Popper, that the original personal hypothesis was of important scientific significance. For students of politics Peirce is central, for rarely can there be realistic testing in politics. Great reliance has to be attached to deductions from the original hypothesis. However, these philosophical issues are dealt with in Chapters 1 and 6.

Thus the ground is prepared for a discussion of some of the many concepts that enter into the theory, such as development, about which Goulet [12] and Azar [4], amongst others, have written. The simplistic economic notion is inadequate: in needs theory, development implies the full development of the individual and identity group, the absence of what Galtung has called 'structural violence' [11]. Then there is the notion of the identity group and its relationship to class and ethnicity, about which Enloe has written [9].

Some consideration of the structures and institutions that frustrate or promote human needs is relevant. The work of Alger is important in this regard [1]. Models of decentralized authority have been neglected, so powerful has been the classical approach which assumed that law and order and peace were best achieved by strong central authorities. Burton [7] has dealt with this to some extent.

Experience shows that once students have grasped the significance of a paradigm shift and have been introduced to the consequent re-conceptualizations, the theoretical framework does not present difficulties. It has been articulated by Burton [6] and by Mitchell [17, 18]. Wedge has written from the point of view of a psychiatrist [22]. Articles and books by Kelman [14] and by Pruitt [20] offer different but related perspectives. There are special aspects that need to be considered, for example the difference between negotiable interests and non-negotiable needs, which Azar has dealt with [3], and the relationship between domestic and international tensions, dealt with by Burton [7]. The processes of conflict resolution are the end point of the curriculum, but this is covered in Chapter 9.

When dealing with human behaviour at any social level, everything relates to everything else. The task is to be selective without destroying the image of the whole. A curriculum should seek to do this. The danger is that a too extensive bibliography can destroy the purposes of the curriculum. Selection is important if there is to be effective communication. However, selection implies a theory. It also implies the view that there is a good deal of past literature, even classical literature, that need not be included in a bibliography about the shift in thinking on world society.

Bibliography to Chapter 3

1. Alger, C. 'Role of People in the Future Global Order'. *Alternatives*, vol. IV, no. 1, 1978, pp. 233–62.
2. Azar, E. 'Peace Amidst Development: A Conceptual Agenda for Conflict and Peace Research'. *International Interactions*, vol. 6, no. 2. 1979, pp. 123–43.
3. _____ 'Theory and Practice of Conflict Resolution'. Paper presented to Council for the Facilitation of International Conflict Resolution, 1984, Center for International Development, University of Maryland.
4. _____ The Theory of Protracted International Conflict and the Challenge of Transforming Conflict Situations. In *Conflict Processes and the Breakdown of International Systems*, ed. D.A. Zinnes. Mirrian Seminar on Research Frontiers, Denver, CO, Denver University Press, 1983.
5. _____ (ed.) *The Theory and Practice of Conflict Resolution*. Brighton, Wheatsheaf and College Park, MD, Center for International Development, University of Maryland, 1985.
6. Burton, J.W. *Deviance, Terrorism and War: The Process of Solving Unsolved Social and Political Problems*. Oxford, Martin Robertson and New York, St. Martin's, 1979.
7. _____ *Global Conflict: The Domestic Sources of International Crisis*. London, Wheatsheaf Books and College Park, MD, Center for International Development, University of Maryland, 1984.
8. Davies, J.C. (ed.) *When Men Revolt and Why*. London, Collier-Macmillan and New York, Free Press, 1971.

9. Enloe, C. *Ethnic Conflict and Political Development*. Boston, Little, Brown, 1973.
10. Fisher, R. *Basic Negotiating Strategy*. London, Allen Lane, 1970. (Published in the USA as *International Conflict for Beginners*, New York, Harper & Row, 1970.)
11. Galtung, J. 'A Structural Theory of Aggression'. *Journal of Peace Research*, vol. 1, no. 2, 1964, pp. 95–119.
12. Goulet, D. *The Cruel Choice*. London & New York, Atheneum, 1973.
13. Gurr, T.R. *Why Men Rebel*. Princeton, NJ & Guildford, Princeton University Press, 1970.
14. Kelman, H.C. The Problem-Solving Workshop in Conflict Resolution. In *Communication in International Politics*, ed. R.L. Merritt. Urbana, IL & London, University of Illinois Press, 1972.
15. Kuhn, T.S. *The Structure of Scientific Revolutions* (International Encyclopaedia of Unified Science). Chicago & London, University of Chicago Press, 1970.
16. Levi, I. Induction in Peirce. In *Science, Belief and Behaviour*, ed. D.H. Mellor. London & New York, Cambridge University Press, 1980.
17. Mitchell, C.R. *Peacemaking and the Consultant's Role*. Farnborough, Hants, Gower and New York, Nichols, 1981.
18. _____ *The Structure of International Conflict*. London, Macmillan and New York, St. Martin's, 1981.
19. Popper, K.R. *The Poverty of Historicism*. London, Routledge & Kegan Paul, 1960 and New York, Harper & Row, 1977.
20. Pruitt, D.G. *Negotiating Behavior*. New York & London, Academic Press, 1982.
21. Sites, P. *Control: The Basis of Social Order*. New York, Associated Faculty Press, 1973.
22. Wedge, B. 'A Psychiatric Model for Intercession in Intergroup Conflict'. *Journal of Applied Behavioral Science*, vol. 6, no. 4, 1971, pp. 733–61.
23. Wilson, E.O. *Sociobiology: The New Synthesis*. Cambridge, MA, & London, Harvard University Press, 1980.

4 Development and Dependency

Chris Brown

University of Kent at Canterbury

Introduction

Apart perhaps from the development of weapons of mass destruction, the most important change in international relations since the Second World War has been the emergence of a greatly enlarged, and for the first time truly global, international system. For the last four hundred years the European state system has gradually extended its control over the whole world; the system remains intact but the agents of its expansion, the European empires, have divided into over a hundred new political entities. Real power has changed in a less dramatic way, but in formal terms the system has been transformed. By using their voting power in the United Nations and elsewhere, the new states have been able to effect a substantial change in the international political agenda. It seems safe to assert that the successful functioning of the international system in the decades ahead will depend on the adequacy of its response to this new situation.

The new agenda centres on the most salient feature of the new international system: the contrast between formal political equality and actual economic inequality. The combination of the socio-economic differences to be found in the modern world with the notion of formal equality is unique to the modern international system. The system has become inclusive, but the reality of the newcomer's membership in the international society lacks meaning in the absence of the political, social and economic resources required for full participation in the political structure. The demands of the 'South' are largely demands that the *political* structure makes a reality of their membership of it, even if the most characteristic form these demands take is for a new international *economic* order. From the perspective of the South, decolonization is an uncompleted process, which must be extended so that political power is genuinely redistributed. First and foremost this redistribution requires a change in the economic conditions prevailing in the South.

This chapter does not address the detailed issues raised by the demands for a New International Economic Order (NIEO), which are outlined and put in the wider context of the politics of contemporary international economic relations in a number of excellent textbooks such as Blake & Walters [17], Spero [64], and Hoogvelt [42]. The concern here is with the impact of the new system on the theory of international relations. How are we to conceptualize relations between the newcomers and the established world order?

Development

What has been said above implies that 'North–South' relations are at least in part antagonistic. Yet in the 1950s when these issues first arose, it was expected that North–South relations would be essentially co-operative. The Southern 'less developed countries' (LDCs) would develop with the assistance of the already developed countries, removing substantial material inequalities. But what constitutes 'development'?

The most convincing and coherent answer to this question came from the American structural–functionalist school, as exemplified by the work of Almond and his associates [1, 2 and 3]. A developed political system is one in which the processes of decision-making are secularized and rationalized, and in which political institutions are structurally differentiated. This process is of course tied up with economic development as Lipset emphasizes [51]. The economic problems of LDCs lie in the combination within each society of a small modern sector and a large traditional sector making them 'dual economies' [50]. Good policy plus economic aid would enable LDCs to enter the *Stages of Economic Growth* [61] and, in particular, reach the 'take-off' point through which the developed Western economies had passed, and after which the impetus to growth would be self-sustaining. Northern countries would assist in this as a public duty and as a concrete act in the fight against communism.

It is clear that this influential body of work takes a number of assumptions about development more or less for granted: that development equals westernization, that the existing 'advanced industrial nations' have arrived and constitute a model for LDCs, and that the end result of the process of development will be the emergence of an homogenous world culture on Western lines. Although later writers have criticized this definition of development as being too tied up with Western-style industrialization, nevertheless the alternative, more spiritually satisfying, definitions of development may be impossible to achieve in the absence of industrialization. Thus the ethnocentrism of orthodox development theorists may be more apparent than real; moreover, its guilt is shared by many of its critics. Although Marxist writing on development in the 1950s was often bitterly critical of this body of work [47], Western bias is equally to be found in the works of Marx and Engels. Marx's stages of economic growth are different (and more subtle) than those of Rostow, but the idea of progress in a quasi-Victorian sense was present in his work – and indeed the Preface to *Capital*, vol. 1 most explicitly suggests that the more advanced countries show the less advanced a picture of their own future [52].

None the less the 1950s concept of development is now widely scorned. Many writers doubt that the Western path is a *desirable* path, and many more doubt that it is a *possible* route to development. The key alternative concept is dependency. It is argued that the commitment to industrialization on a Western model is based on a false assessment of the Western achievement and, moreover, that the mere existence of the developed capitalist economies of the West prevents the LDCs from taking the Western road.

Dependency

There is no single coherent body of thought that can accurately be described as 'dependency theory'. Instead various theories stress the key notion that some countries (or economies) are conditioned in their development by their dependence on other countries (economies), and that this dependence is structural and deeper than the dominance relationship between societies that differ in size, but not in level of socio-economic development. Thus the relationship between Brazil and the United States could be, and usually is, described as dependent, but that between Denmark and West Germany would not be so described. Dependence is different from dominance. This is not simply a question of multinational capital and ownership: it is structure that is crucial. The general notion of dependency subsumes several different theories including (i) dependencia, (ii) centre–periphery analysis, and (iii) world-system analysis.

Dependencia

Dependencia originated in Latin America in the 1950s and 1960s. Given the premise that dominance and exploitation can be sustained without formal Empire and political control, dependency effects, if they exist, are likely to be most visible in Latin America – the oldest of the decolonized areas. The dependencia theorists – or 'dependendistas' – were able to draw upon the experiences of 150 years of formal independence in formulating their ideas. The key role in formulating dependencia was probably played by the UN's Economic Commission for Latin America (ECLA) under the Argentinian economist Raul Prebisch. The ECLA analysis emphasized Latin America's role as a supplier of primary products which it exchanged for the manufactures of the industrial world, and argued that the 'terms of trade' were moving over the long term against primary products. In these circumstances, development could take place only slowly if at all. The ECLA remedy was import substitution industrialization (ISI) – the construction of an industrial base, behind tariff barriers, which would meet the internal need for manufactured products. A brief guide to the work of the ECLA and ISI is Roxborough [62]. A key issue is whether the terms of trade are actually moving against primary products: the most that can be said is that the evidence is inconclusive [17, 64].

While ISI met both the emerging interests of the United States and the 'Alliance for Progress', and fitted in with the position of orthodox communist policy with its emphasis on the alliance of 'progressive' forces against the reactionary feudal interests, the 'dependendistas' argued in the early 1960s that it was demonstrably failing. The essence of the dependencia critique of the ECLA is that ISI cannot work, because the internal market for consumer goods is too limited and the nature of demand is determined by elite tastes oriented to the products of the developed world and because it tends to be based on capital-intensive industries, which have low employment effects and therefore do little to create demand. Moreover, it is based on imported capital goods, components and materials which, therefore, does little to assist the balance of payments and may even cause crises, and it increases dependence on multinational capital and on foreign technology. These arguments are drawn from the work of 'dependendistas' such as Dos Santos, Cardoso and Furtado, and can be found in collections such as Bernstein [15], Wilber [72] as well as in Furtado [39]. The central point is that while the ECLA approach correctly identifies the root of the problem as lying in the position of Latin American economies in the international division of labour, ISI fails to follow through the implications of this position, and leaves the Latin American economies firmly tied to their unfavourable world status. It is this that needs to be changed.

Assessment of the dependencia argument is not easy because, as is also the case with other variants of dependency theory, it is not always possible to work out in advance exactly what sort of evidence would count as refutation or confirmation of the approach. Followers of the 'dependendistas' in the 1960s might be forgiven for assuming that development in Latin American countries was simply impossible, unless some attempt was made to cut their links with the present international division of labour. If so, then the quite remarkable growth rates achieved in, say, Brazil in the late 1960s and most of the 1970s would count as disconfirmation of the theory: however Cardoso [22], Evans [26] and other sympathetic writers such as Kemp [46] argue that this is a case of 'dependent development'. Brazilian economic growth is seen as still dependent on trends in the major industrial countries rather than independently determined; the power relation is unchanged. Possibly so, but how is this to be measured? How can the dependencia position be tested? What counts as *in*dependent development? We will return to this point later, but now turn to a more ambitious and radical version of 'dependencia'.

'Centre-Periphery' Analysis

An early 'dependencia' writer was Frank, whose case studies of Brazil and Chile [27] set the tone for a variant of dependency theory, here called 'centre-periphery' relations, by adding a number of features to the original model.

The key theoretical notion of his earlier work is that of a 'chain of exploitation linking centres and peripheries'. In his vision of the world, the capitalist world economy reaches to the ends of the earth, with the chain of exploitation beginning in the villages of the Andes and reaching to the corporate headquarters of New York and London. Latin American countries do not develop, because this chain drains them of the resources they need for development. Indeed these countries have been 'underdeveloped' over the centuries, their condition deteriorating by comparison with their original '*un*developed' state. Development is achievable only via revolution and a breaking of links with the developed world. The situation is desperate and no limited 'economistic' strategy will work.

The dependendistas had some Marxist roots, but Marxist thought dominates Frank's work (although he denies the label, much in the spirit of Marx's own rejection of the term). His Marxism is heterodox and eclectic and, in spite of his frequent use of Leninist terminology, owes more to Baran's reformulations [12] than to Marxist classics. It is also directed against the official communism of Moscow-line Latin American communist parties of the 1960s. Orthodox Marxism works with a 'stages' model of economic development and sees the mode of production as crucial, which Frank contests. For him Latin America has been 'capitalist' since the sixteenth century and this is the root cause of its underdevelopment. This highly unMarxist notion of capitalism, as Brenner [20] and Laclau [49] have pointed out, defines capitalism as integration in the world division of labour. In classical Marxism, capitalism is 'generalised commodity production' where labour is itself a commodity, and the serf or slave plantations of old Latin America cannot be seen as capitalist simply because they produce for a world market.

The third feature of Frank's work that distinguishes him from the dependencia school is his willingness to generalize beyond Latin America, by attacking orthodox development studies, and by widening his concerns to include the whole of the third world. He accuses the 'development' school of acting as ideological mentors of monopoly capital [36]. He extends and refines his original insights in [32, 33] and provides an historical account of the operation of the world economy over the centuries [31, 37], concentrating on the present in [28, 29, 35]. In his most recent works [30, 34] he again returns to a theoretical defence of his basic position.

Almost as prolific, and developing his argument on the same general lines but from an African base is the Egyptian scholar Amin. He set out a similar centre–periphery analysis in [4, 5, 6, 7, 8]. In the same school, Rodney [59] is valuable, and there are a number of useful collections of Frankian analysis and its critics [54, 58, 55, 23, 24]. Although this analysis does not rest crucially on the ownership of capital, the role of multinational corporations (MNCs) is relevant, and Barnet & Müller [13] and Radice [56] are valuable here.

Frank outlines the fact of exploitation but is unclear on explanation. For Marx, exploitation takes place through the extraction of surplus value, but this answer does not fit centre–periphery relations. The centre is not a capitalist employer of the periphery (although some capitalists of the centre may be via MNCs). Exploitation must take place through 'unequal exchange', but what is 'unequal exchange' given Marx's assumption that commodities exchange at their values? Frank does not answer this, but another important theorist, Emmanuel, does [25]. For Emmanuel wages are the key independent variable. The price at which a product enters the market is largely determined by the wage level that constitutes the historically determined minimum subsistence level in the country of origin. As a result of class struggle, wages are higher in some countries than in others. The effect is that exchanges between high wage and low wage countries work to the benefit of the former. Effectively Emmanuel is elaborating the 'terms of trade' argument of the dependendistas, but in terms of the products of particular (low wage) countries rather than in terms of particular commodities. His account is of great value because almost alone amongst the dependency theorists he provides an explanation rather than a description. But this explanation is not without problems – apart from its questionable empirical basis (see earlier references on terms of trade), his argument leads to the conclusion that the working classes of the centre are the agents and beneficiaries of the exploitation of the peripheries. This is highly unMarxist (see Bettleheim's polemic [16]) and it is also not what the dependency theorists want to say.

World-System Analysis

The third variant of dependency to be examined is termed 'world-system analysis' and is focused on the work of Wallerstein, Director of the Fernand Braudel Center at the State University of New York (SUNY). The Center produces a journal, *Review* [57], and a series of Yearbooks [e.g. 40, 43, 45].

Wallerstein's early career in the sociology of development in Africa led him to develop a critical analysis similar to that of Frank and other centre-periphery theorists of conventional development sociology. This critical analysis can be found in two clear and thought-provoking collections of essays [66, 70], with their distinctive insistence that any account of the present structure of the world economy must be based on a long-run study of the capitalist world system seen as a totality. This insistence characterizes his *magnum opus*, a projected four volume study of *The Modern World System* (MWS) the first two volumes of which have appeared [68, 69].

The MWS is a dense work, rich in scholarly insights. Any attempt to reproduce the argument briefly is doomed to be inadequate. All that will be attempted here is to pick out some important themes. Wallerstein distinguishes between World Empires, hierarchical polities where economic transactions over long distances take the form of tribute, and World Systems, or World Economies, where diverse forms of independent political organizations interact via trade. He argues that a world economy emerged in the 'long' sixteenth century, with the establishment of an international division of labour and core, peripheral and semi-peripheral regions. The emergence of cores, peripheries and semi-peripheries is partly a function of the nature of state structures, strong states having the ability to structure the international division of labour to their own advantage, and partly a question of the form of labour control. Wage labour is characteristic of cores, share cropping of semi-peripheries and forms of slavery or serfdom of peripheries. This threefold pattern has persisted since the sixteenth century through a series of waves of contraction and expansion and a concurrent series of successive 'hegemonies' as Holland, England and the United States have in turn occupied the 'core' role within the structure.

Wallerstein insists that the international political system and the international economic system are two ways of looking at the same thing and, equally, that such categories as 'class', 'nation', 'race' and 'ethnic group' are again different ways of viewing the same phenomena – namely divisions created by the structuring of the world system. This gives a considerable degree of coherence to Wallerstein's analysis, albeit making him argue a rather mechanistic view of the world in which dominant groups alter their strategies in response to changes in the system in seemingly implausibly neat ways. Another strong feature of Wallerstein's analysis is his straightforward approach to Marxist critiques of his position. Dependency theorists are often accused of ignoring the improvements in productivity and overall growth in wealth of the last four centuries. Whereas Frank's response to this is unclear, Wallerstein simply denies that 'development' in the orthodox Marxist sense has taken place. His latest work [67] – a brief essay that forms an excellent introduction to his work as a whole – specifically denies that the liberal/Marxist notion of progress is relevant for the vast majority of humanity, even if a small privileged group in the 'core' are 'better off'. This view is hard to accept but does have the merit of coherence, and allows Wallerstein to treat the history of the last 400 years as more a question of the distribution of a surplus than the triumphant march of technical progress. However, his historical generalizations need to be carefully examined in the light of other recent large scale studies covering his period like Tilly [65] and Anderson [10, 11].

It should be stressed that these three categories of 'dependency theory' are by no means exclusive or necessarily hostile to one another. In a collection of essays by Amin, Arrighi, Frank and Wallerstein [9] differences do emerge, but there is a high degree of consensus. Furthermore, Furtado, one of the leaders of the 'dependencia' school, has recently produced a work [38] which discusses limits of technical progress in a similar way to Wallerstein [67]. There are distinctive schools within the dependency approach, but the differences are possibly less striking than the similarities.

Assessment

How are dependency theorists to be assessed bearing in mind that dependency theorists are not simply arguing that 'economic development' is impossible in the Third World'? It would be simple to assess this argument by reference to economic indicators like those collected by the World Bank [73]. Even a fairly cursory examination of these statistics indicates that during the last twenty years real living standards in the Third World have grown in general at rates that are, historically, quite impressive; and that despite the recent stagnation in the world economy – and not a few countries having been left behind completely in this process – 'development' has taken place. If these considerations were crucial, the dependency theorists could argue that much of the growth has been wiped out by population growth, that poverty has not been eradicated and that the gap between rich and poor remains, and often is increasing. But they could not argue that the dependent status of Third World nations has prevented development. Their position would be similar to the international Keynesianism of the 'Brandt Reports' [18, 19].

Unfortunately, things are not that simple. Challenges to the relevance of a statistical definition of development and the notion of 'dependent development' provide a double obstacle to this kind of assessment of the dependency argument. There is considerable value in the sort of analytical criticisms to be found in the special issue of *International Organisation* devoted to dependency theory [44], or by Smith [63] or Rosen & Kurth [60], but at root the issue cannot be settled by less than a reappraisal of the theory as a whole.

A good starting point for this is Warren's polemic [71]. This splendidly vigorous assault on dependency ideas is written from the perspective of a Marxism so 'orthodox' in its assumptions that it could easily be mistaken for a 'capitalist apologia'. Warren identifies two problems. First he accuses the dependency proponents of 'romantic' anti-capitalism: the dependency school's vision of the ills of the present world system is coloured by a reaction against industrial civilization as such, a position he characterizes as fundamentally unMarxist and wrong. But second, and perhaps more telling, he accuses the dependency approach of acting as a shield for nationalism, a theoretical device to cast the ills of developing countries at the door of the foreigner, rather than to be acknowledged honestly as inevitable, or, in some cases, due to poor local management. His point is that the historical role of capitalism is to develop the world and make socialism possible. This may not be a pleasant process, but to talk of a 'cruel choice' [41] is misleading. There is no choice. Warren overstates his case (as his critics have pointed out in [53]), but his basic position has much to commend it, and can be found in rather more temperate language in Kitching [48], Brewer [21] and in many of the essays in Radice [56]. Even a cursory examination of the actual record of different developing countries confirms the view that policy *does* matter and that the fatalism of a view that developing countries are conditioned to remain in the shadows of the rich is unsustainable. Of course, many small developing countries will inevitably find their prospects determined from the outside – but this takes us back to the original idea that there is a distinction between the position of a small country 'dominated' by a larger country, and a small, less-developed country 'dependent' on a large developed country. Warren and other critics from the 'left' would largely deny the relevance of this distinction, while from the 'right' critics such as Bauer [14] would deny the relevance of either term. In the last resort, dependency is more convincing as a critique

70   *Chris Brown*

of naive developmentalism than as a substantive alternative view of
the world, but its role as the stimulant to a new and better
understanding of the international system should not be under-
estimated. The emergence in recent years of a genuine global
political economy owes much to the work of Frank, Wallerstein and
others, even if the specifically dependency oriented side of their work
is being left behind. Quite probably the next edition of this book will
not contain a chapter on 'dependency' as such, but it will most
certainly address the issues dependency theorists have put on the
agenda.

Bibliography to Chapter 4

1. Almond, G.A. & Powell, G.B. Jr. *Comparative Politics: A Developmental Approach*. Boston, Little, Brown, 1978.
2. Almond, G.A. & Verba, S. *The Civic Culture*. Boston, Little, Brown, 1965.
3. Almond, G.A. & Coleman, J.S. (eds), *The Politics of the Developing Areas*. Princeton, NJ, Princeton University Press and London, Oxford University Press, 1960.
4. Amin, S. *Accumulation on a World Scale* (2 volumes). London and New York, Monthly Review Press and Hassocks, Harvester Press, 1978.
5. _____ *Class and Nation, Historically and in the Current Crisis*. London, Heinemann Educational and New York, Monthly Review Press, 1980.
6. *Imperialism and Unequal Development*. New York, Monthly Review Press, 1977 and Hassocks, Harvester, 1978.
7. _____ *The Law of Value and Historical Materialism*. New York and London, Monthly Review Press, 1980.
8. _____ *Unequal Development: An Essay on the Social Formations of Peripheral Capitalism*. Hassocks, Harvester, 1978 and New York, Monthly Review Press, 1977.
9. _____ *et al., Dynamics of Global Crisis*. London, Macmillan and New York, Monthly Review Press, 1982.
10. Anderson, P. *Lineages of the Absolutist State*. London, Verso Editions and New York, Schocken, 1979.
11. _____ *Passages from Antiquity to Feudalism*. London, Verso Editions and New York, Schocken, 1978.
12. Baran, P.A. *The Political Economy of Growth*. Harmondsworth, Middx, Penguin, 1973 and New York, Monthly Review Press, 1957.
13, Barnet, R.J. & Müller, R.E. *Global Reach: The Power of Multinational Corporations*. New York, Simon and Schuster and London, Cape, 1975.

14. Bauer, P.T. *Equality, the Third World and Economic Delusion*. London, Methuen, 1982 and Cambridge, MA, Harvard University Press, 1983.
15. Bernstein, H. (ed.) *Underdevelopment and Development*. Harmondsworth, Middx, Penguin, 1973.
16. Bettelheim, C. 'Theoretical Comments', Appendix 1 of Emmanuel, A. *Unequal Exchange: A Study in the Imperialism of Trade*. London, New Left Books and New York, Monthly Review Press, 1972.
17. Blake, D.H. & Walters, R.S. *The Politics of Global Economic Relations*. Englewood Cliffs, NJ & London, Prentice-Hall, 1983.
18. The 'Brandt Commission' I. Report of the Independent Commission on International Development Issues. *North–South: A Programme for Survival*. London, Pan and Cambridge, MA, MIT Press, 1980.
19. The 'Brandt Commission' II. Report of the Independent Commission on International Development Issues. *Common Crisis*. London, Pan and Cambridge, MA, MIT Press, 1983.
20. Brenner, R. 'The Origins of Capitalist Development: A Critique of Neo-Smithian Marxism'. *New Left Review*, no. 104, 1977, pp. 25–92.
21. Brewer, A. *Marxist Theories of Imperialism: A Critical Survey*. London, Boston and Henley, Routledge & Kegan Paul, 1980.
22. Cardoso, F.H. Associated-Dependent Development: Theoretical and Practical Implications. In *Authoritarian Brazil: Origins, Policies, Futures*, ed. A. Stepan. New Haven, CT & London, Yale University Press, 1973.
23. Cockcroft, J.D. *et al.*, *Dependence and Underdevelopment*. New York, Doubleday, 1972.
24. de Kadt, E. & Williams, G. (eds), *Sociology and Development*. London, Tavistock and New York, Methuen, 1974.
25. Emmanuel, A. *Unequal Exchange: A Study in the Imperialism of Trade*. London, New Left Books and New York, Monthly Review Press, 1972.
26. Evans, P. *Dependent Development*. Princeton, NJ, & Guildford, Princeton University Press, 1979.
27. Frank, A.G. *Capitalism and Underdevelopment in Latin America*. New York, Monthly Review Press, 1969 and Harmondsworth, Middx, Penguin, 1971.
28. _____ *Crisis: In the Third World*. London, Heinemann Educational Books and New York, Holmes & Meier, 1981.
29. _____ *Crisis: In the World Economy*. London, Heinemann Educational Books and New York, Holmes & Meier, 1980.
30. _____ *Critique and Anti-Critique: Essays of Dependence and Reformism*. London, Macmillan, 1984.
31. _____ *Dependent Accumulation and Underdevelopment*. London, Macmillan and New York, Monthly Review Press, 1979.
32. _____ *Latin America: Underdevelopment or Revolution*. New York, Monthly Review Press, 1971.

33. _____ *Lumpenbourgeoisie – Lumpendevelopment*. New York, Monthly Review Press, 1973.

34. _____ *On Capitalist Underdevelopment*. New York, Bombay, Oxford, Oxford University Press, 1975.

35. _____ *Reflections on the World Economic Crisis*. London, Hutchinson Education and New York, Monthly Review Press, 1981.

36. _____ *Sociology of Development and Underdevelopment of Sociology*. London, Pluto Press, 1971.

37. _____ *World Accumulation 1492–1789*. London, Macmillan and New York, Monthly Review Press, 1980.

38. Furtado, C. *Accumulation and Development*. Oxford, Martin Robertson and New York, St. Martin's, 1983.

39. _____ *Economic Development of Latin America*. London and New York, Cambridge University Press, 1977.

40. Goldfrank, W.L. (ed.) *The World-System of Capitalism: Past and Present*. Beverly Hills, CA & London, Sage, 1979.

41. Goulet, D. *The Cruel Choice*. London & New York, Atheneum, 1973.

42. Hoogvelt, A.M.M. *The Third World in Global Development*. London, Macmillan and Atlantic Highlands, NJ, Humanities Press, 1982.

43. Hopkins, T.K. & Wallerstein, I. (eds), *Processes of the World-System*. Beverly Hills, CA & London, Sage, 1979.

44. *International Organization*. 'Dependence and Dependency in the Global System', ed. J.A. Caporaso, vol. 32, no. 1, 1978.

45. Kaplan, B.H. (ed.) *Social Change in the Capitalist World Economy*. Beverly Hills, CA & London, Sage, 1978.

46. Kemp, T. *Industrialisation in the Non-Western World*. London & New York, Longman, 1983.

47. Kiernan, V.G. *Marxism and Imperialism*. London, Edward Arnold, 1974 and New York, St. Martin's, 1975.

48. Kitching, G. *Development and Underdevelopment in Historical Perspective*. London & New York, Methuen, 1982.

49. Laclau, E. *Politics and Ideology in Marxist Theory: Capitalism, Fascism, Populism*. London, Verso Editions and New York, Schocken, 1979.

50. Lewis, W.A. *The Theory of Economic Growth*. London & Edison, NJ, Allen & Unwin, 1955.

51. Lipset, S.M. *Political Man*. London, Heinemann, 1959 and New York, Doubleday, 1960.

52. Marx, K. *Capital: A Critique of Political Economy, Vol. I*. Harmondsworth, Middx., Penguin, 1976 and Totowa, NJ, Bibliographic Distribution Centre, 1978.

53. *New Left Review*. 'The End of The Third World?' no. 132, March/April 1982.

54. Oxaal, I. *et al.* (eds), *Beyond the Sociology of Development: Economy and Society in Africa and Latin America*. London & Boston, MA, Routledge & Kegan Paul, 1975.

55. Petras, J. & Zeitlin, M. (eds), *Latin America: Reform or Revolution.* Greenwich, CT, Fawcett, 1968.
56. Radice, H. (ed.) *International Firms and Modern Imperialism.* Harmondsworth, Middx, Penguin, 1979.
57. *Review.* Journal of the Fernand Braudel Center for the Study of Economies, Historical Systems and Civilizations. vol. 1, no. 1, 1977.
58. Rhodes, R.I. (ed.) *Imperialism and Underdevelopment.* New York & London, Monthly Review Press, 1970.
59. Rodney, W. *How Europe Underdeveloped Africa.* Dar es Salaam, Tanzania Publishing House, 1971, London, Bogle-L'Ouverture Publishers, 1972 and Washington, DC, Howard University Press, 1982.
60. Rosen, S. & Kurth, J. (eds), *Testing the Theory of Economic Imperialism.* Lexington, MA, D.C. Heath & Co., 1974.
61, Rostow, W.W. *The Stages of Economic Growth: A Non-Communist Manifesto.* Cambridge & New York, Cambridge University Press, 1971.
62. Roxborough, I. *Theories of Underdevelopment.* London, Macmillan and Atlantic Highlands, NJ, Humanities Press, 1979.
63. Smith, T. 'The Underdevelopment of Development Literature: The Case of Dependency Theory'. *World Politics,* vol. XXXI, no. 2, 1979, pp. 247–88.
64. Spero, J.E. *The Politics of International Economic Relations.* London, Allen & Unwin, 1982 and New York, St. Martin's, 1985.
65. Tilly, C. (ed.) *The Formation of National States in Western Europe.* Princeton, NJ & London, Princeton University Press, 1975.
66. Wallerstein, I. *The Capitalist World Economy.* Cambridge & New York, Cambridge University Press, 1979.
67. _____ *Historical Capitalism.* London, Verso (New Left Books) and New York, Schocken, 1983.
68. _____ *The Modern World System: Capitalist Agriculture and the Origins of the European World-Economy in the Sixteenth Century.* London & New York, Academic Press, 1974, reissued in 1981.
69. _____ *The Modern World System II: Mercantilism and the Consolidation of the European World Economy 1600–1750.* London & New York, Academic Press, 1980.
70. _____ *The Politics of the World Economy.* Cambridge & New York, Cambridge University Press, 1984.
71. Warren, B. *Imperialism: Pioneer of Capitalism.* London, Verso, 1980 and New York, Schocken, 1981.
72. Wilber, C.K. (ed.) *The Political Economy of Development and Underdevelopment.* New York, Random House, 1978.
73. World Bank. *World Development Report 1984.* Washington, D.C., World Bank, 1984.

5 Structuralism and Neo-Realism

Richard Little
University of Lancaster and CAC

A fascinating recent development in International Relations (IR) has been the recovery of realism. At the beginning of the 1970s, having dominated the discipline for twenty years, realism showed every sign of being in retreat. Attacks were taking place on all sides, from behaviouralists for employing flawed methodological tools, from pluralists for presenting an outdated view of the world and from radicals for perpetrating an ideology which preserved the status quo and distorted the past. Although these attacks were sustained, indeed intensified, during the course of the 1970s, the realists regrouped their forces and manned a counter-attack under the flag of what is now frequently referred to as 'neo-realism'. Far from falling into oblivion, realism or neo-realism, shows every sign of recovering its former position of pre-eminence.

A recent critic, Ashley [6], has argued, however, that neo-realism displays very different characteristics from traditional realism. These differences arise because the neo-realists have adopted a structural mode of analysis, antithetical to traditional realism and exported from Europe, where its failings have been exposed and demonstrated to be beyond repair. At first sight Ashley's argument appears perverse, because although there is a complex and extensive literature on a structural approach to social science, it has been scarcely mentioned during methodological and epistemological debates in IR. This apparent neglect seems unlikely to be the result of ignorance, since advocates of structuralism, such as Levi-Strauss in anthropology and Chomsky in linguistics, are household names in the social sciences. But there are few references to either writer in IR.

The absence of discussion does not, however, necessarily mean that the approach has been eschewed. An alternative explanation is that in IR, analysts, like Molière's M. Jourdain, who never knew he spoke prose, have proceeded on the basis of unacknowledged methodological assumptions. It will be suggested in this review that structuralism is not a new development, although its recent articulation has played a role in the renaissance of realism.

Structuralism and Social Science

Ashley's attack and the response to it [30] reflects a certain amount of confusion about what structuralism entails. The confusion is eminently understandable because there is substantial disagreement even amongst its supporters. Some authors such as Piaget [67] identify a common methodology influencing the work of all structuralists; others, Boudon [9] and Runciman [75] for example, only observe specific structural theories which vary from one discipline to another. A compromise, formulated by Keat & Urry [50], states that common features run through almost all structural analyses, and the differences reflect competing conceptions of science. This formula is accepted here, although the implications for IR of divergent views of science, while important, are not examined.

The origins of structuralism have also been a source of controversy. In an analysis of Levi-Strauss, Clarke [21] argues that Durkheim [25] established the foundations when he developed a collectivist form of analysis. Alexander [2], on the other hand, traces structuralism back to the nineteenth century revolt by Bentham against prevailing individualist and instrumental explanations of social action; although he goes on to suggest that Marx represents the most important thinker working within this tradition before the twentieth century. Finally, Boudon [9] argues that if structuralism is associated with holism, then this mode of analysis can be traced all the way back to Aristotle.

A historical survey of methodology suggests that social activity has always been examined from one of two broad avenues, defined by holism and individualism. In the twentieth century this has led to a fierce debate about their respective merits. O'Neill [66] has drawn together the seminal articles. Individualists insist that there are no social laws which operate independently of human understanding; all explanations can be reduced to the level of the individual and couched in terms of the nature and intentions of these actors. Holists, on the other hand, argue that when people interact, they create systems. These systems are defined by enduring characteristics.

Individuals may come and go, but the structures of the system persist. The task of the social scientist is to identify these structures and determine how they affect social action. They must also be concerned with the development and transformation of these structures.

Holists, therefore, are dealing with theoretical or metaphysical properties of the social system, since these properties are not amenable to direct inspection. Far from rendering their analysis unscientific, however, holists insist that social science can only advance on this plane. They point to the central importance of theoretical concepts such as gravity in natural science. Because holism is also associated with metaphysical speculation, however, social scientists operating from a holistic perspective have tended to be referred to as structuralists.

Structuralists assume that human behaviour cannot be understood simply by examining individual motivation and intention because, when aggregated, human behaviour precipitates structures of which the individuals may be unaware. By analogy, when people walk across a field, they may unintentionally create a path. Others subsequently follow the path and in doing so 'reproduce' the path. The process of reproduction, however, is neither conscious nor intentional. Structuralists characterize language in similar terms. No-one consciously establishes the rules of language, nor would it be possible for any individual to change the rules. Nevertheless, by using language, its structure is reproduced for the future.

Behind the mêlée of social activity it is also possible to identify structures which, as with language and the path, were never consciously established, and yet are continuously being reproduced. Marxists, for example, accept that technological change and the emergence of a capitalist mode of production established a pattern of social relations which constituted a class structure. Once in existence individuals unconsciously reproduce the structure, despite its repressive character. Marxists, like all structuralists, believe it is necessary to probe beneath the surface manifestations of human motivation to identify the invisible but powerful structures which mould and guide behaviour. Other characteristics distinguishing a structural approach have been identified [7, 50, 55], but these features are sufficient to discuss its role in IR.

In mainstream social science it is now often accepted that structuralism and individualism represent complementary rather than competitive approaches. There is growing support for the idea that social action needs to be understood on two distinct levels [8].

No such reconciliation has taken place amongst radical social scientists, where a fierce debate continues to rage.

This polemical wrangle may appear strange at first to those operating outside the radical's paradigm, because structuralism is considered to be synonymous with radicalism. Marx, for example, is often cited as one of the first major structural thinkers. However, the harness joining these two 'isms' obscures the acrimonious debate in radical thinking about the role of structuralism. Although the debate initially seems to concern rather opaque methodological and epistemological issues, further investigation suggests that the hostility generated derives primarily from its practical significance. Radicals are a distinctive group because they are dissatisfied with contemporary society. Invariably, therefore, they are committed to a programme of change. Structuralism divides radicals because of its implications for the way change can be brought about. If it is the case that established structures dictate how society operates, and that structures change only as the result of impersonal forces, then individuals can only affect society by violent intervention and an overthrow of the existing structures – if at all. But many radicals do not endorse this conclusion. E.P. Thompson, for example, does not accept that the course of history is determined by vast forces which lie beyond the control of human beings. He argues that structuralists have a dehumanized view of the world, where 'systems and subsystems, elements and structures are drilled up and down the pages pretending to be people' [82]. Far from providing a radical interpretation of society, structuralism is an ideology that inhibits attempts to bring about change. The debate is complex and runs throughout the radical literature, impinging upon virtually every issue, although the consequences are not always confronted. For example, Althusser, a major French structuralist, is condemned by Callinicos for his failure to examine the unity of theory and practice, or to show how to 'detonate an explosion that would bring down capitalists' [20]. Those, like Thompson, who want to use existing political structures to implement radical change, inevitably shy away from an approach which suggests that fundamental change can only take place on a revolutionary basis. Following Stretton [81], it seems as if methodological and epistemological choices are profoundly influenced by the values of the analyst. This debate is important, because Ashley draws on the radical critics of structuralism when attacking neo-realism.

Structuralism and IR

It is often assumed that structuralism has played no role in IR. Allison [3] argues in his influential study of the Cuban Missile Crisis that the discipline has traditionally been studied from the perspective of an individualist rational choice model. A decade later, Waltz, an advocate of structuralism, maintained that IR specialists have failed to appreciate the essential characteristics of structural explanations: only by default have they produced individualist or reductionist explanations [90].

Finally, Ashley has asserted that structuralism has only recently been introduced into the discipline by American neo-realists who have failed to appreciate its fatal flaws. This assessment has been endorsed by Ruggie [74] who considers that Waltz has revived the flagging fortunes of Durkheim by resurrecting structuralism. In contrast to Ashley, who wishes to see this influence expunged, Ruggie is anxious to shore up the inadequacies in Waltz' analysis.

Despite this consensus, it is not difficult to find evidence of a structural perspective in realism. Although Ashley and Allison assert that Morgenthau used an individualist approach, it is hard to sustain this argument if his views are taken as a whole. The basic theme of *Politics Among Nations* is that the structure of the international system has been transformed during the twentieth century. Bipolarity has replaced multipolarity. For Morgenthau [62] this has very serious consequences because the balance of power, crucial to the maintenance of international stability, functions best in a multipolar world.

Morgenthau was not alone among traditional realists in suggesting that we are living through a period of structural upheaval. Herz [36] predicted the demise of the sovereign state and the emergence of continental blocs. He later revised this view [38], but it is evident that the emphasis on structure and its impact on state behaviour runs throughout the traditional realist literature. This is not to deny that realists also adopt an individualist perspective; in fact, structuralism and individualism are normally woven together in a complex multi-layered analysis. When Ashley [6] identifies an individualist's tenor in Morgenthau's voice, he is failing to acknowledge the diversity and richness of the approach. Traditional realists adopt an eclectic, unself-conscious attitude to methodology. The complementarity of individualism and structuralism is taken for granted, and partisan affiliation is thereby avoided. In the past, however, this catholic approach to method tended to discourage discussion of methodology.

Behaviouralism and the Realist Revival

Formal attempts to examine methodology only began to take place in the late 1950s, with the development of behaviouralism. Attention was initially focused on systems theory, quickly identified by Kaplan [46], McClelland [58] and others as the methodology most likely to develop a theory of international politics. For more than a decade, the discipline was inundated with systems terminology. Indeed, critics argued that the language was used as a substitute for theoretical insight. Weltman [92] was not alone in claiming that there was nothing distinctive about a systems approach because it denoted no more than interaction. This conclusion could not have been reached if the analysis had been informed by the mainstream debate between structuralists and individualists in social science where, despite fundamental disagreement, no one doubted that a real issue was at stake. Both systems thinking and structuralism appealed to holism and in Piaget [67], the line between these methodologies seems very faint indeed. Yet there are discernible differences in emphasis. Systems thinking, for example, finds its origins in the natural sciences and represents an attack on atomistic and mechanistic modes of thinking. Structuralism, on the other hand, was developed in the social sciences and represents an alternative to ahistorical and individualist ways of analysing social activity.

Traditional realists, already schooled in structuralism, were quite ready to adopt the holistic message of the new systems theorists. Herz [36], for example, drew on Kaplan's work. The neo-realists, however, have gone further and made a self-conscious attempt to integrate systemic and structuralist ideas. Waltz [91], for example, who, despite trenchant criticism [11, 47, 71, 74], has provided the best discussion of a holistic approach to IR, draws upon both camps, identifying a debt to Buckley [13] for his ideas on systems and to Nadel [65] for his ideas on structuralism. He does not, however, acknowledge that these sets of ideas come from different traditions. But he does argue that it is structure which makes it possible to think of a system as a whole and he defines political structure by (a) an ordering principle, (b) the functions of differentiated units, and (c) the distribution of capabilities across these units.

Systems thinking, however, was only one dimension of the putative behavioural revolution. In practice, the revolution was more commonly associated with the introduction of numerical analysis to the discipline. Realists made no secret of their distaste for the statistical side of behaviouralism [16, 61] and their attack precipitated the so-called Great Debate. During the course of this debate the structural aspects of realism became obscured. Realists argued that in order to employ statistical techniques, it was necessary to make extraordinarily crude and naive assumptions about international politics. In developing this attack, they drew largely on arguments reflecting the individualist side of their methodoogy. This resulted in a distorted conception of realism, but it also promoted the solecism that behaviouralists were only concerned with what was pejoratively referred to as 'number-crunching'. In reality, numerical analysis was as alien to many behaviouralists as to traditional realists. The distortions perpetrated during the Great Debate were only revealed after the largely unseeing eye of this methodological storm had passed over the discipline.

Vasquez [85] correctly pointed out later that many behaviouralists were firmly imbued with fundamental realist assumptions about international politics. But he was mistaken in suggesting that these were their only assumptions. What the behaviouralists disliked about traditional realism was the unsystematic approach to model building. Realists were seen to draw, in an *ad hoc* fashion, on a range of potent but largely untested hypotheses. The behaviouralists were particularly interested in those hypotheses which reflected the structural aspects of realist thinking.

A rich seam of empirical propositions was identified which analysed, albeit often in inconsistent terms, the structural properties of the international system. The propositions centred on Morgenthau's assertion that multipolarity is more stable than bipolarity. The behaviouralist attempts to examine this relatively straightforward proposition in a systematic fashion demonstrate some of the difficulties associated with behavioural research. The early efforts reached conflicting conclusions, with some researchers linking stability to bipolarity [89] and others to multipolarity [24]. Reassessing this research, it has become clear that bipolarity was operationalized in two quite different ways. One associates bipolarity with the emergence of two conflicting alliance systems, the other with the emergence of two states of disproportionate power in the system [70, 79]. The debate, which began in the 1960s, is proving to be just as lively in the 1980s. Behaviouralism, therefore, is not incompatible with realism. Moreover, neo-realists have taken the methodological lessons of behaviouralism on board and also reasserted the importance of structuralism. Although Waltz has categorically denied that he is a structural determinist [90], he has argued forcefully that a theory of international politics can only be formed at the structural level. For most neo-realists, a structural approach has taken priority [54]. But the importance of structuralism for the realists was also reinforced by the criticism levelled by pluralists and radicals.

Pluralism and the Realist Revival

The pluralist approach in international politics emerged during the 1960s and 1970s in response to the ostensible inadequacies of realism. It was accepted that realists could provide an acceptable characterization of the international system prior to the twentieth century. But, according to Morse [63], Brown [12] and others, a technological revolution has taken place with consequences realism cannot accommodate. The difficulty is related to the realist's belief that international politics involve, as Wolfers [95] explained, relations among states of strikingly similar character and behaviour. This 'billiard ball' view of international politics [19] was considered deficient.

Pluralists at first characterized the international system in terms of transnational relations [52], conducted amongst a kaleidoscope of non-state actors [59]. This meant, as Burton [19] observed, that the boundaries of the state were being dissolved and, as Hanrieder [34] noted, the divide between domestic and international politics was breaking down. This development, Fox [27] demonstrates, had already been anticipated in the 1920s and 1930s by Charles Merriam [60] – one of the fathers of American pluralism. The readiness of Americans to believe in the vulnerability of the state and its boundaries to transnationalist forces was a product of being schooled in pluralism and socialized in a country where, as Dyson [26] so clearly demonstrates, the role of the state had always been minimized.

During the 1970s realists attempted to reassert the primacy of the state and the centrality of power in international politics. A forceful restatement came from Tucker [84] in a frontal assault on the pluralists. In strictly structuralist terms, he argued that international decisions which failed to reflect the existing distribution of power would not only be unsuccessful, but also precipitate disorder by violating the logic of an anarchic arena. Even his critics had to admit the force of his arguments [1]. More restrained, although still focusing on the structural idea of order, Bull [15] rehearsed again the realist reasons for the dominance of the Great Powers in an anarchic arena. Bull acknowledged the need to take account of transnationalism, but he undermined the pluralist picture by pointing to the declining influence of transnationalism over the past three hundred years. The pluralists began to give ground if not to the arguments of the realists, then at least to the requirements of structuralism. It was easy enough, from an individualist perspective, to describe the emergence of non-state actors. It was considerably more difficult to imagine the mode of organization relating this plethora of new actors in the absence of a structural principle. The re-emergence of realism took place, in part, because its renewed emphasis on structure gave a coherence which was very evidently lacking in the pluralist perspective. The main advocates of transnationalism retreated, resurrected the state, and drew upon the idea of interdependence [51] as a means of characterizing contemporary relations among states.

An extensive literature on interdependence developed during the 1970s, comprehensively reviewed by Rosecrance [72, 73]. But as Holsti [43] noted, this literature lacked a structural focus and seemed to be operating in a void. In recent years, therefore, pluralists have been struggling to develop a structural framework. At the heart of this endeavour is the belief that the realists have over-estimated the role of power in international politics. The pluralists have been impressed by evidence that, in many instances, relationships amongst states are not determined by the distribution of power. As a consequence there have been attempts to develop a structural perspective which excludes this dimension. In a pioneering effort, Burton [17] contrasted two structural models, one dominated by power distribution and the other by cybernetics. Puchala [69] and Winham [94] have followed in this direction, while Keohane & Nye [51] have distinguished between power- and regime-governed structures. The collective goods literature has also been a fertile source of ideas [63]. It is apparent, however, that the pluralists have some way to go before they develop a structural approach which matches the theoretical elegance of realism.

The Radicals and the Realist Revival

Until recently radicals were not considered by the realists to have made any contribution worthy of comment. Although there have been attempts to develop a radical interpretation of imperialism [14, 49, 56], realists such as Cohen [22] have been almost contemptuous of this literature. Moreover, Holsti [44] demonstrated that when the New Left in the United States endeavoured to develop a revisionist interpretation of the Cold War, they continued to rely, like the mainstream interpreters, on an essentially realist model of international politics.

Since the end of the Second World War, however, radicals in economics and sociology have been developing a structural model of the international system which represents a serious challenge to realism. Instead of identifying the world economy by the transactions among a set of autonomous national economies, radical economists began to think of the economy in terms of an integrated centre and a decentralized, exploited periphery. Prebisch [68], one of the first to define the world economy in centre–periphery terms, was soon followed by others [28, 64]. It was argued that Third World economies had no autonomy and had been organized to satisfy interests at the centre. Although some of the peace researchers, particularly Galtung [29], made use of this literature, its effect on the discipline overall was slight.

In the 1970s, however, Wallerstein [87, 88], a sociologist, picked up the idea of centre–periphery relations and used it as an organizing device for looking at world history. In contrast to the earlier economic models, Wallerstein argued that to understand world history a structural model which embraces political and economic elements is required. History demonstrates, he argues, that centralized empires have been the dominating mode of economic and political organization. Although after collapsing empires have been replaced briefly by decentralized world systems, these have soon disintegrated when a political unit seized control and created a new empire. Modern history since the sixteenth century is unique, according to Wallerstein, because a world system has survived. He accounts for this development by identifying a concentration of factors in the sixteenth century which permitted certain states to operate a system of unequal exchange. This created a set of strong states and permitted the emergence of a world economy defined in terms of a core and a periphery. This has persisted because of the balance of power amongst the strong states.

Wallerstein's model has come in for a welter of criticism [5, 10, 31, 78, 80, 83]. Furthermore, Vasquez [85] has argued that the model has not made serious inroads into the discipline. In fact, he underestimates the interest in extending the model into the discipline [42] and the influence that this work has had on realism. In conjunction with Anderson's work [4], it has forced realists to re-examine their easy acceptance of a homogenized, ahistorical view of the state. Realists have started to examine Wallerstein's explanation of how the modern state came into existence. Zolberg [96] and Gourevitch [31, 32] have noted, for example, that he takes insufficient account of the international political system and the role of the balance of power on the way states have emerged. This point has also been appreciated in the field of comparative politics, where more attention is now focused on the international system in explanations of domestic developments such as revolutions [77].

In the process of examining the task of state-building, neo-realists have come to realize that they are, in fact, simply re-emphasizing an interest already established by earlier realists. Working within a tradition which can be traced back to Ranke and the early nineteenth-century historicists, Hintze [39] argued at the beginning of the twentieth century that the internal political organization of the state could in part be accounted for in terms of its position in the international system. A similar argument is now being made in the context of state-building in Africa [45].

The consequences of this development are only beginning to become apparent. Realists like Krasner [53] appreciate that it is not at all easy to account for the emergence of the state and that the realists are a long way from forming an adequate theory. It is also becoming clear that the realists need to revise radically their homogenized view of the state. Ruggie [74] only partially recognizes this fact when he attacks Waltz for eliminating unit differentiation from his analysis of international structure. Ruggie wants this element reintroduced so that structuralists can explore the medieval period. But this misses the point that it must also be acknowledged that even in the modern world, states play different roles in the international system – a point understood by the pluralists [71] and by traditional realists who have developed an interest in middle powers [40, 41] and small states [33].

Structuralism, therefore, can be seen to play an important role in the way pluralists and radicals are endeavouring to analyse IR. It has always played an important role in the way traditional realists have examined the international arena. What the neo-realists have done is to bring its significance back into focus.

Bibliography to Chapter 5

1. Ajami, F. 'The Global Logic of the Neo Conservatives'. *World Politics,* vol. XXX, no. 3, 1978, pp. 450–68.
2. Alexander, J.C. 'Social Structural Analysis: Some Notes on its History and Prospects'. *Sociological Quarterly,* vol. 25, no. 1, 1984, pp. 5–26.
3. Allison, G.T. *Essence of Decision.* Boston, Little, Brown, 1971.
4. Anderson, P. *Lineages of the Absolutist State.* London, Verso Editions and New York, Schocken, 1979.
5. Aronowitz, S. 'A Metatheoretical Critique of Immanuel Wallerstein's *The Modern World System'. Theory and Society,* vol. 10, no. 4, 1981, pp. 503–20.
6. Ashley, R.K. 'The Poverty of Neo Realism'. *International Organization,* vol. 38, no. 2, 1984, pp. 225–86.
7. Assiter, A. 'Althusser and Structuralism'. *British Journal of Sociology,* vol. XXXV, no. 2, 1984, pp. 272–96.
8. Barry, B. *Sociologists, Economists and Democracy.* London and Chicago, University of Chicago Press, 1979.
9. Boudon, R. *The Uses of Structuralism* (translated by M. Vaughan). London, Heinemann, 1971.
10. Brenner, R. 'The Origins of Capitalist Development: A Critique of Neo-Smithian Marxism'. *New Left Review,* no. 104, 1977, pp. 25–92.
11. Brown, C. 'International Theory: New Directions'. *Review of International Studies,* vol. 7, no. 3, 1981, pp. 173–86.
12. Brown, S. *New Forces in World Politics.* Washington, Brookings, 1974.
13. Buckley, W. *Sociology and Modern Systems Theory.* Englewood Cliffs, NJ, Prentice Hall, 1967.
14. Bukharin, N.I. *Imperialism and the World Economy.* London, The Merlin Press, 1972 and New York, London, Monthly Review Press, 1973.
15. Bull, H.N. *The Anarchical Society: A Study of World Order.* London, Macmillan and New York, Columbia University Press, 1977.
16. _____ 'International Theory: The Case for the Classical Approach'. *World Politics,* vol. XVIII, no. 3, 1966, pp. 361–77.
17. Burton, J.W. *International Relations: A General Theory.* Cambridge, Cambridge University Press, 1965.
18. _____ *Systems, States, Diplomacy and Rules.* Cambridge & New York, Cambridge University Press, 1968.

19. _____ *World Society*. London & New York, Cambridge University Press, 1972.

20. Callinicos, A. *Althusser's Marxism*. London, Pluto Press, 1980 and New York, Urizen Books, 1976.

21. Clarke, S. *The Foundations of Structuralism: A Critique of Levi-Strauss and the Structural Movement*. Brighton, Harvester Press, 1981.

22. Cohen, B.J. *The Question of Imperialism: The Political Economy of Dominance and Dependence*. London, Macmillan, 1974 and New York, Basic Books, 1973.

23. Dean, P.D. 'From Power to Issue Politics: Bipolarity and Multipolarity in Light of a New Paradigm'. *Western Political Quarterly*, vol. 29, no. 1, 1976, pp. 7–28.

24. Deutsch, K.W. & Singer, J.D. 'Multipolar Power Systems and International Stability'. *World Politics*, vol. XVI, no. 3, 1964, pp. 390–406.

25. Durkheim, E. *The Rules of Sociological Method* (edited by S. Lukes). London, Macmillan, 1982. (Published in the USA as *The Rules of Sociological Method and Selected Texts on Sociology and its Method*. New York, Free Press, 1982.)

26. Dyson, K. *The State Tradition in Western Europe*. Oxford & New York, Oxford University Press, 1980 and Oxford, Martin Robertson, 1982.

27. Fox, W.T.R. 'Pluralism, the Science of Politics and the World System'. *World Politics*, vol. XXVII, no. 4, 1975, pp. 597–611.

28. Frank, A.G. *Latin America: Underdevelopment or Revolution*. New York, Monthly Review Press, 1971.

29. Galtung, J. 'A Structural Theory of Imperialism'. *Journal of Peace Research*, vol. 8, no. 1, 1971, pp. 81–117.

30. Gilpin, R.G. 'The Richness of the Tradition of Political Realism'. *International Organization*, vol. 38, no. 2, 1984, pp. 287–304.

31. Gourevitch, P. 'The International System and Regime Formation'. *Comparative Politics*, vol. 10, no. 3, 1977–8, pp. 419–38.

32. _____ 'The Second Image Reversed: The International Sources of Domestic Politics'. *International Organization*, vol. 32, no. 4, 1978, pp. 881–911.

33. Handel, M. *Weak States in the International System*. London, Frank Cass, 1981.

34. Hanrieder, W.F. 'Dissolving International Politics: Reflections on the Nation State'. *American Political Science Review*, vol. LXXIV, no. 4, 1978, pp. 1276–1287.

35. _____ 'The International System: Bipolar or Multipolar?'. *Journal of Conflict Resolution*, vol. IX, no. 3, 1965, pp. 299–308.

36. Herz, J.H. *International Politics in the Atomic Age*. New York, Columbia University Press, 1962.

37. _____ 'Rise and Demise of the Territorial State'. *World Politics*, vol. IX, no. 4, 1957, pp. 473–93.

38. _____ The Territorial State Revisited: Reflections On the Future

of the Nation-State. In *International Politics and Foreign Policy: A Reader in Research and Theory*, ed. J.N. Rosenau. New York, Free Press, 1969.

39. Hintze, O. Military Organization and the Organization of the State. In *The Historical Essays of Otto Hintze*, ed. F. Gilbert. London & New York, Oxford University Press, 1975.

40. Holbraad, C. *Middle Powers in World Politics*. London, Macmillan and New York, St. Martin's, 1984.

41. _____ 'The Role of Middle Powers'. *Cooperation and Conflict*, vol. 6, no. 2, 1971, pp. 77–90.

42. Hollist, W.L. & Rosenau, J.N. 'World Systems Debate'. Special Issue of *International Studies Quarterly*, vol. 25, no. 1, 1981.

43. Holsti, K.J. 'A New International Politics? Diplomacy in Complex Interdependence'. *International Organization*, vol. 32, no. 2, 1978, pp. 513–30.

44. Holsti, O.R. 'The Study of International Politics Makes Strange Bedfellows: Theories of the Radical Right and the Radical Left'. *American Political Science Review*, vol. LXVIII, no. 1, 1974, pp. 217–42.

45. Jackson, E.H. & Rosebury, C.G. 'Why Africa's Weak States Persist: The Empirical and the Juridical in Statehood'. *World Politics*, vol. XXXV, no. 1, 1982, pp. 1–24.

46. Kaplan, M.A. Bipolarity in a Revolutionary Age. In *The Revolution in World Politics*, ed. M.A. Kaplan. New York, Wiley, 1962.

47. _____ The Genteel Art of Criticism. In *Towards Professionalism in International Theory*, ed. M.A. Kaplan. London, Collier-Macmillan and New York, Free Press, 1979.

48. _____ *System and Process in International Politics*. New York, Krieger, 1975.

49. Kautsky, K. 'Ultra-Imperialism'. *New Left Review*, no. 59, 1970, pp. 40–8.

50. Keat, R. & Urry, J. *Social Theory as Science*. London & Boston, MA, Routledge & Kegan Paul, 1982.

51. Keohane, R.O. & Nye, J.S. *Power and Interdependence: World Politics in Transition*. Boston, Little, Brown, 1977.

52. _____ (eds), *Transnational Relations and World Politics*. Cambridge, MA & London, Harvard University Press, 1973.

53. Krasner, S.D. 'Approaches for the State: Alternative Conceptions and Historical Dynamics'. *Comparative Politics*, vol. 16, no. 2, 1984, pp. 223–46.

54. _____ 'Regimes and the Limits of Realism: Regimes as Autonomous Variables'. *International Organization*, vol. 36, no. 2, 1982, pp. 497–510.

55. Lane, M. (ed.) *Structuralism: A Reader*. London, Jonathan Cape, 1970.

56. Lenin, V.I. 'Imperialism, The Highest Stage of Capitalism'. *Collected Works*, vol. 22, Moscow, Progress Publishers and London, Lawrence &

88   *Richard Little*

Wishart, 1964.
57. Lentner, H.H. 'The Concept of the State: A Response to Stephen Krasner'. *Comparative Politics*, vol. 16, no. 3, 1984, p. 367.
58. McClelland, C.A. 'System and History in International Relations'. *General Systems Yearbook*, vol. 3, 1958, pp. 221–47.
59. Mansbach, R.W. *et al.*, *The Web of World Politics: Non State Actors in the Global System*. Englewood Cliffs, NJ, Prentice Hall and London, Prentice Hall International, 1976.
60. Merriam, C.E. *New Aspects of Politics*. London & Chicago, Chicago University Press, 1970.
61. Morgenthau, H.J. International Relations: Quantitative and Qualitative Approaches. In *A Design for International Relations* (Monograph 10), ed. N.D. Palmer. Philadelphia, The American Academy of Political and Social Science, 1970.
62. _____ *Politics Among Nations: The Struggle for Power and Peace*. New York, Alfred Knopf, 1985.
63. Morse, E.L. *Modernization and the Transformation of International Relations*. New York, Free Press and London, Collier-Macmillan, 1976.
64. Myrdal, G. *Economic Theory and Underdeveloped Regions*. London, Methuen, 1963.
65. Nadel, S.F. *The Theory of Social Structure*. Glencoe, IL, Free Press, 1957.
66. O'Neill, J. (ed.) *Modes of Individualism and Collectivism*. London, Heinemann and New York, St. Martin's, 1973.
67. Piaget, J. *Structuralism* (translated by C. Maschler). London, Routledge & Kegan Paul and New York, Basic Books, 1971.
68. Prebisch, R. *The Economic Development of Latin America and its Principal Problems*. New York, United Nations, 1950.
69. Puchala, D.J. 'Of Blindmen, Elephants and International Integration'. *Journal of Common Market Studies*, vol. X, no. 3, 1972, pp. 267–84.
70. Rapkin, D. *et al.*, 'Bipolarity and Bipolarization in the Cold War Era'. *Journal of Conflict Resolution*, vol. 23, no. 2, 1979, pp. 261–95.
71. Rosecrance, R. 'International Theory Revisited'. *International Organization*, vol. 35, no. 4, 1981, pp. 691–713.
72. Rosecrance, R. & Stein, A. 'Interdependence: Myth or Reality?' *World Politics*, vol. XXVI, no. 1, 1973, pp. 1–27.
73. Rosecrance, R. *et al.*. 'Whither Interdependence?' *International Organization*, vol. 31, no. 3, 1977, pp. 425–72.
74. Ruggie, J.G. 'Continuity and Transformation in the World Polity: Towards a Neorealist Synthesis'. *World Politics*, vol. XXXV, no. 2, 1983, pp. 260–85.
75. Runciman, W.G. 'What is Structuralism?' *British Journal of Sociology*, vol. 20, no. 2, 1969, pp. 253–65.
76. Singer, J.D. *et al.*, Capability Distribution, Uncertainty, and Major Power War – 1816–1965. In *Peace War and Numbers*, ed. B. Russett. Beverly Hills, CA, Sage, 1972.

77. Skocpol, T. 'France, Russia, China: A Structural Analysis of Social Revolutions'. *Comparative Studies in Society and History*, vol. 18, no. 2, 1976, pp. 175–210.
78. _____ 'Wallerstein's World Capitalist System'. *American Journal of Sociology*, vol. 82, no. 5, 1977, pp. 1075–90.
79. Stall, R.J. 'Bloc Concentration and the Balance of Power: The European Major Powers 1824–1914'. *Journal of Conflict Resolution*, vol. 28, no. 1, 1984, pp. 25–50.
80. Stinchcombe, A.L. 'Review Essay: The Growth of the World System'. *American Journal of Sociology*, vol. 87, no. 6, 1981/2, pp. 1389–95.
81. Stretton, H. *The Political Sciences: General Principles of Selection in Social Science and History*. London, Routledge & Kegan Paul, 1972.
82. Thompson, E.P. *The Poverty of Theory and Other Essays*. London, Merlin Press, 1978 and New York, Monthly Review Press, 1980.
83. Trinberger, E.K. 'World Systems Analysis: The Problem of Unequal Development'. *Theory and Society*, vol. 8, no. 1, 1979, pp. 127–37.
84. Tucker, R.W. *The Inequality of Nations*. New York, Basic Books and Oxford, Martin Robertson, 1977.
85. Vasquez, J.A. *The Power of Power Politics*. London, Frances Pinter and New Brunswick, NJ, Rutgers University Press, 1983.
86. Wallerstein, I. *The Capitalist World Economy*. Cambridge & New York, Cambridge University Press, 1979.
87. _____ *The Modern World System: Capitalist Agriculture and the Origins of the European World-Economy in the Sixteenth Century*. London & New York, Academic Press, 1974, reissued in 1981.
88. _____ *The Modern World System II: Mercantilism and the Consolidation of the European World Economy 1600–1750*. London & New York, Academic Press, 1980.
89. Waltz, K.N. 'International Structure: National Force and the Balance of World Power'. *Journal of International Affairs*, vol. 21, no. 2, 1967, pp. 215–31.
90. _____ 'Letter to Editor'. *International Organization*, vol. 36, no. 3, 1982, pp. 679–81.
91. _____ *Theory of International Politics*. Reading, MA & London, Addison-Wesley Publishing Co., 1979.
92. Weltman, J.J. *Systems Theory in International Relations: A Study in Metaphoric Hypertrophy*. Lexington, MA, Lexington Books, 1973.
93. Winham, G.R. 'International Negotiation in an Age of Transition'. *International Journal*, vol. XXXV, no. 1, 1979–1980, pp. 1–20.
94. _____ 'Negotiation as a Management Process'. *World Politics*, vol. XXX, no. 1, 1977, pp. 87–114.
95. Wolfers, A. *Discord and Collaboration: Essays in International Politics*. Baltimore, Johns Hopkins University Press, 1966.
96. Zolberg, A.R. 'Origins of the Modern World System'. *World Politics*, vol. XXXIII, no. 2, 1980–1981, pp. 253–81.

6 Methodology

Michael Nicholson
Netherlands Institute for Advanced Study

In most disciplines there are a group of scholars who ask questions about the fundamental nature of the activity which is being followed. Thus, while mathematicians do mathematics, some people ask questions such as 'What is valid proof?' In the natural sciences, scientists try to establish theories, while a few ask what a theory is. Similarly, in the social sciences most people carry out the activity in question, but a few will ask such questions as 'What do explanations in the social sciences consist of?' These sorts of problems are the subject matter of the 'philosophy' of the various disciplines.

For this reason 'methodology' is a slightly unfortunate term, for this chapter is not intended to be a discussion of 'how' to do international relations (IR) in the practical sense. Its purpose is not a description of the statistical techniques, mathematical models, psychological experiments, and so on, which may possibly be useful in the analysis of international phenomena. It is to draw attention to the literature which debates whether the nature of international relations is such that these techniques may even in principle be applicable, irrespective of the practical issues which may attend such work.

I shall concentrate on those authors who address the issue of whether IR is a social science, even if they conclude that it is not. If it is agreed that IR is a form of social behaviour, then the issues involved in its study are shared by students of any other form of social behaviour. The disagreements mirror some basic disagreements in the philosophy of the social sciences as a whole and, while there is some literature on the specific issues raised by political science, and a little specifically in IR, the fundamental problems are common to the social sciences a a whole.

The major disagreement concerns the legitimacy of using scientific methods in the analysis of social behaviour. Any analysis of the philosophy of the social sciences has to be discussed in the context of the philosophy of the natural sciences: the would-be scientists regard this as the obvious starting point, while their opponents commonly take it as the point of attack. It is convenient to divide the following note into three fairly arbitrary parts. First, mention is made of some books on the philosophy of science in general – primarily that of natural science. The second part consists of works on the philosophy of social science in general, including especially relevant works on particular social sciences other than IR. The third part deals with the philosophy of political science, in particular IR.

The Philosophy of Science

There are a large number of books on the philosophy of science, with a variety of emphases and some substantial disagreements. Personal taste is a significant factor in choosing, but introductory books with rather different emphases are Harré [32], Hempel [35], and Toulmin [78].

Rather more difficult, but rewarding for those who are prepared to stay the course, is Braithwaite [8] who provides a clearer and more thorough knowledge of the nature of laws and explanations in science than would a more superficial reading of a wider range of books. Popper is a name which is quickly brought into any discussion of scientific method [63]. He is particularly renowned for his belief that falsifiability is the principle which demarcates scientific from non-scientific statements. This is regarded as too strong a criterion by some philosophers (e.g. Ayer [5], discussing a more general topic than the philosophy of science alone). Readable, witty, but profound, is Russell [69].

The dependence of perception on changing conceptual frameworks is emphasized by Kuhn in one of the most widely quoted books in this area [43]. Kuhn is interested in scientific change and discovery and is less clinical and detached than Popper. The concept of a *paradigm*, that fruitful but ill-defined term, was introduced by Kuhn. At times difficult, but rewarding and elegant, Hanson [31] writes in a related vein.

Some of the disputes within the philosophy of science have been edited by Lakatos & Musgrave [44], a symposium in which both Popper and Kuhn have substantial contributions. An important, even seminal, essay here is Lakatos' own paper 'Falsification and the Methodology of Scientific Research Programmes' which, if only for the frequency of its citation, should be read by anyone seriously interested in the philosophy of science.

This brief list of salient contributions will help anyone interested in the foundations of the philosophy of science. For anyone who believes that, in the last analysis, our knowledge of social behaviour is of the same form as our knowledge of inanimate behaviour, it is prudent, to say the least, to have some acquaintance with the way that scientists interpret the world – or at least, how the philosophers of science believe that scientists interpret the world. Obviously, the more one knows about natural science, particularly physics, the easier it is to understand the implications of these books. However, apart from Hanson, the arguments can be followed without any scientific training.

The Philosophy of the Social Sciences

Attitudes to the philosophy of social science are divided into totally inconsistent viewpoints. Very crudely there are those who hold that social phenomena can be analysed, generally speaking, in a manner closely parallel to those of the natural sciences, and those who insist that this is totally out of the question. The first of these views is sometimes referred to as 'behaviouralism', although 'empiricism' is becoming an increasingly popular term and has a somewhat broader connotation.

The core of the problem is that social behaviour is conscious and intentional behaviour. People perform acts in a social context, and it is only in those social contexts that these actions are meaningful. Thus, if we talk of a 'War of National Independence' we refer not merely to a set of physical activities of people who fight each other (even 'fight' has some interpretative overtones, though we might overlook them). We are talking of a complex set of interpretations and understandings which include concepts, for example, such as 'nation' and 'state', quite apart from 'war' itself. These are not as readily reducible to observable events as observations of the inanimate world are, even when the observations may be a very long way from experience (as is often the case with physics). The question, then, becomes whether we can reduce a concept such as 'War of National Independence' to a set of observations which we can relate to other concepts, which are at least understandable in the same way by people of vastly different ideologies. The empiricists argue that we can. Their opponents argue that social life is inherently so impregnated with values and with individual rather than public understandings of phenomena, that the exercise of trying to find generalizations is either impossible or, at best, trivial. Although this is an over-simplification of the differing approaches, the essence of the problem lies here.

Two introductory books on the philosophy of the social sciences are Ryan [71] and Rudner [67]. A defiant assertion of the validity of the scientific school is made by Hempel in 'The Function of General Laws in History' in [36]. This paper is well worth reading since it has the twin virtues of being a clear exposition of the 'Covering Law Model' of explanation, while applying it to history, the discipline which by common consent is one of the hardest to fit into this framework. If the model applies in history, then it applies to the rest of social science without additional assumptions. The issues concerning explanation in history are argued in two excellent short books: Gardiner [22] argues for scientific explanations in history, while Dray [15] offers the counter-argument. A collection of essays edited by Gardiner [23] provides a good survey of the controversies.

The most vigorous, almost strident exponent of the view that social science cannot be modelled on natural science is Winch [83]. In some respects a curiously similar argument is presented from a Marxist point of view by Goldmann [26]. Taylor's more sober work [76] is obligatory for anyone other than the dilettante. The hardest, but by far the most intellectually convincing version of the argument against modelling social science on natural science is by Von Wright [80].

Economists have been greatly concerned with the problem of explanation and tend to be more cheerfully empiricist than political scientists. A classic statement of the extreme empiricist case influential in much of social science was made by Friedman [20]. A more recent work which takes later developments into account is Blaug [7]. In a series of essays edited by Latsis [45], an effort is made to apply the 'Research Programme' concept to economics though with limited success.

While hard cases may make bad law, it is arguable that they make good philosophy. Perhaps the most tendentious field to which an empiricist approach may be applied is psychoanalysis. Here one might consult Sherwood [74] and, rather later, Farrell [17] who apply to that controversial field the principles I have been advocating implicitly with regard to IR. Along with history, it might be thought (incorrectly) that psychoanalysis is the area to which the deductivist or empiricist mode of analysis is least applicable.

Political Science and IR

Whether IR and political science can usefully be separated is arguable. However, they do raise substantially the same methodological problems as those found in the rest of social science except that, historically, their development has been a little different. Rather crudely, the 'traditionalists' uphold a view compatible with Hempel. The issues are stated in a collection of essays edited by Knorr & Rosenau [42]. The classical or traditional view is defended in a well known essay in the collection by Bull. Reynolds [66] confines himself to IR, while Gregor [28] deals with the political sciences as a whole. Shapiro [73] provides an excellent critique of the empiricist position from a philosophically sophisticated standpoint. Nicholson [56] uses IR and economics as a base to try to bring some of the objections to empiricist explanations into the empiricist fold, with a success which it is for others to judge.

Amongst those who are in some sense 'scientific' in their approach to IR there are inevitable controversies about method, even if there is broad agreement about the nature of the end product. There is a question of emphasis on whether our relative lack of understanding of the international system is due to a shortage of data, or whether there is a shortage of theory. In particular, there is disagreement about the significance of quantitative studies. The two contending attitudes are clearly stated by Young [84] and Russett's reply [70]. Whatever the merits of these arguments, however, and while philosophical predispositions show through, it would be a mistake to confuse the justification of an empiricist approach with a justification of statistical approaches. These debates, though important, are debates about priorities, not about the nature of social knowledge.

Bibliography to Chapter 6

1. Almond, G. & Genco, S.J. 'Clouds, Clocks and the Study of Politics'. *World Politics*, vol. XXIX, no. 4, 1977, pp. 489–522.
2. Andreski, S. *Social Science as Sorcery*. New York, St. Martin's, 1973 and Harmondsworth, Middx, Penguin, 1974.
3. Archibald, G.C. 'Refutation or Comparison'. *British Journal For Philosophy of Science*, vol. XVII, no. 4, 1966, pp. 279–96.
4. Ayer, A.J. Man as a Subject for Science. In *Philosophy, Politics and Society*, ed. P. Laslett & W.G. Runciman, Oxford, Basil Blackwell, 1967 and New York, Barnes & Noble Books, 1972.
5. _____ *The Problem of Knowledge*. Harmondsworth, Middx, Penguin, 1971.
6. Blaug, M. 'Kuhn versus Lakatos, or Paradigms versus Research Programmes in the History of Economics'. *History of Political Economy*, vol. 7, winter 1975, pp. 399–433.
7. _____ *The Methodology of Economics or How Economists Explain*. Cambridge & New York, Cambridge University Press, 1980.
8. Braithwaite, R.B. *Scientific Explanation*. Cambridge & New York, Cambridge University Press, 1953.
9. Brodbeck, M. (ed.) *Readings in the Philosophy of the Social Sciences*. New York, Macmillan, 1968.
10. Brown, R. *Explanation in Social Science*. Chicago, Aldine Press, 1963.
11. Charlesworth, J.C. (ed.) *The Limitations of Behavioralism in Political Science*. Philadelphia, American Academy of Political and Social Science, 1962
12. Clarkson, G.P.E. *The Theory of Consumer Demand: A Critical Appraisal*. Englewood Cliffs, NJ & London, Prentice Hall, 1963.
13. Cyert, R.M. & Grunberg, E. Assumption, Prediction and Explanation in Economics. In *A Behavioral Theory of the Firm*, ed. R.M. Cyert & J.G. March. Englewood Cliffs, NJ & London, Prentice Hall, 1964.
14. Deutsch, K.W. 'On Political Theory and Political Action'. *American Political Science Review*, vol. LXV, no. 1, 1971, pp. 11–27.
15. Dray, W.H. *Laws and Explanations in History*. London & Westport, CT, Greenwood Press, 1979.
16. Elster, J. *Logic and Society: Contradictions and Possible Worlds*. Chichester & New York, Wiley, 1978.
17. Farrell, B.A. *The Standing of Psychoanalysis*. Oxford & New York, Oxford University Press, 1981.
18. Feyerabend, P. *Against Method: Outline of an Anarchistic Theory of Knowledge*. London, Verso Editions and New York, Schocken Books, 1978.
19. Frank, P.G. (ed.) *The Validation of Scientific Theories*. New York, Collier Books, 1961.
20. Friedman, M. *Essays in Positive Economics*. Chicago & London,

University of Chicago Press, 1966.

21. Gallie, W.B. *Philosophy and Historical Understanding.* London, Chatto & Windus, 1964 and New York, Schocken Books, 1969.

22. Gardiner, P.L. *The Nature of Historical Explanation.* London, Oxford University Press, 1965.

23. _____ (ed.) *The Philosophy of History.* London & New York, Oxford University Press, 1974.

24. Giddens, A. *New Rules of Sociological Method.* London, Hutchinson, 1976 and New York, Basic Books, 1977.

25. _____ (ed.) *Positivism and Sociology.* London & Portsmouth, NH, Heinemann, 1974.

26. Goldmann, L. *The Human Sciences and Philosophy* (translated by H.V. White & R. Anchor). London, Jonathan Cape and New York, Grossman, 1969.

27. Goodman, N. *Fact, Fiction and Forecast.* Cambridge, MA & London, Harvard University Press, 1983.

28. Gregor, A.J. *An Introduction to Metapolitics.* London, Collier-Macmillan and New York, Free Press, 1971.

29. Gunnell, J.G. *et al.*, 'Symposium of Scientific Explanation in Political Science'. *American Political Science Review*, vol. LXIII, no. 4, 1969, pp. 1233–62.

30. Hanson, N.R. *Observations and Explanation: A Guide to Philosophy of Science.* New York, Harper & Row, 1971 and London, Allen & Unwin, 1972.

31. _____ *Patterns of Discovery.* Cambridge & New York, Cambridge University Press, 1965.

32. Harré, R. *The Philosophies of Science: An Introductory Survey.* London, Oxford University Press, 1972.

33. Harré, R. & Secord, P.F. *The Explanation of Social Behaviour.* Oxford, Basil Blackwell, 1976 and Totowa, NJ, Littlefield, Adams & Co., 1979.

34. Hempel, C.G. *Aspects of Concept Formation in Empirical Science.* International Encyclopaedia of Unified Science, Chicago, University of Chicago Press, 1967.

35. _____ *Philosophy of Natural Science.* (Foundations of Philosophy Series). Englewood Cliffs, NJ & Hemel Hempstead, Prentice Hall, 1966.

36. _____ (ed.) *Aspects of Scientific Explanation and Other Essays.* London, Collier-Macmillan, 1965 and New York, Free Press, 1970.

37. Hindess, B. *Philosophy and Methodology in Social Sciences.* Atlantic Highlands, NJ, Humanities Press, 1977 and London, Harvester Press, 1980.

38. Hirschman, A.O. 'The Search for Paradigms as a Hindrance to Understanding'. *World Politics*, vol. XXII, no. 3, 1970, pp. 329–43.

39. Homans, G.C. *The Nature of Social Science.* New York, Harcourt & Brace, 1967.

40. Hudson, L. *The Cult of the Fact.* London, Jonathan Cape, 1976.
41. Kalleberg, A.L. 'Concept Formulation in Normative and Empirical Studies: Toward Reconstruction in Political Theory'. *American Political Science Review,* vol. LXIII, no. 1, 1969, pp. 26–39.
42. Knorr, K. & Rosenau, J.N. (eds), *Contending Approaches to International Politics,* Princeton, NJ & Guildford, Princeton University Press, 1969.
43. Kuhn, T.S. *The Structure of Scientific Revolutions* (International Encyclopaedia of Unified Science). Chicago & London, University of Chicago Press, 1970.
44. Lakatos, I. & Musgrave, A. (eds), *Criticism and the Growth of Knowledge: Proceedings of the International Colloquium in the Philosophy of Science.* (International Colloquium in the Philosophy of Science 1965), Cambridge & New York, Cambridge University Press, 1970.
45. Latsis, S. (ed.) *Method and Appraisal in Economics.* Cambridge & New York, Cambridge University Press, 1981.
46. Lessnoff, M. *The Structure of Social Science: A Philosophical Introduction.* London, Allen & Unwin, 1974.
47. Louch, A.R. *Explanation and Human Action.* Oxford, Basil Blackwell and Berkeley, CA, University of California Press, 1966.
48. Macrae, D. *The Social Function of Social Science.* New Haven & London, Yale University Press, 1981.
49. Magee, B. *Popper.* London, Fontana/Collins, 1975 and Lassale, IL, Open Court, 1984.
50. Meehan, E.J. *Explanation in Social Science.* Homewood, IL & London, Dorsey Press, 1968.
51. _____ *The Theory and Method of Political Analysis.* Homewood, IL, Dorsey Press, 1965.
52. _____ *Value Judgement and Social Science: Explanation in Social Science.* Homewood, IL, Dorsey Press, 1968.
53. Miller, F. *et al.,* 'Positivism, Historicism and Political Inquiry'. *American Political Science Review,* vol. LXVI, no. 3, 1972, pp. 796–873.
54. Myrdal, G. *Objectivity in Social Research.* London, Duckworth, 1970 and Middletown, CT, Wesleyan University Press, 1983.
55. Nagel, E. *The Structure of Science: Problems in the Logic of Scientific Explanation.* London, Routledge & Kegan Paul, 1961 and Indianapolis, IN, Hackett, 1979.
56. Nicholson, M.B. *The Scientific Analysis of Social Behaviour: A Defense of Empiricism in Social Science.* London, Frances Pinter, 1983 and New York, St. Martin's, 1984.
57. Nidditch, P.H. (ed.) *Philosophy of Science.* London & New York, Oxford University Press, 1968.
58. Northedge, F.S. *The International Political System.* London, Faber & Faber, 1976.
59. Novak, G. *An Introduction to the Logic of Marxism.* New York, Merit, 1969 and London, Pathfinder Press, 1971.

60. Paskins, B. & Dockrill, M. *The Ethics of War*. Minneapolis, University of Minnesota Press, and London, Duckworth, 1979.
61. Phillips, W.R. 'Where Have All the Theories Gone?' *World Politics*, vol. XXVI, no. 2, 1974, pp. 155–88.
62. Popper, K.R. *Conjectures and Refutations: The Growth of Scientific Knowledge*. New York, Harper & Row, 1968 and London, Routledge & Kegan Paul, 1969.
63. _____ *The Logic of Scientific Discovery*. New York, Harper & Row, 1959 and London, Hutchinson, 1974.
64. _____ *The Poverty of Historicism*. London, Routledge & Kegan Paul, 1960 and New York, Harper & Row, 1977.
65. Ravetz, J.R. *Scientific Knowledge and its Social Problems*. Harmondsworth, Middx, Penguin University Books, 1973 and New York, Galaxy, 1983.
66. Reynolds, C. *Theory and Explanation in International Politics*. London, Martin Robertson, 1975.
67. Rudner, R. *The Philosophy of Social Science*. (Foundations of Philosophy Series). Englewood Cliffs, NJ & Hemel Hempstead, Prentice Hall, 1968.
68. Runciman, W.G. *Social Science and Political Theory*. Cambridge & New York, Cambridge University Press, 1963.
69. Russell, B. *Human Knowledge: Its Scope and Limits*. London, Allen & Unwin, 1948 and New York, Simon & Schuster, 1962.
70. Russett, B.M. 'The Young Science of International Politics', *World Politics*, vol. XXII, no. 1, 1969, pp. 87–94.
71. Ryan, A.P. *The Philosophy of the Social Sciences*. London, Macmillan and New York, Pantheon Books, 1970.
72. _____ (ed.) *The Philosophy of Social Explanation*. London & New York, Oxford University Press, 1973.
73. Shapiro, M.J. *Language and Political Understanding: The Politics of Discursive Practices*. New Haven & London, Yale University Press, 1981.
74. Sherwood, M. *The Logic of Explanation in Psychoanalysis*. New York & London, Academic Press, 1969.
75. Spegele, R.D. 'Deconstructing Methodological Falsification in International Relations'. *American Political Science Review*, vol. LXXIV, no. 1, 1980, pp. 104–22.
76. Taylor, C. *The Explanation of Behaviour*. Atlantic Highlands, NJ, Humanities Press, 1964 and London, Routledge & Kegan Paul, 1980.
77. Todd, W. *History as an Applied Science*. Detroit, Wayne State University Press, 1972.
78. Toulmin, S. *Philosophy of Science*. London, Hutchinson, 1953 and New York, Harper & Row, 1977.
79. Van Dyke, V. *Political Science: A Philosophical Analysis*. Stanford, CA, Stanford University Press, 1960.

80. Von Wright, G. *Explanation and Understanding*. London, Routledge & Kegan Paul and New York, Cornell University Press, 1971.
81. Walsh, W.H. *An Introduction to Philosophy of History*. London, Hutchinson, 1977.
82. Weber, M. *The Methodology of the Social Sciences*. New York, Free Press, 1950.
83. Winch, P. *The Idea of a Social Science*. London, Routledge & Kegan Paul and Atlantic Highlands, NJ, Humanities Press, 1970.
84. Young, O.R. 'Professor Russett: Industrious Tailor to a Naked Emperor'. *World Politics*, vol. XXI, no. 3, 1969, pp. 486–511.

7 A Personal Synthesis

A.V.S. de Rueck

University of Surrey and CAC

Contrary to received impressions, international relations (IR) does not merely comprise a multitude of disconnected 'islands' of theory. A substantial proportion of IR literature today, implicitly or explicitly, is devoted to exploring, circumnavigating, attacking or defending a theoretical 'continent' whose outline is just beginning to emerge [see 6–11, 37, 47].

This note is intended to sketch that emerging perspective – so called in order to leave open the question of whether it constitutes a distinct paradigm in itself – which represents not a set of settled conclusions but a programme for future research in the discipline. It subsumes some aspects of present paradigms and supplants others. It starts from four sets of premises.

The first premises assert that the proper unit of analysis in IR is the *relationship*, which takes the form of exchanges, and that the totality of these reciprocal transactions, whether within or across the national boundaries, forms a network spanning the globe [8, 23].

The second set of premises asserts that this trading network constitutes a global *system* [29] which comprises interdependent economic, political and cultural *subsystems* [36, 33]. The degrees of interdependence, historical development [34, 44] and geographical extent [31, 45, 46] of this system and its subsystems are matters for empirical enquiry and controversy [26–29, 42, 44–47]. At this point, however, an inference is possible, namely that the global subsystems, being networks of exchanges, have substantially the forms and functions of *markets*, which result in market distributions of both resources and roles among the states around the world [23].

The third set of premises asserts, as a consequence, that international relations are functions of the relative positions and movements (and therefore of any ambiguities in those locations and movements) of the related actors within the global system [20]. It also asserts that *changes in relationships* (which broadly speaking is what is meant by *behaviour* in IR) are functions of *change* in the systemic structure [2]. Behaviour is viewed as systemic activity arising from context rather than from the idiosyncracies of actors. This is not to deny the validity of other levels of analysis – the individual, the group, the nation or the state – but merely to emphasise the pervasive influence of structural constraints at all levels. Such collectivities are not theoretical givens; they have to be derived empirically from the interaction patterns, as microsystems within macrosystems in 'cascading interdependence' [37].

A fourth premise asserts that ultimately all values depend upon or inhere in relationships [6–11]. Legitimized human relations are the keys to personal and national identities, to moral systems and to self-respect; they may well be valued above life itself [7]. *Legitimacy rather than power is the fundamental concept in politics* [6]. Ever since the Enlightenment, political development has been synonymous with enhanced legitimacy.

The first three premises form the basis of the theory that is interpreted in human terms by the fourth. They jointly establish the connections between the three modes of relations distinguished by Boulding [4], which he calls the threat system, the exchange system and the integrative system. Threat and exchange correspond to negative and positive reciprocity, of 'bads' and 'goods' respectively, to be compared with Chance's agonistic and hedonic modes [12]. Together they give rise to a more or less stable behavioural configuration which represents the acting out of the cultural pattern of the moment; as it were, an embodied collective 'frame of mind'. So reciprocity distributes roles and resources, functions and connections through an ever-changing structure derived from a productive as well as an exploitative division of labour – Boulding's integrative system.

To recapitulate, the unit of analysis is the *exchange relationship between roles* [13, 14, 15, 21]; and the network of relationships forms a *market system* which defines both the roles and the constraints on the actors concerned. Their roles may be governmental or non-governmental, individual or institutional, intra-, inter- or supra-national, in IGOs, INGOs or MNCs, churches or corporations, in the PLO, WCC, ICRC, or UNO . . . [31]. Every actor is enmeshed in one or other subsystem of interlocking roles whose relationships are expressed as exchanges, political, economic or cultural, as the case may be.

These interlocking roles provide implicit expectations concerning their interactions. The ground rule is that of reciprocity both in the perceived value or intensity of exchange and in its quality (of amity or enmity). This is not a moral injunction: it is self-interest. We pay our debts in order that we may be able to borrow again. Positive reciprocity sustains valued relations, negative reciprocity seeks to repudiate unsatisfactory ones. Balanced reciprocity is, however, rarely attained. Those who exchange on a basis of equality can 'turn the tables' of advantage at the next transaction so that things even out; but those who must bargain from a subordinate position are apt to find themselves at a constant disadvantage.

'Rational' actors are supposed to behave strategically so as to increase their gains and reduce their costs in trading networks which persist only so long as they provide advantages to one or both of the parties concerned [14, 21]. By definition, actors in economic roles seek solvency, political roles optimize legitimacy, cultural roles pursue prestige and defence roles seek security through military capacity and alliances [33, 36]. The subsystem or role to be activated at any time has also to be negotiated, usually tacitly, and the 'rules of the game' are not immutable, but are themselves subject to continuous renegotiation. They combine co-operative (Lockeian) and competitive (Hobbesian) elements in proportions dependent on the degree to which their values are fulfilled or frustrated by the operation of the system.

International structure corresponds to the network of exchanges. *Structure* is the more or less persistent pattern of transactions which retains its general form while continually changing in content (like a waterfall) [24, 35]. The system is therefore to be regarded as a process rather than an entity, and that process, as we have suggested, shares many of the structural and dynamic properties of a market. For example, it displays the imperfections of a market, and Pareto distributions of inequality may be expected, in wealth, in power and in prestige. Any advantage may be exploited to create further advantage and so tends to growth and self-perpetuation (*Matthew* 13:12). In the international free-for-all, the unintended consequence of multitudes of self-interested interactions is a market allocation of resources, political as well as economic. With due caution, one may hope to apply to this model such market concepts as supply and demand, elasticity and marginality, concentration and monopoly, and inflation or deflation [13, 33, 40]. The structure also shares with a market a tendency to become divided into sub-markets (segments on blocs) employing different currencies.

As a result, each of the subsystems – political, economic and cultural – is both stratified and segmented. In each, those who interact frequently and intensely are in close relationships; those who interact less are politically, economically and culturally more distant. Thus relations and the distance between actors may be mapped either upon a centre–periphery model or alternatively on a stratified cone of which the centre–periphery is a contour map, a radial plot, close and intense in the middle, sparse and attenuated around the margins. It is important to appreciate that in this way *structure is defined and mapped interactively*. It is not defined statically in terms of the attributes of actors, which are then invoked to explain their behaviour. It is defined in terms of systemic relationships, the dynamics of which actually constitute behaviour [31].

Alternatively the system can be mapped in terms of attention structure [12]. Attention is directed preferentially upward in the hierarchy: those who receive attention are regarded as having superior status; those who accord attention are defined as subordinate. Therefore those at the top generally receive more than they give – in other words, those of high rank generally enjoy a favourable balance of trade in all classes of exchange – political, economic or cultural. The international structure is thus mapped in a behavioural space. A change in structure implies a change in behaviour and *vice-versa*.

So it appears that the global political subsystem is distinctly hierarchical in form and stratified into superpowers at the apex or centre, major powers in the middle or core and small powers below or on the periphery; and on the other hand it is segmented into Western, Eastern and Southern (Nonaligned) blocs [29].

At the centre are mapped those actors involved in dense and extensive networks; they are most active because they are best endowed or most productive. At the periphery (lower strata) lie those less well connected in trade, in alliances or in cultural exchanges, because they are ill-endowed and so have least to offer in transactions. The superpowers at the centre of the segmented political subsystems are each surrounded by a core of client states which in turn overlie a peripheral stratum of developing countries [23].

As Parsons [36] has emphasized, exchange entitlement is based upon credit tacitly accorded to each actor by others depending on his reputation. Legitimate authority and cultural prestige are both forms of 'credibility', forms of political and cultural credit employed in those respective subsystems, homologous with monetary credit in the economic subsystem. They are based upon a combination of (a) a particular actor's endowment from the past (including natural resources, cultivated skills and industrial base), (b) his present reputation for productivity – politically, economically or culturally, and (c) on consequent expectations of future rewarding transactions with him. The centre and core enjoy high reputations for political, military, economic and cultural performance; their credit in all sectors is good. Those on the periphery have no such reputations, their exchange entitlement is low, and so they are politically, economically and culturally impoverished. Thus it arises that those below in all sectors tend to be at a disadvantage in any exchange with those above: unequal exchange is systematized between centre and periphery [1, 16, 18].

Power, whether political, military, economic or cultural, arises out of an incapacity of some to give as good as they get [33, 36]; most power is exercised over debtors unable either to discharge or to repudiate their debts [3]. To put the matter differently, legitimate power is the capacity to secure compliance from others to whom one is indispensable. OPEC is a case in point.

The differentiation of roles among states within the international system accords with their capabilities. Both capabilities and the international division of labour are also systemically distributed throughout the global structure. Peaceful relations are nourished by legitimate role differentiation and conflict by its absence [6–11].

The centre is distinguished by the dominant roles of economic creditor, political suzerain and cultural patron over the peripherals' subordinate roles of debtor, dependency and client [26, 27, 28]. In the economic division of labour, the centre is characterized by tertiary (service) activities, the core by secondary output (capital-intensive manufacturing), and the periphery by primary production (labour-intensive agriculture and mining) [1, 17]. Urban industrial specialization renders the centre *gesellschaftlich*: the rural agrarian periphery is relatively *gemeinschaftlich* [22, 24].

It is evident that the stratification represents a developmental sequence. But since no two actors occupy identical locations in the structure, and since the structure itself is constantly evolving, so it appears that no upwardly mobile society ever actually recapitulates the developmental history of a predecessor. There are no universal stages of economic growth.

The currency of political exchange is legitimacy (Parsons uses the word 'authority') [36], i.e. a political credit resting upon a reputation for honouring political debts, for executing political threats, and above all for productivity in the organization of collective goods. International collective goods include peace (disarmament?), security (deterrence?), territorial and maritime rights, and the stability of the global economy: public services on which the hegemonies of the superpowers are allegedly based. Governments need legitimacy among their constituents to secure authority at home; they need legitimacy among other governments to secure compliance abroad [6–10]. The Soviet government lacked legitimacy abroad for a generation after 1917 and was a pariah among nations; the Shah's government enjoyed much legitimacy abroad but lacked it in Iran. Both are needed to secure effective compliance. Legitimacy, we said, is a value placed upon a relationship. Valued relationships, resulting from acceptable role behaviour, motivate and sustain the ordinary commerce of daily life.

Naked power politics arises when legitimacy fails [9, 25]. And naked power in the long run is liable to be self-defeating.

Those at the top command a surplus which they can 'invest' (in long-term projects like space research or star wars); those in the middle can prudentially afford the premiums on 'insurance' policies (like the EC or CMEA), while those below having no assured surplus are reduced to 'gambling' on quick returns (Israel, Libya). Policy at the centre is pragmatic, in the core prudentially conservative and on the periphery radical and ideological.

Thus the situation, the problems, the resources, the strategies and the *mentalité* of actors go with their location in the global structure [5]. Those who are most active, and thus at the centre or core, are so on the basis of a resource endowment inherited from the past and on a reputation for present productivity (politically as well as economically and culturally speaking). Those lacking endowment and productivity are forced into the relatively passive periphery.

The top in all sectors is preferable to the bottom. The dynamic of the system arises from the imperative to rise (or at least not to fall) in the structure. There is then a general striving toward the top because even those with little ambition to imitate those above them in the structure find it necessary to struggle for development and 'progress' in order to avoid being surpassed by their peers. There is a general tendency to envy and to emulate those above in the structure which acts as a constant engine of 'progress' and change, of economic growth, of political development and of technical advance. And of conflict [2].

However, since the relative distribution of wealth, power and prestige in the system over several generations is remarkably stable (Pareto's Law), those that rise are often compensated by a downward displacement of others, relatively if not absolutely, so that the overall structure changes only slowly, although the mobility of actors across strata is relatively high (cf. displacement of UK by USA, changing positions of the USSR, India, China, OPEC and the NIC economies, all within one generation).

International actors are not necessarily aware either of the structure of the system or of their location in it, but they are aware of movement in their locality, through their connections in the exchange network and of changes in transaction patterns that correspond to movement in location. Actors are thus enabled to compare themselves with others in their (structural) vicinity. Actors measure their performance, or their costs and benefits in political, military, economic or cultural dimensions against so-called reference groups [39, 43]. It is generally the case that superior performers are at the same time economically productive, politically influential, militarily powerful and culturally prestigious. By the same token, subordinate actors tend to poverty, and to lack of influence, power and prestige. Both of these categories are said to be *congruent* [30, 20].

Actors that rank relatively high on some dimensions and low on others are *incongruent*. They suffer role strain since their location in the international structure taken as a whole is ambiguous. Their internal leadership is likely to experience cognitive dissonance as a result of a natural inclination to adopt as a reference group those congruent with their highest dimension, but to be evaluated by others in terms of their lower dimensions. A sense of injustice is liable to be engendered [39, 43].

After a time-lag that calls for empirical study, but which may be of the order of 15 years, governments that are not congruent grow highly motivated to become so, generally by using the resources with which they are well endowed (e.g. the economic resource of oil) to raise their standing in other dimensions on which they are low (e.g. political influence or military capacity). Failure in this ambition is a source of aggressive self-assertion in some, though others retreat into quietism depending upon structural factors and resource availability [32].

It is thus neither absolute deprivation nor inequality in the system that is the prime source of dissatisfaction, but deprivation relative to vicinal reference groups.

Relative deprivation of wealth or power tends to move state actors to the political left (Soviet Union); relative deprivation of prestige or status mobilizes to the right (Third Reich). Incongruent nations are fertile revolutionary soil domestically (e.g. Iran). Incongruence among developing countries may be expected to be correlated with revisionist foreign policies (e.g. Chinese People's Republic).

The boundaries of the various subsystems, of course, neither coincide nor remain static; and marginal roles develop between them in which brokers flourish. Nationalism as a political ideology since the French Revolution has brought political, economic and ethnic (or cultural) frontiers in Europe into some sort of coincidence so that they operate temporarily to reinforce one another. But demographic, technological and economic developments have tended to render such alignments obsolete and damaging. New aggregative and adaptive processes are working simultaneously toward upward integration for 'high' political functions (defence and economics) and downward devolution for 'lower' cultural and welfare functions that call for more active popular participation. The rate-constants for development in the various subsystems are very different, however (being of the order of years for the economy, generations for the polity and centuries for the ethnic subsystem), which inserts further parameters into the equations of change [14, 37]; 'cascading inter-dependence' in Rosenau's phrase [37].

Conflict is a symptom of movement in the system. It occurs between those who seek new relationships or fresh terms of trade and those who prefer the *status quo*. It may be an attempt by the strong to pass the burdens of adjustment on to the weak. So conflict begets change and most change leads to more conflict. Violent conflict is symptomatic of an attempt to break a web of intolerable and otherwise inescapable relations. Conflict is a decision process: it decides between alternative future structural connections. Since such change is universal and inevitable, so conflict is endemic and unavoidable; but it can be creative. It heralds the demise of the outworn and the birth of the new. Conflict resolution relies upon attempts to decide such outcomes by more rational and less costly means than violence, seeking accommodations that are less arbitrary and more acceptable than a temporary balance of power [2].

It is evident that national goals and interests, political values and perspectives, foreign policies and strategies, as well as economic resources and capabilities, all depend upon location in the system. The theory implies a concomitant dependence of detailed behaviour on position and movement.

Continuity of behaviour is not a problem: it is the natural outcome of stable structure. Behavioural change is the problem: movement begets change in behaviour and change in behaviour results in structural movement. It is this that interests policy makers. These are the areas of detailed dependence between behaviour, position and movement with which the perspective is ultimately concerned.

Bibliography to Chapter 7

1. Amin, S. *Unequal Development: An Essay on the Social Formations of Peripheral Capitalism*. Hassocks, Harvester, 1978 and New York, Monthly Review Press, 1977.
2. Banks, M. (ed.) *Conflict in World Society: A New Perspective on International Relations*. Brighton, Wheatsheaf and New York, St. Martin's, 1984.
3. Blau, P. *Exchange and Power in Social Life*. Chichester & New York, Wiley, 1964.
4. Boulding, K.E. *Ecodynamics: A New Theory of Societal Evolution*. Beverly Hills, CA & London, Sage, 1981.
5. Bourdieu, P. *Outline of a Theory of Practice*. London & New York, Cambridge University Press, 1977.
6. Burton, J.W. *Deviance, Terrorism and War: The Process of Solving Unsolved Social and Political Problems*. Oxford, Martin Robertson and New York, St. Martin's Press, 1979.
7. _____ *Global Conflict: The Domestic Sources of International Crises*. Brighton, Wheatsheaf and College Park, MD, University of Maryland Center for International Development, 1984.
8. _____ *International Relations: A General Theory*. Cambridge, Cambridge University Press, 1965.
9. _____ *Systems, States, Diplomacy and Rules*. Cambridge, Cambridge University Press, 1968.
10. _____ *World Society*. London & New York, Cambridge University Press, 1972.
11. _____ *et al.*, *The Study of World Society: A London Perspective*. Pittsburgh, PA, ISA Occasional Paper no. 1, 1974.
12. Chance, M.R.A. & Larsen, R.R. (eds), *The Social Structure of Attention*. New York & London, Wiley, 1976.
13. Curry, R.L. & Wade, L.L. *A Theory of Political Exchange: Economic Reasoning in Political Analysis*. Englewood Cliffs, NJ & Hemel Hempstead, Prentice Hall, 1968.

14. Deutsch, K.W. *Nationalism and Social Communication: An Inquiry into the Foundations of Nationality.* Cambridge, MA & London, MIT Press, 1966.
15. Ekeh, P.P. *Social Exchange Theory.* London, Heinemann and Cambridge, MA, Harvard University Press, 1974.
16. Emmanuel, A. *Unequal Exchange: A Study in the Imperialism of Trade.* London, New Left Books and New York, Monthly Review Press, 1972.
17. Finkle, J.L. & Gable, R.W. *Political Development and Social Change.* New York & Chichester, Wiley, 1971.
18. Frank, A.G. *Dependent Accumulation and Underdevelopment.* London, Macmillan and New York, Monthly Review Press, 1979.
19. Galtung, J. *Peace and Social Structure.* Copenhagen, Christian Ejlers and Atlantic Highlands, NJ, Humanities Press, 1978.
20. _____ *Peace and World Structure.* Copenhagen, Christian Ejlers and Atlantic Highlands, NJ, Humanities Press, 1980.
21. Homans, G.C. *Social Behaviour: Its Elementary Forms.* New York & London, Harcourt Brace Jovanovich, 1974.
22. Hoogvelt, A.M.M. *The Sociology of Developing Societies.* London, Macmillan, 1978.
23. Hopkins, T. & Wallerstein, I. *World System Analysis.* Beverly Hills, CA & London, Sage, 1982.
24. Inkeles, A. 'The Emerging Social Structure of the World'. *World Politics,* vol. XXVII, no. 4, 1975, pp. 467–95.
25. Kaplan, M.A. *System and Process in International Politics.* New York, Krieger, 1975.
26. Keohane, R.O. & Nye, J.S. *Power and Interdependence: World Politics in Transition.* Boston, Little, Brown, 1977.
27. _____ (eds), *Transnational Relations and World Politics.* Cambridge, MA & London, Harvard University Press, 1973.
28. Knorr, K. *Power and Wealth: The Political Economy of International Power.* New York, Basic Books and London, Macmillan, 1973.
29. Knorr, K. & Verba, S. (eds), *The International System: Theoretical Essays.* London & Westport, CT, Greenwood Press, 1982.
30. Lenski, G.E. & J. *Human Societies: An Introduction to Macrosociology.* Maidenhead, McGraw-Hill, 1981 and New York, McGraw-Hill, 1982.
31. Mansbach, R.W. *et al., The Web of World Politics: Non State Actors in the Global System.* Englewood Cliffs, NJ, Prentice Hall & London, Prentice Hall International, 1976.
32. Merton, R.K. *Social Theory and Social Structure.* New York, Free Press and London, Collier-Macmillan, 1968.
33. Mitchell, W.C. *Sociological Analysis and Politics: The Theories of Talcott Parsons.* Englewood Cliffs, NJ & London, Prentice Hall, 1967.
34. Olson, M. *The Rise and Decline of Nations: Economic Growth, Stagflation and Social Rigidities.* New Haven & London, Yale University Press, 1984.

110   *A.V.S. de Rueck*

35. Park, G.K. *The Idea of Social Structure.* New York, Anchor Books, 1974.
36. Parsons, T. *Politics and Social Structure.* New York, Free Press, 1969.
37. Rosenau, J.N. 'A Pre-Theory Revisited: World Politics in an Era of Cascading Interdependence'. *International Studies Quarterly*, vol. 28, no. 3, 1984, pp. 245–306.
38. _____ (ed.) *Linkage Politics: Essays on the Convergence of National and International Systems.* New York, Free Press, 1969.
39. Runciman, W.G. *Relative Deprivation and Social Justice: A Study of Attitudes to Social Inequality in Twentieth Century England.* London, Routledge & Kegan Paul, 1966 and Boston, Routledge & Kegan Paul, 1980.
40. Russett, B.M. (ed.) *Economic Theories of International Politics.* Chicago, Markham, 1968.
41. Strange, S. (ed.) *Paths to International Political Economy.* London & Winchester, MA, Allen & Unwin, 1984.
42. Thompson, W.R. (ed.) *Contending Approaches to World Systems Analysis.* Beverly Hills, CA & London, Sage, 1983.
43. Urry, J. *Reference Groups and the Theory of Revolution.* London & Boston, MA, Routledge & Kegan Paul, 1978.
44. Wallerstein, I. *The Capitalist World Economy.* Cambridge & New York, Cambridge University Press, 1979.
45. _____ *The Modern World System: Capitalist Agriculture and the Origins of the European World-Economy in the Sixteenth Century.* London & New York, Academic Press, 1981.
46. _____ *The Modern World System II: Mercantilism and the Consolidation of the European World Economy 1600–1750.* London & New York, Academic, 1980.
47. Waltz, K.N. *Theory of International Politics.* Reading, MA & London, Addison-Wesley, 1979.

Part Two:
Partial Theories

8 Power, Influence and Authority

A.V.S. de Rueck

University of Surrey and CAC

It has been held that as wealth is to economics, so power is to politics, and Morgenthau expressed the classical view that 'International politics, like all politics, is a struggle for power'. Nevertheless, power has proved as difficult to conceptualize as it is to quantify.

Power Politics in International Relations (IR)

The 'realist' school of thought developed the use of power as the key explanatory concept in the study of IR, and many scholars accepted power as the organizing principle for the whole discipline of political science. The most comprehensive and systematic treatment of international studies within this framework is by Morgenthau [30]. To this one should add the works of Aron [1], Schwarzenberger [38], and the Sprouts [44, 45] and Wight [48] as well as the penetratingly critical assessment of the whole 'power politics' school of international theorists carried out by Claude in his well-known study [13]. The classical concept of the 'balance of power' has been subjected to systems analysis by Kaplan [22] and Rosecrance [35], and to game theory analysis by Schelling [37], while Singer has made a sustained attempt both to establish an historical quantitative data bank and to test empirically the propositions derived from balance of power theory, with inconclusive results [43]. He finds, for example, that during the nineteenth century peace depended on parity between coalitions, whereas in the twentieth century, preponderance of the leading coalition was the condition for international stability [40, 41].

For those interested in reviewing the range of power approaches in IR, a number of useful surveys exist [7, 8, 31, 46]. The recent literature on the modern doctrine of nuclear deterrence is reviewed in Chapter 10.

The primacy of power both as motivating principle and as explanatory concept in political theory has been challenged by some (but not all) authors of the 'behavioural' school, who treat 'legitimacy' (in the sociological rather than the juridical sense) as the prime concept. They regard power politics as the pathological outcome of failures of legitimacy, both in domestic and in international affairs. Pre-eminent among these authors is Burton [10, 11, 12]. The greater complexity of the legitimacy paradigm and the fact that much history has been written, implicitly or explicitly, in the power political mode, renders these works difficult to grasp, but the power political position, whether as a policy prescription or as a theoretical framework, is now on the defensive and may in due course be relegated to an aspect of strategic studies.

Power nevertheless remains one of several concepts of central importance in political science in general and IR in particular. It is remarkable that although power was for so long accorded pride of place at the political table, it is to sociology rather than to political science that one must go for the most significant analyses of the nature of power. The remainder of this chapter will be devoted to tracing a path through this branch of the literature, toward a better understanding of the modern concept of power compatible with the newer behavioural paradigm. It will be shown that a coherent thread runs through what at first sight appears as a bewildering array of disparate notions.

Community Power

A classical paper by Bachrach and Baratz [4] attempted a semantic clarification. They noted that the word 'power' had been used indiscriminately by different authors to describe the capacity of actors to secure compliance from other actors by a variety of means, and urged that the following vocabulary (given in parenthesis) should be adopted in order to distinguish instances where compliance is sought by threat of sanctions (power), by persuasion or expectation of reward (influence), by violent coercion (force), by covert misdirection or misinformation (manipulation), or by consent in the joint pursuit of common aims (authority). Note that whereas power (threat), if it succeeds in its objective is costless in the short term, successful influence (reward) involves debts to be paid. On the other hand, threats that fail are unlikely to be cost free, since they then call for sanctions which are usually costly to impose. In the longer term, the exercise of power, force or manipulation breeds enmity and destroys legitimacy, whereas influence and authority, rewardingly exercised, breed trust and enhance legitimacy and compliance for the future.

Traditional analysis proceeds to describe power (to threaten credible sanctions) as the possession by an actor of capability, assessed in terms of tangible assets such as military forces, manpower potential, productive capacity, resource endowment and geographical situation; together with intangible factors which include strategic situation, national morale, levels of technical skill, and political and economic stability.

In a later paper Bachrach and Baratz [2] expanded the concept of power to embrace control over the agenda and processes of decision-making; and introduced the concept of the 'non-decision' to indicate situations where no overt exercise of authority, influence, power or force is necessary to achieve desired ends, as no challenge to those ends is contemplated by potential adversaries (see also [24]).

Both the above papers, as well as the same authors' study of the exercise of political power in a US city [3], were originally intended to challenge Dahl's efforts to conceptualize an operationalized version of political power [14] as a basis for empirically delineating 'the powerful' in the US community of New Haven [15]. The debate between 'pluralists' and 'neo-elitists' in the analysis of community power has centred around the crucial matter of the existence of a permanent and self-perpetuating power elite in US society, a debate that has its roots in Wright Mills' original enquiry into that topic [28]. For those interested in following the debate there are a number of papers that usefully summarize and augment this inconclusive series of exchanges [2, 4, 14, 15, 16, 19, 20, 21, 24, 26, 27, 31, 33, 34, 43, 50].

Exchange and Power

Talcott Parsons [32] draws attention to power as a generalized medium of exchange in political transactions, analogous to credit in economic affairs – an admirable account by Mitchell [29] contains an exhaustive bibliography. Parsons' detailed and sophisticated exploration of this homology in the domestic polity is briefly outlined in Deutsch's chapter 7 [18]. To comprehend its international significance two points must be appreciated. First, it refers as much or more to legitimate power (rewarding influence) as to the power of threat, so that henceforth the traditional emphasis on power as military credibility must be replaced by an even stronger emphasis on influence derived from proven capability to provide collective satisfactions. Second, power, like credit, depends upon past performance and present reputation both to execute threats and to reward compliance. The traditional analyses of capability remain relevant as a checklist of assets that render credible both threats and promises, expressed or implied. But it also requires inclusion of the past record of reliability of the actor concerned – a point indeed never neglected by traditional analysts.

Parsons' analysis [32] brings out two further aspects of the nature of power. Firstly, power, like credit, is a relational attribute rather than a possession of an actor and since it inheres in the attitudes of the related actors, it may be highly specific to the context and issues involved. Secondly, power, like credit, injudiciously overextended, may result in political inflation, homologous in most respects with economic inflation, arising from similar causes and subject to similar remedies. This is one of the most important insights offered by the new conceptualization, and it is capable of extensive elaboration. It promises to lead to a more rigorous explication of the consequences of 'exports' and 'imports' between the economic and political systems, i.e. to their interdependence. The crucial importance of political legitimacy is another aspect of the concept of power as political credit.

Blau [9] made a valuable but superficially contradictory formulation of the concept of power as arising from a monopolistic situation. If actor A is in a position to grant or withhold (political) services from actor B which the latter considers essential and does not know how to obtain elsewhere, then A has power over B, particularly if B commands nothing that A vitally needs in return. In general, the party less dependent on an exchange relationship is in the more powerful position.

Again, this emphasizes that power is an attribute of a structural relationship rather than a possession of an actor, although universal needs afford universal power to monopolists of 'essential' services (e.g. nuclear powers). Blau shows that the theory of monopoly (or of oligopoly) applies to the resulting relationships. For example:

1.   if the service supplied is inelastic, the introduction of new

    clients will enhance the power of the supplier (Malta's
    relations with NATO and the Warsaw Pact),
2. suppliers who club together to create a monopoly increase
    their power (OPEC),
3. clients' ignorance of alternative sources of supply enhance the
    power of the supplier, in whose interest it is therefore to keep
    clients separated and ignorant (divide and rule).

Subordinate actors can escape from the powerful only by learning to do without the 'essential' service, or by finding viable substitutes or alternative suppliers.

Parsons and Blau are not inconsistent; they are complementary. For Parsons, power inheres in unequal exchanges. For Blau, powerlessness arises from an inability to repay one's debts. Whereas Parsons conceptualizes power in a competitive 'market', resulting from a combination of a reliable reputation, a productive base, good (legitimate) relationships and scarce political talents, Blau emphasized oligopolistic power *over* a 'market'; that is to say, the power to dictate one's own terms in transactions. Political 'markets' of both sorts exist. The oligopolistic situation more closely resembles the international system, although as the number of actors increases, whether they be states or transnational agencies or corporations, the competitive market model becomes increasingly relevant. Power as political credit rests upon legitimacy; monopoly power stresses threat.

The task of reducing this concept of power, whether *in* or *over* a 'market', to an operational definition, so that it may be measured on an ordinal or (ultimately) an interval scale, has not been completed. Deutsch (in chapter 3 of [17]) distinguishes the following dimensions: power potential (material and human resources capable of mobilization to secure compliance), weight (the probability that a decision will be followed by the appropriate outcome), domain (the institutional actors, persons, territory or resources controlled), scope (the number of sectors, e.g. political, military, economic, social or cultural, subject to control), and range (the difference between the highest reward or 'indulgence' and the worst penalty or 'deprivation' which the powerful actor can bestow or inflict within his domain). Deutsch (in [18]) remarks that since power affords an ability to impose the costs of change on others and to resist the attempts of others to impose the costs of change on oneself, the net power differential between pairs of actors may be assessed as the ratio of costs imposed to costs accepted.

No discussion of legitimate power can neglect Weber's classical analysis in terms of traditional, legal-rational and charismatic modes of authority [47]. Charismatic authority tends to arise when either the traditional 'divine right' or the rational 'bureaucratic' modes break down in crises. Some men are born great, some achieve greatness and some have greatness thrust upon them. Notwithstanding all appearances to the contrary, charisma lies in the eye of the beholder and is thrust upon leaders in times of crisis. But in the final analysis all (legitimate) authority is conferred by those over whom it is exercised.

Bibliography to Chapter 8

1. Aron, R. *Peace and War: A Theory of International Relations.* London, Weidenfeld & Nicholson, 1967 and Melbourne, FL, Krieger, 1981.
2. Bachrach, P. & Baratz, M.S. 'Decisions and Non-Decisions: An Analytic Framework'. *American Political Science Review*, vol. LVII, no. 3, 1963, pp. 632–42.
3. _____ *Power and Poverty: Theory and Practice.* London & New York, Oxford University Press, 1970.
4. _____ 'Two Faces of Power'. *American Political Science Review*, vol. LVI, no. 4, 1962, pp. 947–52.
5. Baldwin, D.A. 'Foreign Aid, Intervention and Influence'. *World Politics*, vol. XXI, no. 3, 1969, pp. 425–47.
6. _____ 'The Power of Positive Sanctions'. *World Politics*, vol. XXIV, no. 1, 1971, pp. 19–38.
7. Barry, B. (ed.) *Power and Political Theory: Some European Perspectives.* London & New York, John Wiley, 1976.
8. Bell, R. *et al.* (eds), *Political Power: A Reader in Theory and Research.* New York, Free Press, 1969 and London, Collier-Macmillan, 1970.
9. Blau, P.M. *Exchange and Power in Social Life.* Chichester & New York, John Wiley, 1964.
10. Burton, J.W. *Deviance, Terrorism and War: The Process of Solving Unsolved Social and Political Problems.* Oxford, Martin Robertson and New York, St. Martin's, 1979.
11. _____ *International Relations: A General Theory.* Cambridge, Cambridge University Press, 1965.
12. _____ *Systems, States, Diplomacy and Rules.* Cambridge, Cambridge University Press, 1968.

13. Claude, I.L. *Power and International Relations*. New York, Random House, 1962.
14. Dahl, R.A. 'The Concept of Power'. *Behavioral Science*, vol. 2, no. 3, 1957, pp. 201–15.
15. _____ *Who Governs? Democracy and Power in an American City*. New Haven, CT & London, Yale University Press, 1961.
16. Debnam, G. 'Non-decisions and Power: The Two Faces of Bachrach and Baratz'. *American Political Science Review*, vol. LXIX, no. 3, 1975, pp. 889–99.
17. Deutsch, K.W. *The Analysis of International Relations*. Englewood Cliffs, NJ, Prentice Hall, 1978.
18. _____ *The Nerves of Government*. New York, Free Press, 1963.
19. Eisenstadt, S.N. & Lemarchand, R. *Political Clientism, Patronage and Development*. Beverly Hills, CA & London, Sage, 1981.
20. Flathman, R.E. *The Practice of Political Authority*. Chicago & London, University of Chicago Press, 1980.
21. Frey, F.W. 'On Issues and Non-issues in the Study of Power'. *American Political Science Review*, vol. LXV, no. 4, 1971, pp. 1081–101.
22. Kaplan, M.A. *System and Process in International Politics*. New York, Krieger, 1975.
23. Keohane, R.O. & Nye, J.S. *Power and Interdependence: World Politics in Transition*. Boston, Little, Brown, 1977.
24. Knorr, K. *Power and Wealth: The Political Economy of International Power*. New York, Basic Books and London, Macmillan, 1973.
25. Lockett, M. & Spear, R. (eds), *Organizations as Systems*. Milton Keynes, Open University Press, 1979 and Philadelphia, PA, Taylor & Francis, 1980.
26. Martin, R. *The Sociology of Power*. London & Boston, MA, Routledge & Kegan Paul, 1977.
27. Merelman, R.M. 'On the Neo Elitist Critique of Community Power'. *American Political Science Review*, vol. LXII, no. 2, 1968, pp. 451–60.
28. Mills, C.W. *The Power Elite*. London & New York, Oxford University Press, 1956.
29. Mitchell, W.C. *Sociological Analysis and Politics: The Theories of Talcott Parsons*. Englewood Cliffs, NJ & London, Prentice Hall, 1967.
30. Morgenthau, H.J. *Politics Among Nations: The Struggle for Power and Peace*. New York, Alfred Knopf, 1985.
31. Olsen, M.E. (ed.) *Power in Societies*. New York, Macmillan and London, Collier-Macmillan, 1970.
32. Parsons, T. *Politics and Social Structure*. New York, Free Press, 1969.
33. Polsby, N.W. *Community Power and Political Theory*. New Haven, CT & London, Yale University Press, 1980.
34. Riker, W.H. 'Some Ambiguities in the Notion of Power'. *American Political Science Review*, vol. LVIII, no. 2, 1964, pp. 341–9.
35. Rosecrance, R.N. *Action and Reaction in World Politics*. Westport, CT,

Greenwood, 1977.

36. Russell, B. *Power: A New Social Analysis*. New York, Norton, 1969 and London, Allen & Unwin, 1975.

37. Schelling, T.C. *The Strategy of Conflict*. Cambridge, MA & London, Harvard University Press, 1980.

38. Schwarzenberger, G. *Power Politics: A Study of World Society*. London, Stevens, 1964.

39. Singer, J.D. 'Inter-Nation Influence: A Formal Model'. *American Political Science Review*, vol. LVII, no. 2, 1963, pp. 420–30.

40. Singer, J.D. *et al.*, Capability Distribution, Uncertainty and Major Power War, 1816–1965. In *Peace, War and Numbers*, ed. B.M. Russett. Beverly Hills, CA, Sage, 1972.

41. Singer, J.D. & Small, M. 'National Alliance Commitments and War Involvement'. *Peace Research Society (International) Papers*, vol. V, 1966, pp. 109–40.

42. _____ 'Patterns of International Warfare; 1816–1965'. *Annals of the American Academy of Political and Economic Science*, vol. 391, September 1970, pp. 145–55.

43. _____ *The Wages of War, 1816–1965. A Statistical Handbook*. New York, John Wiley, 1972.

44. Sprout, H. & M. *The Ecological Perspective in Human Affairs*. London & Westport, CT, Greenwood Press, 1979.

45. _____ *Foundations of International Politics*. London & Princeton, NJ, Van Nostrand, 1962.

46. Taylor, T. (ed.) *Approaches and Theory in International Relations*. London & New York, Longmans, 1978.

47. Weber, M. *The Theory of Social and Political Organization*. New York, Free Press, 1964.

48. Wight, M. *Power Politics*. Leicester, Leicester University Press and New York, Holmes & Meier, 1978.

49. Wolfinger, R.E. 'Non-decisions and the Study of Local Politics'. *American Political Science Review*, vol. LXV, no. 4, 1971, pp. 1063–80.

50. Wrong, D.H. *Power*. Oxford, Blackwell and New York, Harper & Row, 1979.

9 Conflict, War and Conflict Management

C.R. Mitchell

The City University, London and CAC

It has been a tradition in international relations (IR) to treat war as unique and, hence, as a subject of study isolated from other forms of collective human behaviour. While there is some justification for this assumption – the sheer scale of lethal damage and destruction involved even in relatively 'minor' wars seems to make the phenomenon unlike any other – recent study has tended to see war as one example of a more general form of human behaviour, namely *social conflict*. The basic assumptions of 'conflict research' are, therefore, that while wars and civil wars may be the most obvious examples of organized human behaviour in situations where salient goals are perceived as incompatible, none the less there are enough similarities among ostensibly different types of human conflict (including war), to make worthwhile their study as a class. Escalation and de-escalation occur in strikes and inter-factional conflicts as well as in wars; as do threats and warnings and negotiation processes. Conflict research, therefore, hopes to illuminate our understanding of various types of human conflict by studying, comparing and contrasting all such types, rather than examining each in isolation from others. In this chapter, we examine the general field of 'conflict research', move on to studies dealing specifically with war, and end by reviewing various ways of coping with, or 'managing', conflict at different levels of global and domestic society.

Conflict Research

Recent literature has, to some degree, tended to reflect the convergence of interest among those who study war and those whose main focus of interest has previously been conflict within societies (a distinction that has become empirically more difficult to justify, given the increasing number of 'transnational' conflicts – the

Lebanon, Namibia, Cyprus, El Salvador in our contemporary world). Different writers have different emphases depending upon whether they approach the subject of conflict from the background of IR, on the one hand, or sociology or comparative politics on the other. The works of the first group tend to start by examining the nature and processes of domestic conflict and then proceed to consider war in the light of findings from these 'lower level' disputes. Of this group of writers, the most distinguished works are those by Himes [65] (particularly valuable in its analysis of racial and ethnic conflict) and Kriesberg's recent updating of his well-known 1973 study [80]. Wehr's book [144] on the 'regulation' of conflict contains a great deal of useful material on conflicts over the environment.

The second group of scholars comes from a background of IR and, starting from the opposite end of the war–social conflict continuum, attempts to understand general human conflict by applying findings from conflict in one of the most unstructured social systems – global society – to others where conflicts are (relatively) less destructive and often more regulated. The most readable of this group remains Rapoport [106], although Nicholson's work [96] may be preferable for those wanting a clear introduction to formal, mathematical analyses. My own textbook [94] is an attempt to gather together ideas about conflict between humans from a wide range of examples and disciplines. Works of this genre which deserve to be better known include those by Prosterman [102] and Dedring [36], although many scholars working in the field would still argue that the best overall introduction to conflict research remain the classic articles in the *Journal of Conflict Resolution* by Mack & Snyder [85] and by Fink [47], together with Bernard's paper written in 1957 for UNESCO and Thomas's more recent review [13, 136]. For those with a taste for collections of journal articles, both Smith's and Brickman's readers are worth dipping into [126, 22], and those interested in formal analysis could start with Boulding [19] and move on to Isard & Smith's difficult but rewarding survey [72].

Most of the survey works mentioned above devote at least some space to the main topics for research within the field. What are the origins of collective human conflict? What are the common identifiable processes as conflicts arise and are played out? How do people behave in conflicts as they try to achieve goals being blocked by an adversary? How do people – leaders and led – feel and perceive when engaged in one of the more stressful of human activities? In turn, each of these separate topics has generated a varied literature of its own. Of all the major questions to do with human conflict, that concerning the origins of the phenomenon has given rise to the greatest controversy and hence a literature seeming to lack coherence. At the individual level, much work has been devoted to analysing the nature and causes of human aggressiveness as a basic cause of human conflict. One school of thought, including Storr, Lorenz and others [132, 83], argues that aggressive behaviour is innate and biologically programmed into the human species, while another, such as Dollard or Scott [41, 119], takes the view that aggression is the result of the frustration (by other humans or circumstances) of goal-seeking behaviour. A third school holds that aggressive behaviour is essentially learned or modelled behaviour which is usually (but not necessarily) copied by the young from their elders in both formal and informal socialization processes. The best introduction to this particular controversy and to the whole field remains the set of readings by Megargee & Hokansen [87], although Gunn's deceptively simple book [57] is also a useful way into the debate, linking ideas of individual human aggressiveness with more general social violence. Anyone then interested in pursuing the topic could consult the work of Dollard and Tajfel [41, 133], proceeding thence to consider broader issues of the biology of political behaviour raised a few years ago by sociobiologists such as Wilson [148].

Sociological and political explanations of the origins of human conflict emphasize social structure and the maldistribution of resources (material and symbolic) as the source of much conflict between human groups and collectivities. Neo-Marxist analysis continues to be based upon the assumption of 'objective' conflicts of interest between haves and have-nots within society. This idea is interestingly extended by Dahrendorf's work [34] on a class conflict based upon possession of rights to manage and command; by Hechter's ideas on internal colonialism [63], and by the whole school of writing on international stratification, global systems analysis and underdevelopment led by Galtung, Wallerstein [54, 141], Chase-Dunn [29] and many others.

A number of writers have attempted to synthesize ideas about the origins of discontent, protest and social conflict into a multi-level framework to explain the origin and development of collective social conflict. Best known of such attempts is that by Gurr, who has taken the conception of a widespread sense of *relative* deprivation as the engine for growing discontent, and tried to show how this can become generalized and mobilized under the right combination of social, economic and political circumstances [58, 59, 60]. Even though operationalizing 'relative deprivation' has proved to be a tricky matter, Gurr's work remains an impressive effort at a general explanation of why and how conflicts arise within a society.

Literature on the *development* of social conflicts and common processes noticeable in particular cases is sparser and less satisfactory than work in most other parts of conflict research. Deutsch [40] has made a number of interesting observations about the nature of benign and malign conflict spirals and factors contributing to each. Similarly, there has been general interest in the processes of escalation of conflicts to the point of overt coercion, although less on the concomitant process of de-escalation. However, little has been written systematically on how and why conflicts become 'polarized' or on the effects of an external struggle on intra-party relationships and political processes. (For the latter, one still has to rely upon the insights provided by Coser's work [31, 32].) On the other hand, one recent interesting development in looking at conflict processes has taken the form of work on the process by which leaders find themselves increasingly committed to a line of policy which is more and more counter-productive, but from which they perceive they cannot escape. Work on this process of 'entrapment' by such scholars as Rubin [111] and Teger [134] has again emphasized the contribution that social psychology can make to our understanding of what happens in a conflict. It has also helped to clarify why leaders find it difficult to make U-turns, especially in conditions of intense conflict with a disliked and distrusted adversary.

In contrast to the somewhat patchy consideration of processes and interaction patterns in conflict, the work on both how people behave (i.e. their *tactics* and *strategies*) and how they feel in conflicts (i.e., the *psychology of being in conflict*) is much richer and more systematic. Efforts of parties to influence, compel and deter an adversary have been well described and analysed. Schelling's works on deterrence and compellence [117, 118] are well known, as are Morgan's conceptual analysis of deterrence [95] and Milburn's contribution to the same subject from a psychological perspective [90, 91].

Less familiar approaches to the complex and varied way in which people behave when engaged in a dispute involve some consideration of the use of non-violent strategies as a way of influencing an adversary. Sharp's works in this field repay study [120], while Boserup & Mack's book on the subject is succinct but full of useful ideas [18]. Similarly, Baldwin's work [5, 6] on the nature and use of positive sanctions as a means of gaining one's ends has rescued this aspect of behaviour in conflicts from relative neglect, and emphasized that rewards can also be employed successfully, even in the most intractable of disputes. Finally, the large literature on the behaviour of decision-makers during crises – the points at which a conflict crosses some threshold and enters a new, more dangerous phase necessitating quick response – has continued to grow apace with distinguished studies of Israeli crisis decision-making by Stein and Tanter [129] to add to Brecher's work in that area [20, 21]. For those coming new to this branch of conflict research, crisis behaviour can best be surveyed in the reader edited by Hermann [64] and the empirical and conceptual studies by McClelland [84] or the Stanford Group led by North [67, 68 and in 88].

Finally, the psychology of actually being in conflict and the concomitant perceptual changes (and attitudinal changes brought about by attendant stresses) are all widely considered in the available literature which deals with such topics as misperceptions, mirror images, dehumanization, identification, repression and much more. The best introduction to this field is Nye's *Conflict among Humans* [99], a succinct but thorough introduction that deserves to be better known. Stagner's older study [127] is more immediately attractive (if obtainable) and makes an interesting contrast with his earlier work on the psychology of industrial conflicts [128]. It has recently been challenged by a good introductory survey by Eldridge [44]. (See Chapter 14.)

War Studies

While conflict research has been using insights from a wide variety of academic disciplines – psychology, economics, political science, mathematics – to illuminate the general phenomenon of collective human violence and conflict, many other scholars have continued to analyse the more particular problems of war in global society. Much of this work has occurred as part of conventional efforts to understand how countries and their governments behave while at war, what tactics are used, how new weapons systems affect the conduct of war (and of 'no-war situations', where lethal violence is absent but the threat is not), and how defence and deterrence in partnership with others differs from defence and deterrence alone.

In other words, it forms part of the sub-discipline of strategic studies. (See Chapter 10).

Other writers have concentrated upon broader questions of war and peace, paying particular attention to questions such as the origins of particular wars and of war in general; domestic sources and effects of war; structural conditions in global society that are conducive to war or its absence; and the problems and difficulties of bringing war to an end. Many of these studies have involved massive research efforts and produced a wide range of publications, but there are a number of short introductions to the topic which are well worth reading, both as introductions and in their own right. The most readable of these remains Blainey's enjoyable study *The Causes of War* [14], while Howard's long essay on the same subject is also lucid and stimulating [69]. Waltz's classic needs no recommendation [143]. For those wanting a robustly power political approach, Stoessinger's short book [131], now in its second edition, will prove useful, as will Buchan's work on war in society [24].

One major feature of research into the nature and causes of war over the last two decades has been the impact of the computer, with its ability to handle large amounts of data and to search systematically for associations within a data set. The availability of this new tool has enabled a number of scholars, chiefly in the United States, to build upon the early, pioneering work of people such as Wright [149] and Richardson [110] who in the 1930s and 1940s launched research projects which compared a large number of wars in an effort to discover patterns in their origins. Probably the most carefully prepared and executed of these projects was that begun at Michigan by Singer, entitled the 'Correlates of War' Project (COW). Singer and his colleagues are now well into the second decade of their project and have published over 100 articles, books and dissertations based upon the 'hard data' that they have collected on the incidence of international war from 1815 onwards. Perhaps their best-known publication is a summary of these data, originally brought out under the title of *The Wages of War* [123], but revised and republished in 1982 as *Resort to Arms* [122]. An examination of either of these works will give a reader some idea of the care and intellectual rigour that Singer's team have devoted to the collection and analysis of data.

One distinguished exception to the group of scholars who use big machines for a big subject is Beer, although he is at home with the use of large amounts of quantitative data as his early works on the periodicity of wars demonstrate [8]. Beer's recent book *Peace Against*

War [9] represents the author's attempt to synthesize both quantitative and qualitative findings about what he terms the 'ecology' of war – why it occurs and what might be done to predict, and even to prevent, its occurrence. Beer draws ideas and information from a wide variety of disciplines and sources and his book must be counted as the most coherent account of the nature and causes of war presently available, as well as one of the most stimulating – although not the easiest to read.

If COW might be characterized as a large scale cross-sectional and diachronic study of wars during (roughly) the last two centuries, then another line of work has been opened up by the intensive study of a single case of war – the First World War – by Choucri & North [30]. Originally interested in the crisis of July/August 1914 that, through major miscalculations, led to an unwanted and feared war, the Stanford Studies broadened their focus to longer-term trends leading up to that war. These researchers have developed the concept of 'lateral pressure' on countries and within the system to explain why countries have, throughout history but in different, specific historical circumstances, engaged in war. In the major work on this case, North has tried to develop specific, long-term indices of lateral pressure to indicate where and when major points of friction (possibly leading to war) might develop, although one of his major arguments is that lateral pressure takes different forms depending on the historical circumstances of an epoch. This idea has been taken up by others, for example Ashley, who has applied North's basic ideas to the US–Soviet–CPR rivalry of the 1950s and 1960s in a complex but interesting work [2] which seeks to marry ideas of lateral pressure and 'historical relativism' with others from the world system school, headed by Wallerstein.

Finally, a major growth area in war studies during the last few years has been concerned with questions of how wars begin and how they end. One major line of thought has concerned decision-making calculations that attend choices of continued war versus negotiation and peace, and an effort to provide both formal and informal models that can embrace these (ostensibly very different) choice situations. Most formal of these approaches is Bueno de Mesquita's attempt to explain how decision-makers can become locked into a process whereby war might seem the optimum course of action [25]. *The War Trap* is an interesting attempt at a formal, general theory but it has weaknesses and, indeed, much of this new work sometimes seems a reversion to rational-actor, 'national interest' assumptions about how policy choices are made. One needs to read such research in tandem with the older work on crisis behaviour to obtain a clearer idea of the factors likely to work against the applicability of formal 'rational' models, with assumptions of stable preference orderings, decision-makers tolerably in agreement and generally agreed estimates of probabilities.

At the other end of the process of lethal coercion by war, the literature on how to end wars grows slowly but steadily. Randle's survey [105] remains the best general work on how wars have ended, while Iklé's older work [71] has stayed lively, readable and full of useful insights. Of the newer works, Pillar's subtle and compre-hensive analysis draws on much of the recent literature on negotiation theory [100].

Conflict Management

Whether one persists in the conventional view that war is so different that it is a unique phenomenon, or adopts the approach that it is 'merely' the most violent and lethal form of collective human conflict, there is still the problem of what to do about it, either by way of prevention before it arises or of management once it has become overt. Many scholars would argue that one tried and tested way of preventing conflict is through the deterrent threat, or demonstrative use, of military force, so that all of the vast literature on deterrence theory – whether analytical, by Morgan [95] or critical, by Green [55] – is relevant to conflict management. Similarly, a case could be made that much of the work on arms control or disarmament should, of right, form a part of any review of conflict management techniques. However, in the one case, deterrence strategy is merely a way of suppressing a conflict while disarmament attempts to remove the most dangerous tools for prosecuting an existing dispute. In both cases, the conflict is still there in the form of mutually incompatible goals and (probably) hostile and fearful emotions. Mere suppression or modification of conflict behaviour can hardly be counted as true 'management'. For these intellectual reasons, as well as for purely practical reasons of space, we leave these topics to be discussed in Chapter 10.

On the other hand, it does seem legitimate to consider that efforts to create structures, rules and processes to avoid or channel conflict into acceptable (or less damaging) ways of arriving at a solution do form part of the general field of conflict management. Relatively peaceful societies appear to be those which manage their conflicts well, rather than those which experience no conflict. Possibly the most interesting ideas in this area are from those writers who deal with ways of managing conflict in countries split by serious ethnic-religious or linguistic divisions, for it is in such societies that conflict management mechanisms are subjected to the greatest strain and are most necessary. In this field, Nordlinger's comparative study of divided societies is a stimulating beginning [97], as is Enloe's work [45] on ethnic politics and its management (or mismanagement). A general survey of the whole problem is contained in Pirages' work [101], while much can be learned by students of international politics from examining the extensive literature on the management of conflict within (and between) organizations. A good introductory collection of papers in this last field is that by Thomas & Bennis [135], while more recent surveys by Tjosfold & Johnson [137] and Bomers & Petterson [16] present a broad-ranging set of papers on how conflicts might best be managed within industrial and other forms of organization.

One interesting development in the purely IR field over the last few years has been the importation of the term 'conflict management' and its application to international and (especially) regional political organizations (both IGOs and INGOs) in the role of 'conflict managers'. The general approach can, of course, be traced back to works such as that by Nye [98] and the excellent short study published by Haas, Nye & Butterworth in the early 1970s [61]; but since that time studies examining various international bodies as 'conflict managers' have been undertaken. The enormous body of work on the United Nations has continued to grow and Bailey's recent two volume survey of UN peacemaking should be mentioned at this point [4]. The last few years have seen the production of numerous single studies of the OAS, the Arab League, the OAU, ASEAN, NATO [152, 62, 121] and the Warsaw Pact [109], all (at least partly) in the role of conflict manager; of comparative studies of a number of such organizations in that role [152]; and of major surveys, such as that by Butterworth [27], of international disputes since 1945 and the ways in which global society has tried (with greater or lesser success) to manage them successfully.

More conventionally, many scholars have continued to work on those aspects of conflict management which fall under the heading of 'institutionalization' – that is, efforts to place the conduct of a conflict and the resultant search for some minimally satisfactory settlement within a framework of norms or rules which parties recognize and which, in favourable circumstances, result in the establishment of some accepted legal system. A good starting point for this subject is Galtung's classic article [53] on institutionalized conflict, which has been reprinted in that author's collected works, themselves a mine of ideas about all aspects of conflict and its management [52]. Many useful ideas can be gained by dipping into some of the anthropological literature on conflict management in tribal societies (see Chapter 13). Particular mention might be made here of Mair's book on 'primitive' government [86] which covers many aspects of the problem of conflict and its management in ostensibly simpler societies than our own. In a similar vein, Gulliver's recent book [56] draws general lessons about negotiation and coping with conflicts from the author's deep experience of such problems in tribally-based societies. It might also be that examination of the manner in which 'rules of the game' developed in industrial societies could enlighten students of the general development of 'conflict within rules'. Flander's old collection of articles in the Penguin Modern Management series [50] is a good starting point for this body of literature and there are many other useful works, for example by Chamberlain & Kuhn [28]. Himes' book [65] has an excellent chapter on this whole issue.

Students of IR start, of course, from the assumption that the 'rules of the game' governing the nature of international conflict are weak and likely to be ignored when interests, defined as vital by national leaders, are at stake. Hence, they look for ways of managing conflicts which depend more upon adversaries acting in their own perceived self-interest than upon those which rely on institutionalized processes and accepted limits on behaviour. Bilateral diplomacy, bargaining and the informal help of third parties are thus of greater moment in the management of international conflict than courts or even the efforts of IGOs. Interestingly enough, it is precisely in these areas in recent years that there has been the greatest scholarly activity on both an analytical and a comparative basis.

Possibly the greatest growth in the study of conflict management has occurred in the analysis of bargaining and negotiation as ways of achieving a compromise ending to a conflict. There were, of course, useful studies before this (e.g. Iklé's work [71]), but recent growth has been phenomenal. To a large degree, this extension of systematic research has been the result of work carried out under the auspices of the Academy for Educational Development and the Harvard Negotiating project, although many other people have contributed to the development. Much of the work started as experimental studies of bargaining in simulated groups and concentrated upon efforts to uncover the impact on 'successful' negotiation of such variables as concession rates, the presence of an audience or the use of delegate negotiators [113]. Similarly, considerable attention was paid by such scholars as Druckman [42] to the psychological aspects of negotiation and negotiators. Work was extended to involve field work with past and present practising negotiators, either reviewing single case studies (such as the Trieste negotiations of 1954 or the Anglo-Maltese negotiations [in 154] over the future of the naval base on the island) or generally distilling the experience of international negotiators to discover how they went about their work and why they thought particular tactics succeeded while others failed [155]. A number of useful symposia resulted from this line of research and from conferences held to discuss varied aspects of the negotiation process [153], while books by Pruitt [103], Raiffa [104] and Gulliver [56] attempt to provide a coherent framework for the whole process, with varied success. Many of these works are interesting and insightful, but one has the feeling that they need to be set in some general framework concerned less with the specifics of negotiation than with the overall problem of terminating a conflict. This latter process involves deciding when to consider compromising; how to signal such a decision successfully to an adversary; pre-bargaining; the actual negotiation stage; and the final process of implementing any agreement. To date many of the important pieces of this process remain under-researched, save some interesting work on concession-making and signalling by Kriesberg [80]. Research remains concentrated upon the processes and practices of negotiation. One sign of this fixation is the emergence of a whole series of 'how to do it' books as guides for 'successful' negotiators. Probably the most interesting of these is Fisher's *Getting to Yes* [48], in which he expounds his approach to obtaining agreement through 'principled negotiation', which he advocates persuasively as an alternative to 'hard' or 'soft' bargaining.'

Finally, there has recently been a parallel growth of interest in informal processes of conflict management that involve third parties in some conciliatory or mediatory role. To a degree, this development has reflected an unusual increase in the use of such techniques in dealing with a wide variety of conflicts and disputes at all levels of society – inter-personal, inter-factional, communal and intra-organizational. In many parts of the world mediation has become a growth industry, particularly in North America where it is being used as a technique to work towards mutually acceptable solutions in familial, neighbourhood, environmental, prison and communal conflicts. In some cases, informal processes of mediation are being seen as an alternative to the criminal law and cases are 'diverted' from courts to undergo a process of mediated settlement. Many of these domestic developments have been admirably summarized in Alper & Nicholls [1].

At the level of international mediation, there have been a number of interesting developments from the pioneering work of Young [151], Jackson [73] and Curle [33]. Interest in informal mediation efforts has been stimulated by the publication of accounts by Jackson [74] himself (his 1956 'shuttle' between Nasser and Levi Eshkol) and by Ashmore & Baggs [3]. Yarrow's book [150] on the Quaker experiences of informal mediation has been supplemented by such works as Berman & Johnson's symposium [12]. 'Quiet diplomacy' (both private and from IGOs) has become the subject of much scholarly interest in recent years.

Accompanying this development has been a revived interest in understanding and analysing the activities of what might be termed 'powerful and interested' intermediaries, although Touval bluntly uses the term 'biased' intermediaries in his work on the topic [138]. This line of research has been stimulated by the ostensible success of such 'superpower intermediaries' as Kissinger and the more recent ostensible failures of such figures as Haig and Habib. Moreover, it is undoubtedly the case, as Levine's comparative work [82] showed over a decade ago, that many intermediary efforts to end conflicts are still, in spite of the spectacular growth of IGOs and INGOs, made by interested governments. Hence, the revival of scholarly interest in the powerful go-between is hardly surprising. Most interest to date appears to have been concentrated upon intermediary activity in the Middle East, and work includes studies by Touval [139] of major initiatives in the area from Bernadotte to Camp David, with more detailed consideration, for example by Rubin, of single intermediaries and their activities [112]. Much of the work, however, remains anecdotal and unsystematic but one suspects that, as with the literature on bargaining and negotiation, it will not be long before someone essays a systematic survey of the 'art' of mediation as practised at the level of international conflict, drawing upon the recent work already available and in progress.

One final and related development has been the growth of work and writing about the use of informal 'problem-solving approaches' often utilizing 'workshop' discussions as a way of seeking some solution to intractable conflicts. Once again, these efforts have their origins in similar techniques employed in domestic disputes (particularly within organizations), often associated with the 'organizational development' school of management theorists. However, the approach is now being applied tentatively to international and major inter-communal conflicts, with some success. Two original accounts of such procedures appeared in 1969 by Burton [26] and by Walton [142], but these have now been supplemented by later studies, including my own updating of Burton's work [93] and some useful accounts of the work of Kelman at Harvard [in 88]. Recent reviews and assessments of a promising new approach to conflict management have been written by R.J. Fisher [49], and other relevant work includes articles by de Reuck [37, 38] and Kelman & Cohen [78].

In conclusion, it seems no exaggeration to say that research into conflict, war and conflict management remains an expanding and exciting field, which has benefited from the eclecticism and interdisciplinarity introduced into IR by the behavioural revolution of the 1950s and 1960s. The amount of work going on, and the new lines of thought being pursued is, one suspects, a reflection of the realization that conflict, in its many forms, is a permanent feature of human society, and a highly complex feature at that.

Bibliography to Chapter 9

1. Alper, B.S. & Nicholls, L.T. *Beyond the Courtroom*. Lexington, MA, Lexington Books, 1981.
2. Ashley, R.K. *The Political Economy of War and Peace: The Sino-Soviet-American Triangle and the Modern Security Problematique*. London, Frances Pinter and New York, Nichols, 1980.
3. Ashmore, H.S. & Baggs, W.C. *Mission to Hanoi*. New York, G.P. Putnam's Sons, 1968.
4. Bailey, S.D. *How Wars End* (2 volumes). London & New York, Oxford University Press, 1982.
5. Baldwin, D.A. 'Power and Social Exchange'. *American Political Science Review*, vol. LXXII, no. 4, 1978, pp. 1229–42.
6. _____ 'The Power of Positive Sanctions'. *World Politics*, vol. XXIV, no. 1, 1971, pp. 19–38.

7. Barringer, R.E. *War: Patterns of Conflict* (2 volumes). Cambridge, MA, & London, MIT Press, 1972.

8. Beer, F.A. *How Much War In History: Definitions, Estimates, Extrapolations and Trends.* Beverly Hills, CA & London, Sage, 1974.

9. _____ *Peace Against War.* San Francisco & Oxford, W.H. Freeman, 1981.

10. Bercovitch, J. *Social Conflicts and Third Parties.* Boulder, CO, Westview, 1984.

11. Berkowitz, L. *Aggression: A Social-Psychological Analysis.* New York & Maidenhead, McGraw Hill, 1962.

12. Berman, M.R. & Johnson, J.E. (eds), *Unofficial Diplomats.* New York & Guildford, Columbia University Press, 1977.

13. Bernard, J. The Sociological Study of Conflict. In *The Nature of Conflict.* Paris, UNESCO, 1957, pp. 33–117.

14. Blainey, G. *The Causes of War.* London, Macmillan and New York, Free Press, 1975.

15. Blechman, B.M. & Kaplan, S.S. *Force Without War.* Washington, DC, The Brookings Institute, 1979.

16. Bomers, G.B.J. & Petterson, R.B. (eds), *Conflict Management in Industrial Relations.* The Hague, London, Boston, Kluwer-Nijhof, 1982.

17. Bonoma, T.V. *Conflict, Escalation and DeEscalation.* Beverly Hills, CA & London, Sage, 1976.

18. Boserup, A. & Mack, A. *War Without Weapons: Non-violence in National Defence.* London, Frances Pinter, 1974 and New York, Schocken Books, 1975.

19. Boulding, K.E. *Conflict and Defense: A General Theory.* New York, Harper & Row, 1962.

20. Brecher, M. *Decisions in Israel's Foreign Policy.* London, Oxford University Press, 1974 and New Haven, Yale University Press, 1975.

21. _____ (ed.) *Studies in Crisis Behaviour.* New Brunswick, NJ, Transaction Books, 1979.

22. Brickman, P. (ed.) *Social Conflict: Readings in Rule Structure and Conflict Relationships.* Lexington, MA, D.C. Heath, 1974.

23. Bronfenbrenner, U.I. 'The Mirror Image in Soviet–American Relations'. *Journal of Social Issues*, vol. XVII, no. 3, 1961, pp. 45–56.

24. Buchan, A. *War in Modern Society.* London, Collins, 1968.

25. Bueno De Mesquita, B. *The War Trap.* New Haven & London, Yale University Press, 1981.

26. Burton, J.W. *Conflict and Communication.* London, Macmillan and New York, Free Press, 1969.

27. Butterworth, R.L. *Managing Inter-State Conflict, 1945–74.* Pittsburgh, University Center for International Studies, 1976.

28. Chamberlain, N.W. & Kuhn, J.W. *Collective Bargaining.* New York, McGraw Hill, 1965.

29. Chase-Dunn, C. 'Comparative Research on World System Characteristics'. *International Studies Quarterly*, vol. 23, no. 4, December 1979, pp. 601-24.

30. Choucri, N. & North, R.C. *Nations in Conflict: National Growth and International Violence.* San Francisco, Freeman, 1975.

31. Coser, L.A. *Continuities in the Study of Social Conflict.* New York, Free Press and London, Collier-Macmillan, 1970.

32. _____ *The Function of Social Conflict.* London, Routledge & Kegan Paul, 1956 and New York, Free Press, 1964.

33. Curle, A. *Making Peace.* London, Tavistock Publications, 1971.

34. Dahrendorf, R. *Class and Class Conflict in Industrial Society.* London, Routledge & Kegan Paul and Stanford, CA, Stanford University Press, 1959.

35. Davies, J.C. 'Towards a Theory of Revolution'. *American Sociological Review*, vol. 27, no. 1, 1962, pp. 5-19.

36. Dedring, J. *Recent Advances in Peace and Conflict Research.* Beverly Hills, CA & London, Sage, 1976.

37. de Reuck, A.V.S. 'Controlled Communication: Rationale and Dynamics'. *The Human Context*, vol. VI, no. 1, 1974, pp. 64-80.

38. _____ 'A Theory of Conflict Resolution By Problem Solving'. *Man, Environment, Space and Time*, vol. 3, no. 1, 1983, pp. 53-69.

39. _____ & Knight, J. (eds), *Conflict in Society* (A CIBA Foundation Symposium). London, J. & A. Churchill, 1966.

40. Deutsch, M. *The Resolution of Conflict.* New Haven, CT & London, Yale University Press, 1973.

41. Dollard, J. *et al.*, *Frustration and Aggression.* London & Westport, CT, Greenwood Press, 1980.

42. Druckman, D. *Human Factors in International Negotiations.* Beverly Hills, CA & London, Sage, 1973.

43. Edmead, F. *Analysis and Prediction in International Mediation.* New York, UNITAR, 1971.

44. Eldridge, A.F. *Images of Conflict.* New York, St. Martin's, 1979.

45. Enloe, C. *Ethnic Conflict and Political Development.* Boston, Little, Brown, 1973.

46. Farrell, J.C. & Smith, A.P. (eds), *Image and Reality in World Politics.* New York, Columbia University Press, 1968.

47. Fink, C.F. 'Some Conceptual Difficulties in the Theory of Social Conflict'. *Journal of Conflict Resolution*, vol. XII, no. 4, 1968, pp. 412-60.

48. Fisher, R. & Ury, W. *Getting to 'Yes'.* London, Hutchinson and New York, Penguin, 1983.

49. Fisher, R.J. 'Third Party Conciliation'. *Journal of Conflict Resolution*, vol. XVI, no. 1, 1972, pp. 67-94.

50. Flanders, A. (ed.) *Collective Bargaining.* Harmondsworth, Middx, Penguin, 1971.

51. Fromm, E. *The Anatomy of Human Destructiveness*. New York, Fawcett, 1978 and Harmondsworth, Middx, Penguin, 1982.
52. Galtung, J. *Essays in Peace Research*. vols. I–V, Copenhagen, Christian Ejlers and Atlantic Highlands, NJ, Humanities Press, 1975–9.
53. _____ 'Institutional Conflict Resolution'. *Journal of Peace Research*, vol. 2, no. 4, 1965, pp. 348–96.
54. _____ 'A Structural Theory of Imperialism'. *Journal of Peace Research*, vol. 8, no. 1, 1971, pp. 81–117.
55. Green, P. *Deadly Logic: The Theory of Nuclear Deterrence*. New York, Schocken, 1969.
56. Gulliver, P.H. *Disputes and Negotiations: A Cross-Cultural Perspective*. New York & London, Academic Press, 1980.
57. Gunn, J. *Violence in Human Society*, Newton Abbot, David & Charles and New York, Beckman, 1973.
58. Gurr, T.R. 'A Causal Model of Civil Strife'. *American Political Science Review*, vol. LXII, no. 4, 1968, pp. 1104–24.
59. _____ *Why Men Rebel*. Princeton, NJ & Guildford, Princeton University Press, 1970.
60. _____ (ed.) *Handbook of Political Conflict: Theory and Research*, New York, Free Press and London, Collier-Macmillan, 1981.
61. Haas, E.B. *et al.*, *Conflict Management By International Organisations*. Morristown, NJ, General Learning Press, 1972.
62. Hassouna, H. *The League of Arab States and Regional Disputes*. New York, Oceana and Lancaster, Sijthoff, 1975.
63. Hechter, M. *Internal Colonialism: The Celtic Fringe in the British National Government, 1536–1966*. London, Routledge & Kegan Paul and Berkeley, CA, University of California Press, 1975.
64. Hermann, C.F. (ed.) *International Crises: Insights from Behavioural Research*. London, Collier-Macmillan and New York, Free Press, 1972.
65. Himes, J.S. *Conflict and Conflict Management*. Athens, GA, University of Georgia Press, 1982.
66. Hoglund, B. & Ulrich, J.W. (eds), *Conflict Control and Conflict Resolution*. Copenhagen, Munksgard, 1972.
67. Holsti, O.R. *Crisis, Escalation, War*. Montreal, McGill-Queen's University Press, 1972.
68. _____ 'The 1914 Case'. *American Political Science Review*, vol. LIX, no. 2, 1965, pp. 365–78.
69. Howard, M. *The Causes of War*. London, Temple Smith and Cambridge, MA, Harvard University Press, 1983.
70. Iklé, F.C. *Every War Must End*. New York, Columbia University Press, 1971.
71.   *How Nations Negotiate*. Millwood, NY, Kraus Reprint, 1982.
72. Isard, W. & Smith, C. *Conflict Analysis and Practical Conflict Management Procedures*. Cambridge, MA, Ballinger, 1983.

73. Jackson, E. *Meeting of Minds.* New York, McGraw Hill, 1952.
74. _____ *Middle East Mission.* New York & London, Norton, 1984.
75. Janis, I.L. *Victims of Groupthink.* Boston, Houghton Mifflin, 1982.
76. Jervis, R. *The Logic of Images in International Relations.* Princeton, NJ & Guildford, Princeton University Press, 1970.
77. Kelman, H.C. (ed.) *International Behavior: A Social-Psychological Analysis.* New York, Holt, Rhinehart & Winston, 1965.
78. Kelman, H.C. & Cohen, S.P. 'The Problem-Solving Workshop'. *Journal of Peace Research*, vol. 13, no. 2, 1976, pp. 79–90.
79. Kolb, D, *The Mediators.* Cambridge, MA & London, MIT Press, 1984.
80. Kriesberg, L. *Social Conflicts.* Englewood Cliffs, NJ & Hemel Hempstead, Prentice Hall, 1982.
81. Lall, A. *Modern International Negotiation.* New York, Columbia University Press, 1966.
82. Levine, E.P. 'Mediation in International Politics: A Universe and Some Observations'. *Peace Research Society (International) Papers*, vol. XVIII, 1972, pp. 23–43.
83. Lorenz, Konrad *On Aggression.* London, Methuen, 1966 and New York, Harcourt Brace and Jovanovich, 1974.
84. McClelland, C.A. 'The Acute International Crisis'. *World Politics*, vol. XIV, no. 1, 1961, pp. 182–204.
85. Mack, R.W. & Snyder, R.C. 'The Analysis of Social Conflict: Towards an Overview and Synthesis'. *Journal of Conflict Resolution*, vol. I, no. 2, 1957, pp. 212–48.
86. Mair, L. *Primitive Government.* London, Scolar Press, 1977 and Indianapolis, Indiana University Press, 1978.
87. Megargee, E.I. & Hokansen, J.E. (eds), *The Dynamics of Aggression.* New York & London, Harper & Row, 1970.
88. Merritt, R.L. (ed.) *Communication in International Politics.* Urbana, IL, & London, University of Illinois Press, 1972.
89. Midlarsky, M. *On War: Political Violence in the International System.* London, Collier-Macmillan and New York, Free Press, 1975.
90. Milburn, T.W. 'The Concept of Deterrence: Some Logical and Psychological Considerations'. *Journal of Social Issues*, vol. XVII, no. 3, 1961, pp. 3–11.
91. _____ 'What Constitutes Effective Deterrence?'. *Journal of Conflict Resolution*, vol. III, no. 2, 1959, pp. 138–45.
92. Milgram, S. *Obedience to Authority: An Experimental View.* London, Tavistock Publications and New York, Harper & Row, 1975.
93. Mitchell, C.R. *Peacemaking and the Consultant's Role.* Farnborough, Hants, Gower and New York, Nichols, 1981.
94. _____ *The Structure of International Conflict.* London, Macmillan and New York, St. Martin's, 1981.
95. Morgan, P. *Deterrence: A Conceptual Analysis.* Beverly Hills, CA &

London, Sage, 1977.

96. Nicholson, M.B. *Conflict Analysis.* London, English University Press, 1970.

97. Nordlinger, E.A. *Conflict Regulation in Divided Societies.* Cambridge, MA, Harvard University, Center for International Studies, 1972.

98. Nye, J.S. *Peace in Parts: Integration and Conflict in Regional Organisations.* Boston, MA, Little, Brown, 1971.

99. Nye, R.D. *Conflict Among Humans.* New York, Springer Publishing Corp, 1973.

100. Pillar, P.R. *Negotiating Peace.* Princeton, NJ & Guildford, Princeton University Press, 1983.

101. Pirages, D. *Managing Political Conflict.* Sunbury on Thames, Middx, Nelson and New York, Praeger, 1976.

102. Prosterman, R.L. *Surviving to 3000: An Introduction to the Study of Lethal Conflict.* Belmont, CA, Duxbury, 1972.

103. Pruitt, D.G. *Negotiating Behavior.* New York & London, Academic Press, 1982.

104. Raiffa, H. *The Art and Science of Negotiation.* Cambridge, MA & London, Harvard University Press, 1982.

105. Randle, R.F. *The Origins of Peace: A Study of Peacemaking and the Structure of Peace Settlements.* New York, Free Press, 1973.

106. Rapoport, A. *Conflict in a Man-Made Environment.* Harmondsworth, Middx, Penguin, 1974.

107. _____ *Fights, Games and Debates.* Ann Arbor, MI, University of Michigan Press, 1974.

108. Ray, J.L. 'Understanding Rummel'. *Journal of Conflict Resolution*, vol. 26, no. 1, pp. 161–87.

109. Remington, R.A. *The Warsaw Pact: Case Studies in Communist Conflict Resolution.* Cambridge, MA, MIT Press, 1971.

110. Richardson, L.F. *Statistics of Deadly Quarrels.* London, Stevens and Ann Arbor, MI, Boxwood Press, 1960.

111. Rubin, J.Z. 'Psychological Traps'. *Psychology Today*, vol. 15, no. 3, 1981, pp. 52–63.

112. _____ (ed.) *Dynamics of Third Party Intervention.* New York, Praeger, 1981.

113. _____ & Brown, B.R. *The Social Psychology of Bargaining and Negotiations.* New York & London, Academic Press, 1975.

114. Rummel, R.J. *Understanding Conflict and War* (vols 1–5). Beverly Hills, CA & London, Sage, 1975–1981.

115. Russett, B.M. *Peace, War and Numbers.* Beverly Hills, CA, Sage, 1972.

116. Schellenberg, J.A. *The Science of Conflict.* Cambridge, MA & London, Harvard University Press, 1980.

117. Schelling, T.C. *Arms and Influence.* London & Westport, CT, Greenwood Press, 1977.

118. _____ *The Strategy of Conflict*. Cambridge, MA & London, Harvard University Press, 1980.
119. Scott, J.P. *Aggression*. Chicago & London, University of Chicago Press, 1976.
120. Sharp, G. *et al.* (eds), *The Politics of Non-Violent Action*. Boston, Porter Sargent, 1980.
121. Simon, S.W. *The ASEAN States and Regional Security*. Stanford, CA, Hoover Institute Press, 1982.
122. Singer, J.D. & Small, M. *Resort to Arms: International and Civil War 1816–1980*. Beverly Hills, CA, Sage, 1982.
123. _____ *The Wages of War, 1816–1965. A Statistical Handbook*. New York, John Wiley, 1972.
124. Singer, J.D. (ed.) *Quantitative International Politics: Insights and Evidence*. New York, Free Press and London, Collier-Macmillan, 1968.
125. Singer, J.D. & Wallace, M.D. (eds), *To Augur Well: Early Warning Indicators in World Politics*. Beverly Hills, CA, Sage, 1979.
126. Smith, C.G. (ed.) *Conflict Resolution: Contributions of the Behavioural Sciences*. Notre Dame, IN & London, University of Notre Dame Press, 1971.
127. Stagner, R. *Psychological Aspects of International Conflict*. Belmont, CA, Brooks/Cole Publishing Co., 1967.
128. _____ *Psychology of Industrial Conflict*. London, Chapman & Hall and New York, John Wiley, 1956.
129. Stein, J.G. & Tanter, R. *Rational Decision-Making: Israel's Security Choices 1967 & 1973*. Columbus, OH, Ohio State University Press, 1980.
130. Steiner, J. 'Nonviolent Conflict Resolution in Democratic Systems: Switzerland'. *Journal of Conflict Resolution*, vol. XIII, no. 3, 1969, pp. 295–304.
131. Stoessinger, J.G. *Why Nations Go To War*. New York, St. Martin's, 1978.
132. Storr, A. *Human Aggression*. New York, Atheneum and Harmondsworth, Middx, Penguin, 1971.
133. Tajfel, H. *Human Groups and Social Categories*. Cambridge & New York, Cambridge University Press, 1981.
134. Teger, A. *Too Much Invested to Quit*. Oxford & New York, Pergamon Press, 1979.
135. Thomas, J.M. & Bennis, W.G. (eds), *Management of Change and Conflict*. Harmondsworth, Middx, Penguin, 1972.
136. Thomas, K. Conflict and Conflict Management. In *Handbook of Industrial and Organisational Psychology*, ed. M.E. Dunnette. Chichester & New York, Wiley, 1983.
137. Tjosvold, D. & Johnson, D.W. (eds), *Productive Conflict Management*. New York, Irvington Publishers, 1983.
138. Touval, S. 'Biased Intermediaries: Theoretical and Historical

Considerations'. *Jerusalem Journal of International Studies*, vol. I, no. 1, 1975, pp. 51–69.

139. _____ *The Peace Brokers: Mediators in the Arab-Israeli Conflict, 1948–1979*. Princeton, NJ & Guildford, Princeton University Press, 1982.

140. Wall, J.A. 'Mediation: An Analysis, Review and Proposed Research'. *Journal of Conflict Resolution*, vol. 25, no. 1, 1981, pp. 157–80.

141. Wallerstein, I. *The Modern World System: Capitalist Agriculture and the Origins of the European World-Economy in the Sixteenth Century*. London & New York, Academic Press, 1981.

142. Walton, R.E. *Interpersonal Peacemaking*. Reading, MA & Wokingham, Berks, Addison Wesley, 1969.

143. Waltz, K.N. *Man, the State and War*. New York, Columbia University Press, 1959.

144. Wehr, P. *Conflict Regulation*. Boulder, CO, Westview, 1979.

145. White, R.K. *Nobody Wanted War: Misperception in Vietnam and Other Wars*. Garden City, NY, Doubleday, 1970.

146. _____ 'Three Not-So-Obvious Contributions of Psychology to Peace'. *Journal of Social Issues*, vol. XXV, no. 4, 1969, pp. 23–40.

147. Wilkenfield, J. (ed.) *Conflict Behavior and Linkage Politics*. New York, David McKay Co., 1973.

148. Wilson, E.O. *Sociobiology: The New Synthesis*. Cambridge, MA, & London, Harvard University Press, 1980.

149. Wright, Q. *A Study of War* (Abridged edition). Chicago & London, University of Chicago Press, 1983.

150. Yarrow, C.H. *Quaker Experiences in International Conciliation*. New Haven, CT & London, Yale University Press, 1978.

151. Young, O.R. *The Intermediaries: Third Parties in International Crises*. Princeton, NJ & Guildford, Princeton University Press, 1967.

152. Zacher, M.W. (ed.) *International Conflict and Collective Security*. New York, Praeger, 1979.

153. Zartman, I.W. (ed.) *The Negotiation Process*. Beverly Hills, CA & London, Sage, 1979.

154. _____ *The 50% Solution*. Garden City, NY, Anchor Press, 1976.

155. Zartman, I.W. & Berman, M.R. *The Practical Negotiator*. New Haven, CT & London, Yale University Press, 1983.

10 Strategy

A.J.R. Groom
University of Kent at Canterbury and CAC

Strategy is concerned with the causes, modalities and effects of power politics and specifically the threat, application, and the effects of overtly coercive measures – the 'sharp end' of power politics. In this volume the subject has been divided into 'conflict' and 'strategy'. The distinction is artificial and reflects the organization of university courses. Thus the chapter on conflict complements this chapter.

Writers of the classical epoch who are read for their insights and historical value knew the importance of relating analyses of the military events of the day to basic political and social processes, thereby ensuring their continued relevance. They addressed themselves to such questions as deterrence, revolution and civil–military relations which are still the concern of contemporary strategists although clearly, then as now, there are important unique aspects of such questions. There is thus a 'classical' literature.

The creation of IR as an academic 'discipline' was a reaction to the horrors of the Great War and owed much to rationalist-progressive thought. It was greatly concerned with the founding and activities of the League of Nations. It is not surprising that the strategists of this period concentrated on collective security and disarmament; in short, on the prevention of war. Later, as the international climate changed, culminating in the Second World War, the concern shifted to waging war. The strategists of the League's activities had an internationalist or pro-League outlook; those that followed wrote about strategic matters more from the standpoint of a particular country. This disturbing trend has continued to the present day as Booth [9] points out. The arms control and disarmament literature, other than that from sources such as SIPRI, also tends to examine problems from the point of view of a participant rather than analyse the phenomenon as a whole. The contemporary literature tends therefore to be *engagé* with a frequent lack of conceptual depth. Indeed, the literature is rich in highly technical analyses of the 'strategic balance', but relatively weak in empirically-based theory dealing with the underlying concepts. This conceptual weakness helps to explain the remarkable waxing and waning of the nuclear deterrence literature. For about a decade from the early 1950s works on nuclear deterrence abounded, inspired by a realization of the enormous power of nuclear weapons, the likelihood of their proliferation and the fact of universal vulnerability. Defence was impossible, so deterrence was the order of the day. Then the flow stopped, not because the issues had been resolved, but because they were not resolvable. The major options of 'massive retaliation' or 'graduated deterrence' had emerged, but there was no empirical theory at any systems level which could decide the issue. Further attempts at conceptual development were futile or, in some cases, frivolous. The basic literature on nuclear deterrence, therefore, dates from the late 1950s and early 1960s, although there has recently been a rekindling of interest in reviewing earlier conceptual work in the light of experience. It seems likely that in the event of further nuclear proliferation, another spate of 'theorizing' will seek to address the modalities and ground rules of systems of regional deterrence and especially the interaction between regional systems and the global system.

There are two other areas of conceptual interest – revolutionary warfare and the arms race and disarmament – which feature prominently in the current literature. A revolution seeks to change the personnel or the policies of a government, the structures of a social unit or, ultimately, its paradigm. It is usually achieved by coercive means, but political, sociological, economic and psychological variables also play important roles and the phenomenon rarely presents itself in a purely military guise. The dramatic success of some revolutionary movements, often at the expense of militarily strong and sophisticated adversaries, has focussed analytical attention on the revolutionary process. There is a renewed interest, too, in arms control and disarmament, especially when they are perceived in the light of new arms race models, new theories of decision-making and analyses of the military-industrial complex. This has also led strategists to give more regard to military sociology.

Strategy is concerned with coercive attempts to promote or to repel change. It is thus one aspect of the political process at all levels of social intercourse. This has not been fully acknowledged in the past. The literature concentrated on the military relations between states and reflected a model of world society depicting states as the major actors hierarchically organized on the basis of power. This view is now questioned as the influence of non-state actors such as multinational corporations or putative state actors such as the Palestinians makes itself felt in power politics. Other systems levels and units of analysis are slowly changing the conceptual framework for the study of strategy. However, the present literature is far from providing an adequate conceptual framework for the analysis of power politics in contemporary world society.

Classical Doctrine and General Works

The extent to which the strategic writings from antiquity to the Second World War are relevant to the contemporary world is a moot point. Writers like Clausewitz [16] still exert an influence, but often need a good editor to sort out the historical chaff from the conceptual wheat. Earle's volume, with a chapter on each major historical figure by a well-known expert, is very useful [22]. In a different vein the Brodies explore the relationships between the defence system and social systems from the *Crossbow to A-Bomb* [12]. Waltz [112] offers an excellent conceptual framework for analysing traditional approaches to war.

Freedman [28] presents a simple overview of post-war 'strategic studies' as it has evolved over nuclear questions, while Lebow [71] and Gilpin [35] have greater depth. Lider [73] somewhat laboriously analyses the Marxist conceptual framework of strategy. The ethical aspects have been given significant attention by Walzer [113], Howard [54], and Hare & Joynt [50] and are discussed in greater detail in Chapter 2. British thought is analysed by Groom [42].

Nuclear Deterrence and Nuclear War

Deterrence involves the manipulation of threats in such a way that the target chooses options which, but for the threat, it would not have chosen. It thus involves a complicated relationship between stake, sanction and the likelihood of the application of the sanction. This raises difficult problems of communication and credibility. At no level of analysis, and especially not at the interstate nuclear level, is deterrence derived from a well-tested empirical theory. Despite the consequent speculative nature of the literature, the manipulation of threat systems is central to power politics and to strategy, and the subject cannot be ignored. Of the general works covering the major traditional aspects of the subject, Garnett's edited volume [32] of well-chosen reprints from the writings of such major nuclear strategists as Schelling and Brodie gives a flavour of the 1950s. Garnett and his colleagues have also produced a volume [6] of original conceptual essays and brief surveys of the defence policies of selected major powers. Students will find that Jones [67] has a felicitious way of meeting their need for a 'quick crib'. Schelling [94] is well worth reading and Bundy's justly celebrated article 'To Cap the Volcano' [13] brings a welcome touch of realism and sanity to a macabre world.

When the nuclear debate developed in the mid-1950s due to hydrogen bomb tests and the beginnings of mutual deterrence, it became evident that there were three broad options – non-nuclear status, massive retaliation and graduated deterrence. Only the latter two were considered seriously by the major powers. The literature reflected this. Unilateralism was treated more as an emotional slogan than as a serious policy option. Unilateralism requires acting in an unreciprocated manner to remove what potential adversaries consider to be a major threat. It involves the risk of easy, costless, and effective exploitation by the adversary against which there can be no real defence. Indeed, it is more effective if it is clear that such a risk is knowingly being taken. The purpose is to change the nature of power relationships by breaking stereotypes, interrupting the cycle of self-fulfilling prophesies of hostility and altering cognitive structures. It may be considered imprudent, but it should not be dismissed. The nuclear debate, however, concentrated on massive retaliation and graduated deterrence. It petered out in the early 1960s, once the major options had been delineated: there was no empirical evidence to settle the argument and it was a futile and boring exercise merely to elaborate ever more complicated scenarios.

The rival advocates of massive retaliation and graduated deterrence touched upon the 'theatre' use of nuclear weapons and its effect on deterrence generally, and credibility and escalation in particular. The question of whether the destructive effects of the 'tactical' use of nuclear weapons would be tantamount to those of a strategic war was raised. Limited nuclear war greatly exercises public opinion, especially in Europe, and the range of academic opinion can be gauged by contrasting SIPRI [98] with Van Cleave & Cohen [107].

The best recent contributions are Clark [15], Smoke [101] and Holst & Nerlich [53].

Nuclear deterrence has been practised as an integral part of 'high politics' between major powers for at least a quarter of a century. A body of experience and impressions is thus available, even if its codification and utilization is difficult. Nuclear proliferation, so long 'promised' horizontally, has sneaked up vertically, as the superpowers have expanded their capabilities at an astonishing and frightening rate. Technological developments may also now presage horizontal proliferation. George & Smoke [33] have examined deterrence theory in the light of US foreign policy since the Second World War. Groom's forthcoming volume puts deterrence theory in a variety of contexts and analyses the nature of limited nuclear war and conventional war in the nuclear shadow [45]. Morgan [80], Jervis [64, 65] and Rosecrance [91] offer useful reassessments of deterrence theory. Finally, there is a vast Soviet literature on the subject, some of which has been translated. Sokolovski [102] provides a useful starting point.

Conventional and Unconventional War

The study of conventional war is usually the separate preserve of military academies. One major exception is conventional war in the nuclear shadow, for which some of the literature on limited nuclear war is relevant. Sea power is considered more frequently than land power, perhaps because a purely conventional war in Europe – the prime area of confrontation – seems unlikely, whereas the great alliances have had some close scrapes at sea. The expansion of Soviet naval power has also focussed attention on sea power, as has the problematic role of conventional sea power in a nuclear war. Booth [8], Cable [14] and the several contributors to the *Adelphi Papers* [86] cover various aspects of these problems. Soviet naval expansion has been given a rationale by Gorshkov [36] and analysed in MccGwire, Booth & McDonnell [75].

The real interest in conventional warfare is in the Third World, where innovations are changing the nature of conventional war and new conventional powers of the first rank have arisen. These developments are only now being thoroughly analysed and incorporated into First and Second World thinking, but Kemp & colleagues [68] provided an early basis for their consideration. Although most of these discussions are empirical and therefore beyond the scope of this volume, they can be followed in the military journals and in *Survival* and the SIPRI *Yearbook*.

Given the unlikelihood of a conventional clash in Europe, the relative frequency of conventional war in the Third World and the historical ties with the former colonial powers, intervention in such wars either through the supply of weapons, actively with troops or perhaps covertly by providing information or air cover, has been and is likely to remain common. Little [74] has analysed cogently this phenomenon and Vincent's work [110] is also relevant. It is a topic on which much work remains to be done.

There has been a renewal of interest in various forms of unconventional warfare. The success of the non-violent techniques of Gandhi and Martin Luther King in the pursuit of their aims is well known. These and analogous experiences are analysed by Sharp [95, 96], who is concerned with the practicality of such techniques. An excellent but less ideological consideration of the practical use of such techniques in the pursuit of power politics can be found in Boserup & Mack [10] and Roberts [89, 90]. Terrorist activities and the more sustained urban guerrilla campaigns have focussed attention on violent unconventional techniques. The literature varies in quality and in ideology, but Wilkinson has attempted a scholarly conceptual framework [114] and Walter provides [111] a brilliant analysis of regimes of political terror. This literature is surveyed in Groom [43]. Chemical and biological warfare has remained 'unconventional' despite its frequent actual use. SIPRI has published work in this field [97].

Revolution and Revolutionary War

The plethora of revolutionary wars have been a striking phenomenon of the post-war world. The types include the strictly anti-colonial, those against a hegemonial power, and those against a local cosmopolitan elite. Clearly, many situations include elements from a wide range of political, economic, psychological and sociological variables. Revolutionary wars can be more or less thoroughgoing, coercive and violent – and changes in personnel, in policies, in structures or even in the paradigm of a social unit may be the goal. In the post-war world the actual violence has been unconventional, involving guerrilla tactics and at a fairly low level, although the intensity has been high. The great engines of war have been comparatively unused and the great military Leviathans have sometimes been muscle-bound. The most effective forms of coercion have often proved not to be the classical military ones. Nevertheless it should not be forgotten that most revolutionary movements fail.

Of the writers on revolutionary war, pride of place must be given to the Asian practitioners. In the light of his experience Mao Tse Tung developed a general framework for revolutionary war [79] which greatly influenced Vietnamese revolutionaries [34]. Equally inspiring but, after the rather fortuitous experience in Cuba, markedly less successful, were the practitioners of Latin America. Ché [46] and Debray [20, 21] are widely read, but the empirical evidence suggests that Mao's rather different precepts have greater validity, even for Latin America. Fanon [26] does not fit easily into a pigeon-hole – Caribbean in origin, working in Algeria, a trained social scientist yet a practitioner – but his analysis and prescriptions are likely to remain seminal, if highly controversial.

The counter-insurgent practitioners' literature includes an early and influential contribution from Thompson [104] who stressed political factors. On the other hand Leites & Wolf [72] lambast the politically oriented 'hearts and minds' approach. Their argument is based on an economic rational actor model, pricing by coercive means the options open to the population. Attitudes are discounted in the belief that behaviour can be coerced successfully, irrespective of value preferences, if the price of pursuing values is made too high. Short-term behaviour is the prime goal. Policies based on such views were unsuccessful in Vietnam.

Leites & Wolf represent a 'half-way house' between the practitioners and the political scientists on revolutionary war, with a scientific pretension underlying a practical strategic purpose. Other political scientists have not been so immediately policy-oriented. Eckstein's edited volume [23] and Gurr's work remain essential reading [47]. The latter has used the notion of 'relative deprivation' as have Davies [19] and Paynton & Blackey [85]. In addition, Gurr's *Handbook of Political Conflict* is a major collection – a 'must' for every library [48]. Cohan [18], Hagopian [49] and Greene [40] provide clear overviews in textbook style. Baldwin's article on positive sanctions [4] should remain on every reading list. The central issue of *Political Order in a Changing Society* [56] is evident. Will society and its institutions adjust and respond or will there be what Johnson termed *Revolutionary Change* [66] as 'multiple dysfunction meets an intransigent elite'? Stone [103] offers an historian's perspective.

When a system no longer responds to feedback and legitimized adjustment procedures are absent, confrontation and coercion become the order of the day. There is often a tendency of one or other party to call upon sympathetic outsiders for help. This is particularly common in revolutionary war situations with results that are, according to classical power politics, sometimes counter-intuitive. Mack suggests [76, 77] why this might be so. The study of revolution takes us away from a conventional and narrow definition of strategy, raising fundamental questions about order and change, the role of the state and social groups. The last decade has seen a flourishing of literature dealing with such questions from diverse and often contradictory points of view. This work is fundamentally and immediately important to strategy because it is about change processes and the role of structures and the often conflictual outcomes which give rise to violent situations. Significant contributions to this literature have recently been made by Skocpol [99], Tilly [105], Trinberger [106], Oberschall [83] and Gamson [30, 31].

Arms Control and Disarmament

The study of disarmament has always been an important element in IR. Arms negotiations and literature about them have been profuse since the beginning of the century. Much of the literature, however, has concentrated on practical contemporary issues and this partly explains the paucity of the conceptual literature, thereby in turn going some way towards explaining the failures of the pragmatic approach. It is a vicious circle.

Much of the literature has been based on an action–reaction model in which the arms race is generated by each state reacting to the actions of another which it interprets as inimical to its security and interests. This model was clearly inadequate at a time when the arms race was going full tilt, yet political *détente* was being consolidated. To some this suggested the malevolent influence of the military-industrial complex and militarism [7, 24]. To others it suggested that procurement processes, once initiated, are self-sustaining. Elements of this debate can be found in Gray [37, 38, 39]. Huntington's classic essay [55] on the arms race and a more recent article by Kohler are essential reading [69]. Richardson pioneered the analysis of the arms race by applying mathematical models and two of his volumes have been published posthumously [87, 88].

Peacekeeping

The considerable literature on peacekeeping has usually concerned itself with particular UN operations. Higgins [52] is invaluable as a reference work on all the UN peacekeeping operations. Of the conceptual treatments, James [59] is representative of the traditional IR approach, whereas Groom [44] pleads for a reconsideration of peacekeeping in the wider context of conflict research, with greater thought being given to the relationship between peacekeeping and peacemaking. This theme has also been examined by Young [115]. In achieving this goal, institutions other than the UN may have a significant role to play.

Civil-Military Relations

The study of strategy cannot ignore the military who interpret conceptual notions in an empirical setting. Thus the sociology of the military is of great interest. Although there are no purely conceptual studies, Janowitz [61] is a pioneering nationally based study. Abrahamsson has produced an excellent more recent study [1]. The psychological literature is relevant (Adorno [2] is an example) and it raises questions on civil-military relations and the military-industrial complex.

Janowitz and Van Doorn [60, 61, 62, 63, 108, 109] are leading figures of an international group who have studied the relationship between the armed forces and society. Interest in the subject generally was sparked by the role of the military, particularly in newly-independent states. Finer [27] had considerable influence, but more recent studies include Albright, Ball and Nordlinger [3, 5, 82]. The role of the military in developed countries cannot be taken for granted, since societal values are changing and moving away from traditional military values; and the military are becoming more professional and so can no longer be perceived as merely a reflection of the nation in arms. In addition (apart, perhaps from US forces), they have mostly lost their colonial role and *raison d'être*. The experience of Communist states is assessed in Herspring & Volgyes [51] and

Kolkowicz & Korbanski [70]. Huntington [56] can be recommended in this context as in others [57, 58]. A little known, but rewarding work is by Coates & Pellegrin, although their empirical examples are limited to the USA [17]. The political performance of military and non-military regimes are beginning to be compared [78]. The military-industrial complex was given great prominence by President Eisenhower in his farewell address to the people of the USA [25]. Since then there has been a variety of studies from many ideological viewpoints, usually confined to the empirical experience of one country – often the USA. Slater & Nardin offer an excellent summary of some of the different conceptual issues [100].

Bibliography to Chapter 10

1. Abrahamsson, B. *Military Professionalisation and Political Power.* Beverly Hills, CA and London, Sage, 1972.
2. Adorno, T.W. *et al.*, *The Authoritarian Personality.* New York and London, Norton, 1983.
3. Albright, D.E. 'A Comparative Conceptualization of Civil-Military Relations'. *World Politics*, vol. XXXII, no. 4, 1980, pp. 553–76.
4. Baldwin, D.A. 'The Power of Positive Sanctions'. *World Politics*, vol. XXIV, no. 1, 1971, pp. 19–38.
5. Ball, N. 'Third World Militaries and Politics: An Introductory Essay'. *Cooperation and Conflict*, vol. XVII, no. 1, 1982, pp. 41–60.
6. Baylis, J.K. *et al.*, *Contemporary Strategy.* London, Croom Helm and New York, Holmes & Meier, 1975.
7. Berghahn, V.R. *Militarism: The History of an International Debate, 1861–1979.* Leamington Spa, Berg Publishers and New York, St. Martin's, 1982.
8. Booth, K. *Navies and Foreign Policy.* London, Croom Helm and New York, Holmes and Meier, 1977.
9. _____ *Strategy and Ethnocentrism.* London, Croom Helm and New York, Holmes and Meier, 1979.
10. Boserup, A. & Mack, A. *War Without Weapons: Non-violence in National Defence.* London, Frances Pinter, 1974 and New York, Schocken Books, 1975.
11. Boulding, K.E. *Conflict and Defense: A General Theory.* New York, Harper and Row, 1962.
12. Brodie, B. & F. *Crossbow to A-Bomb.* Bloomington, IN, Indiana University Press, 1973.
13. Bundy, M. 'To Cap the Volcano'. *Foreign Affairs*, vol. 48, no. 1, 1969, pp. 1–20.

14. Cable, J. *Gunboat Diplomacy*. London, Chatto & Windus, 1971 and New York, St. Martin's, 1981.
15. Clark, I. *Limited Nuclear War*. Oxford, Martin Robertson and Princeton, NJ, Princeton University Press, 1982.
16. Clausewitz, C. Von, *On War* (Edited and translated by M. Howard and P. Paret). Princeton, NJ and Guildford, Princeton University Press, 1976.
17. Coates, C.H. & Pellegrin, R.J. *Military Sociology*. College Park, MD, Maryland Book Exchange, 1965.
18. Cohan, A.S. *Theories of Revolution*. New York, Wiley, 1975 and Wokingham, Van Nostrand Reinhold, 1982.
19. Davies, J.C. (ed.) *When Men Revolt and Why*. New York, Free Press and London, Collier-Macmillan, 1971.
20. Debray, R. *A Critique of Arms*. Harmondsworth, Middx., Penguin, 1977.
21. _____ *Revolution in the Revolution*. London and Westport, CT, Greenwood Press, 1980.
22. Earle, E.M. (ed.) *Makers of Modern Strategy*. New York, Atheneum, 1966.
23. Eckstein, H. (ed.) *Internal War*. London and Westport, CT, Greenwood Press, 1980.
24. Eide, A. & Thee, M. (eds), *Problems of Contemporary Militarism*. London, Croom Helm and New York, St. Martin's, 1980.
25. Eisenhower, D.D. 'President Eisenhower's Farewell to the Nation'. U.S. Dept. of State, *Dept. of State Bulletin*, vol. 44, no. 1128, 1961.
26. Fanon, F. *The Wretched of the Earth*. New York, Grove Press, 1965 and Harmondsworth, Middx., Penguin, 1983.
27. Finer, S.E. *The Man on Horseback*. Harmondsworth, Middx., Penguin, 1976.
28. Freedman, L. *The Evolution of Nuclear Strategy*. London, Macmillan, 1983 and New York, St. Martin's, 1982.
29. Galtung, J. *A Structural Theory of Revolution*. Rotterdam, Rotterdam University Press, 1974.
30. Gamson, W.A. *Power and Discontent*. Homewood, IL, Dorsey, 1968.
31. _____ *The Strategy of Social Process*. Homewood, IL, Irwin-Dorsey, 1975.
32. Garnett, J.C. (ed.) *Theories of Peace and Security*. London, Macmillan and New York, St. Martin's, 1970.
33. George, A.L. & Smoke, R. *Deterrence in American Foreign Policy: Theory and Practice*. New York and London, Columbia University Press, 1974.
34. Giap, V.N. *People's War, People's Army*. New York, Praeger, 1961.
35. Gilpin, R. *War and Change in World Politics*. Cambridge and New York, Cambridge University Press, 1984.
36. Gorshkov, S.G. *Sea Power and the State*. Oxford and New York,

Pergamon Press, 1979.
37. Gray, C.S. 'The Arms Race Phenomenon'. *World Politics*, vol. XXIV, no. 1, 1971, pp. 39–79.
38. _____ *The Soviet–American Arms Race*. Lexington, MA, Lexington Press and Aldershot, Saxon House, 1976.
39. _____ 'The Urge to Compete: Rationales for Arms Racing'. *World Politics*, vol. XXVI, no. 2, 1974, pp. 207–33.
40. Greene, T.H. *Comparative Revolutionary Movements*. Englewood Cliffs, NJ and Hemel Hempstead, Prentice Hall, 1974.
41. Griffiths, S.B. *Mao Tse-Tung on Guerrilla Warfare*. London, Cassell, 1965.
42. Groom, A.J.R. *British Thinking About Nuclear Weapons*. London, Frances Pinter, 1974.
43. _____ 'Coming to Terms with Terrorism'. *British Journal of International Studies*, vol. 4, no. 1, 1978, pp. 62–77.
44. _____ *Peacekeeping*. Bethlehem, PA, Lehigh University International Relations Monograph No. 4, 1973.
45. _____ *Strategy in the Modern World*. Forthcoming.
46. Guevara, C. *Guerrilla Warfare*. New York, Random House, 1968 and Harmondsworth, Middx., Pelican, 1969.
47. Gurr, T.R. *Why Men Rebel*. Princeton, NJ and Guildford, Princeton University Press, 1970.
48. _____ (ed.) *Handbook of Political Conflict: Theory and Research*. New York, Free Press and London, Collier-Macmillan, 1981.
49. Hagopian, M.N. *The Phenomenon of Revolution*. New York, Harper & Row, 1974.
50. Hare, J.E. & Joynt, C.B. *Ethics and International Affairs*. London, Macmillan and New York, St. Martin's, 1982.
51. Herspring, D.R. & Volgyes, I. (eds), *Civil–Military Relations in Communist Systems*. Folkestone, Dawson and Boulder, CO, Westview, 1978.
52. Higgins, R. *UN Peacekeeping 1946–67: Documents and Commentary*. vol. 1: *Middle East*; vol. 2: *Asia*; vol. 3: *Africa*; vol. 4: *Europe*. London and New York, Oxford University Press (issued under the auspices of the Royal Institute of International Affairs), 1966, 1970, 1980, 1981.
53. Holst, J.J. & Nerlich, U. (eds), *Beyond Nuclear Deterrence*. London, MacDonald and Jane's and New York, Crane-Russak, 1977.
54. Howard, M. (ed.) *Restraints on War*. London and New York, Oxford University Press, 1979.
55. Huntington, S.P. Arms Races: Prerequisites and Results. In *Power, Action and Interaction*, ed. G.H. Quester. Boston, Little, Brown, 1971.
56. _____ *Political Order in Changing Societies*. New Haven and London, Yale University Press, 1969.
57. _____ *Soldier and State*. Cambridge, MA, Harvard University Press, 1981.

58. _____ (ed.) *Changing Patterns of Military Politics.* New York. Free Press, 1962.
59. James, A. *Politics of Peacekeeping.* London, Chatto & Windus and New York, Praeger, 1969.
60. Janowitz, M. *The New Military.* New York, Russel Sage Foundation. 1964.
61. _____ *The Professional Soldier.* New York, Free Press, 1960.
62. Janowitz, M. & Van Doorn, J. (eds), *On Military Ideology.* Rotterdam. Rotterdam University Press, 1971.
63. _____ *On Military Intervention.* Rotterdam, Rotterdam University Press, 1971.
64. Jervis, R. 'Deterrence and Perception'. *International Security,* vol. 7. no. 3, 1982/3, pp. 3–30.
65. _____ 'Deterrence Theory Revisited'. *World Politics,* vol. XXXI. no. 2, 1979, pp. 289–324.
66. Johnson, C. *Revolutionary Change.* Stanford, CA, Stanford University Press, 1982 and Harlow, Longman, 1983.
67. Jones, R.E. *Nuclear Deterrence.* London, Routledge & Kegan Paul and Atlantic Highlands, NJ, Humanities Press, 1968.
68. Kemp, G. *et al., The Other Arms Race: New Technologies and Non-Nuclear Conflict.* Lexington, MA and London, D.C. Heath and Lexington, MA. Lexington Books, 1975.
69. Kohler, G. 'Structural-dynamic arms control'. *Journal of Peace Research,* vol. XIV, no. 4, 1977, pp. 315–26.
70. Kolkowicz, R. & Korbonski, A. (eds), *Soldiers, Peasants and Bureaucrats.* London and Edison, NJ, Allen & Unwin, 1982.
71. Lebow, R.N. *Between Peace and War: The Nature of International Crisis.* Baltimore and London, Johns Hopkins University Press, 1981.
72. Leites, N. & Wolf, C. *Rebellion and Authority.* Chicago, Markham, 1970.
73. Lider, J. *Military Force: An Analysis of Marxist-Leninist Concepts.* Aldershot, Hants. and Brookfield, VT, Gower, 1981.
74. Little, R. *Intervention: External Involvement in Civil Wars.* London, Martin Robertson and Totowa, NJ, Rowman & Littlefield, 1975.
75. MccGwire, M. *et al.* (eds), *Soviet Naval Policy: Objectives and Constraints.* New York, Praeger, 1975 (distributed in the UK by Pall Mall, Oxford).
76. Mack, A.J. 'Counterinsurgency in the Third World'. *British Journal of International Studies,* vol. 1, no. 3, 1975, pp. 226–53.
77. _____ 'Why Big Nations Lose Small Wars'. *World Politics,* vol. XXVII, no. 2, 1975, pp. 175–200.
78. McKinley, R.D. & Cohan, A.S. 'Performance and Instability in Military and Non-Military Regime Systems'. *American Political Science Review,* vol. LXX, no. 3, 1976, pp. 850–64.
79. Mao Tse Tung. *Basic Tactics.* New York, Praeger, 1966.

80. Morgan, P. *Deterrence: A Conceptual Analysis.* Beverly Hills, CA and London, Sage, 1977.
81. Myrdal, A. *The Game of Disarmament.* Nottingham, Spokesman Books, 1980 and New York, Pantheon, 1982.
82. Nordlinger, E.A. *Soldiers in Politics.* Hemel Hempstead and Englewood Cliffs, NJ, Prentice Hall, 1977.
83. Oberschall, A. *Social Conflict and Social Movements.* Hemel Hempstead and Englewood Cliffs, NJ, Prentice Hall, 1973.
84. Paskins, B. 'What's Wrong with Torture?' *British Journal of International Studies,* vol. 2, no. 2, 1976, pp. 138–48.
85. Paynton, C. & Blackey, R. (eds), *Why Revolution?* Cambridge, MA, Schenkman, 1971.
86. 'Power at Sea'. *Adelphi Papers,* Part 1, no. 122; Part II, no. 123; Part III, no. 124. London, International Institute for Strategic Studies, Spring, 1976.
87. Richardson, L.F. *Arms and Insecurity.* London, Stevens, 1960 and Ann Arbor, MI, Boxwood Press, 1978.
88. _____ *Statistics of Deadly Quarrels.* London, Stevens and Ann Arbor, MI, Boxwood Press, 1960.
89. Roberts, A. *Nations in Arms.* London, Macmillan, 1978 and New York, Praeger, 1976.
90. _____ (ed.) *The Strategy of Civilian Defence.* London, Faber & Faber, 1967 and Harrisburg, PA, Stackpole, 1968.
91. Rosecrance, R. 'Strategic Deterrence Reconsidered'. *Adelphi Papers,* No. 116. London, International Institute for Strategic Studies, November 1975.
92. Salert, B. *Revolutions and Revolutionaries.* London, Elsevier and London and Westport, CT, Greenwood Press, 1976.
93. Schelling, T.C. *Arms and Influence.* London and Westport, CT, Greenwood Press, 1977.
94. _____ *The Strategy of Conflict.* Cambridge, MA and London, Harvard University Press, 1980.
95. Sharp, G. *Exploring Non-Violent Alternatives.* Boston, Porter Sargent, 1973.
96. _____ *et al.* (eds), *The Politics of Non-Violent Action.* Boston, Porter Sargent, 1980.
97. SIPRI. *C.B. Weapons Today.* London, Paul Elek, 1973.
98. _____ *Tactical Nuclear Weapons.* London, Taylor & Francis, 1978.
99. Skocpol, T. *States and Social Revolutions.* Cambridge and New York, Cambridge University Press, 1979.
100. Slater, J. & Nardin, T. ' "The Military-Industrial" Complex Muddle'. *International Studies Association Conference Paper.* New York, 1973 (mimeograph).
101. Smoke, R. *War: Controlling Escalation.* Cambridge, MA and London, Harvard University Press, 1978.

102. Sokolovski, V.D. (ed.) *Soviet Military Strategy*. London, MacDonald and Jane's for the Strategic Studies Center, Stanford Research Institute and New York, Crane Russak, 1975.
103. Stone, L. 'Theories of Revolution'. *World Politics*, vol. XVIII, no. 2, 1966, pp. 159–76.
104. Thompson, R. *Defeating Communist Insurgency*. London, Macmillan, 1978.
105. Tilly, C. *From Mobilization to Revolution*. Reading, MA and London, Addison-Wesley, 1978.
106. Trinberger, E.K. *Revolutions from Above*. New Brunswick, NJ, Transaction Books, 1978.
107. Van Cleave & Cohen, S.T. *Tactical Nuclear Weapons*. New York, Crane Russak, 1978.
108. Van Doorn, J. (ed.) *Armed Forces and Society*. The Hague, Mouton, 1968.
109. _____ (ed.) *Military Profession and Military Regimes*. The Hague, Mouton, 1969.
110. Vincent, J. *Nonintervention and International Order*. Princeton, NJ and Guildford, Princeton University Press, 1974.
111. Walter, E.V. *Terror and Resistance*. Oxford and New York, Oxford University Press, 1972.
112. Waltz, K.N. *Man, the State and War*. New York, Columbia University Press, 1959.
113. Walzer, M. *Just and Unjust Wars: A Moral Argument with Historical Illustrations*. New York, Basic Books, 1977 and Harmondsworth, Middx., Penguin, 1980.
114. Wilkinson, P. *Political Terrorism*. London, Macmillan, 1974 and New York, Wiley, 1975.
115. Young, O.R. *The Intermediaries: Third Parties in International Crises*. Princeton, NJ and Guildford, Princeton University Press, 1967.

11 Foreign Policy Analysis

Christopher Hill
London School of Economics and Political Science

and

Margot Light
University of Surrey and CAC

Foreign policy analysis has marked time over the last decade, but it has certainly not withered away. The lack of controversy marks the subject's consolidation. While not *the* focal point of International Relations (IR), it is an indispensable level of analysis. But marking time also means less excitement and more modest theoretical ambitions, so that the investigation of state behaviour has been based on ideas and frameworks introduced before 1975, either by testing their validity through various forms of empiricism, or developing their implications. There has been little questioning of basic assumptions, except by those who prefer in any case to work at the systemic or philosophical levels.

Foreign policy analysis has produced a group of theories, the credibility of which is now generally established – bureaucratic politics, misperception, groupthink, and cybernetic decision-making. But no single overarching 'theory of foreign policy' has emerged to match Modelski's effort of 1962 [109]. This is hardly surprising given a sensible reluctance to espouse a 'primacy of domestic policy' paradigm. A common use of the framework and basic concepts discernible ten years ago is evident, based on the distinction made in systems theory between actors and their various environments. The overall environment in which decision-makers operate is divided into the 'external' (or 'international'), the 'domestic', and the 'psychological' environment, an umbrella term for the set of images held by decision-makers of their world, home and abroad, in contrast to its 'operational' reality. These categories are themselves also broken down into the many variables to be found in any process as complex as that of national policy-making. There is broad agreement on the identity of the variables, if not on the boundaries between the respective environments, in particular between what is foreign and what is domestic. The achievement of a taxonomy is exemplified by the way in which the work of Brecher, on Israeli policy-making and on the comparative approach to crisis [18, 19, 20], has been generally accepted and to some extent emulated. But Brecher himself built on the work of others, among them the early texts of Frankel [44] and Rosenau [128], which still stand as good introductions, both more accessible than the pioneering work of Snyder, Bruck & Sapin [149]. Recent equally helpful overviews of the subject are by Bloomfield [14], Clarke & White [25], and Jensen [78]. The British Open University material is also excellent [102, 114].

A central part of foreign policy analysis is the study of decision-making, indicating the multi-disciplinary origins of the subject. The interactions between states or between decision-makers involved in a particular decision can be examined to see whether formal models of bargaining and rational choice express a logic that could be inherent in any process of decision, whatever the mistakes or misperceptions of the actors in practice [148].

Related to theories of rational choice are 'rational-actor' models. They are not favoured by modern students of foreign policy because of their assumption that governments consist of united, purposive strategists who, in possession of full information, calculate and implement actions on the basis of how best to maximize power and security. This assumption ignores possible dissent within the decisional unit, leading to compromise or policies which 'satisfice'. Nor does it allow for disagreements in interpretations of costs and benefits based on ideological and cultural differences. The same is true of the 'billiard-ball' model in which foreign policy positions are seen as being primarily determined by the interplay of international forces. To some extent these models are straw men. It is rare to find statements of overt adherence to their maxims. None the less, most diplomatic historians and many students of current affairs, military strategy and international politics treat states implicitly as if they were calculating individuals and, what is more, individuals calculating on the basis of the currency of power. To some extent this represents an intellectual shorthand to which we all succumb when talking about far-off countries of which we know nothing. Allison and Steinbruner extrapolate the rational paradigm without caricaturing it [2, 155].

This apparent preoccupation with rationality suggests a tie between foreign policy analysis and political philosophy: how can one discuss the reason behind a decision without arguments about the underlying values to be served? In practice the subject has been predominantly positivist (even if individual writers like Waltz [165] and Cohen [26] have continued to work within the normative tradition dealing with the accountability of foreign policy which reaches back to Cobden and Jefferson). But in recent years there has been a revival of political theory in IR generally, which has spilled over into foreign policy analysis. It is reflected in the change in title of the recent edition of Spanier & Uslaner's book on US foreign policy-making [150] and Jones' exploration of the 'principles' at the heart of foreign policy [82]. Indeed, the burgeoning literature on ethics, especially human rights and foreign policy and the just war, exemplifies valuable connections between foreign policy analysis and other mainstream aspects of IR. Ethical discussion has to be related to responsible actors, and states are the most powerful actors in the world system. Walzer [166] and Hoffman [67] each provide a good bridge between foreign policy and international political theory.

Psychology also connects the positivist and normative strands in foreign policy analysis. The concept of misperception, for example, allows debate over whether particular policy decisions represent instances of straightforward error of judgement by decision-makers or the pursuit of policies which are at odds with the observer's values. 'Images' were emphasized by Boulding [15], while Harold and Margaret Sprout combined a concern for perceptions with a more general analysis of causation, in particular the inter-relationship between endogenous perceptions and exogenous constraints such as those deriving from geopolitics [153].

In general, the psychological approach has been one of the most successful lines of investigation undertaken in foreign policy analysis, since its theories generate plausible explanations of actual cases. De Rivera [33] produced an early, but still useful survey of how foreign policy behaviour is susceptible to psychological analysis (if not actual psychoanalysis). Jervis [80] is now the standard text in this field. Janis has also been an important contributor to this cross-disciplinary co-operation, notably in his work on the power of group consensus [76] and in a later, more extensive book with Mann [77], which puts context very much in second place to the intrinsic nature of the process of taking decisions itself. Among other useful works on such subjects as perceptions, groupthink, cognitive dissonance are Dixon [36], on the rigidities and origins of a typical military mindset, and Cottam [27]. Kinder & Weiss [85] provide a critical counter-weight to the whole approach and Hopple [72] offers a quick guide to the literature.

Another important set of theoretical ideas concerns the impact of organizational frameworks on policy outcomes. This is crystallized in the term 'bureaucratic politics', made famous by Allison and Halperin [2, 58]. But whereas these two authors came to subsume a wide range of ideas about bureaucracy under the single heading (in Tanter and Ullman [157]), they started by distinguishing between the impact of routine and the impact of organizational socialization leading to intra-bureaucratic competition. Routine or 'organizational process' suggests that the heavy flow of information into the modern foreign policy system produces standard operating procedures which are difficult to change but which are essential to protect an efficient, regularized administration from whim or partiality. They clearly have serious effects on habits of mind and the collective capacity for flexible response to change, as 'model two' of *Essence of Decision* [2] illustrates. More recently Williamson (in [92]) has applied the concepts to events in 1914. In a closely allied work, Steinbruner outlined the 'cybernetic' and 'cognitive' paradigms [155]. While not perhaps quite so convincing in its relevance to foreign policy processes, it does analyse usefully the way in which both individuals and groups tend to make decisions less on the basis of maximum information than by a highly empirical, even automatic adjustment to the feedback they get from their own actions. The decision-makers are grooved into apparently efficient procedures simply through force of repetition and sufficient positive feedback, even if these procedures prove counter-productive in the long run. Steinbruner's work also links suggestively with that in the psychological field.

The handling of information is central to any study of decision-making and Deutsch's survey of communications theory [35] still repays attention. Here once again the prescriptive realm is not far away. Lindblom's famous idea of 'incrementalism' may be thought to make a virtue of necessity: he concludes that it is sensible to proceed by small, disjointed steps in policy-making given the impossibility of full information or bureaucratic co-ordination [96]. Yet foreign policy decision-makers are always torn between caution in an unpredictable world, and the need to plan against dangerous contingencies through alliances, long-term military research, aid packages, etc. Both George [50] and Rothstein [134] explore these tensions usefully in the context of US foreign policy.

Bureaucratic politics in the main, narrower sense conveyed by Allison and Halperin provoked a wide-ranging critical debate. Smith summarizes the arguments (in [25]) which have largely focussed on whether the model is culture-bound and based on too narrow a definition of politics. Pertinent criticisms have been made by L. Freedman [46], Krasner [89] and Wallace & Paterson [163]. Much work has been done to test the model's main propositions when applied to particular cases [121, 49]. Allison's and Halperin's central argument is that administrative departments develop their own perspectives and vested interests, and tend to socialize those they recruit thereby preventing synoptic views of the national interest or the merits of an issue. Intra-bureaucratic conflicts may thus become almost as problematical as inter-state conflicts. It is, of course, arguable whether this constitutes a fair overall description of the foreign policy process, even in the United States. Nevertheless it focusses on an important dimension of both the formulation and implementation stages of policy-making, and the clashes between successive National Security Advisors and Secretaries of State in the US and the frequent allusions to a 'Foreign Office mentality' in Britain are only the most recent manifestations of their relevance.

One powerful counter-argument maintains that however much departmental infighting distorts policy, its basic thrust is provided by the deeper structure of a society and its ideology. This criticism also cuts at other sub-areas; the concept of cognitive maps [6] hardly discusses ideology, and in general psychologists rarely stray into such difficult territory. Many attempts to analyse Soviet foreign policy, on the other hand, are obsessed with the question of whether Moscow is motivated by Marxism-Leninism or by traditional security concerns. May's widely-read book on how US foreign policy-makers have interpreted the lessons of their own past actions [106] is a model of how to raise such issues, while Frankel's [43] interesting attempt to use the belief-system approach as his basic explanatory framework centres on Britain. Cottam [27] also concentrates on motivations, and the difficulties arising from mutual uncertainty between adversaries about each other's goals. In general, however, the study of ideology in foreign policy contexts has so far been insufficient and unsophisticated.

Foreign policy analysis, especially in the US, has almost been synonymous with 'comparative foreign policy' because any general-ization about decision-making is *ipso facto* a cross-national statement. A 'Californian' comparative school of 'national attribute theory' [156] has flourished [100, 130], moving away from a pre-occupation with the inner workings of a state's system and attempting to generalize across a wide range of states about the kind of behaviour associated with particular attributes. Explicit and detailed hypotheses about the relationships between such pheno-mena as ideology and foreign policy actions have been attempted with predictably trivial results. Enthusiasts for this methodology find large questions about broad national characteristics easier to manage, returning to the old questions which interested de Tocque-ville, Lippman, and Kissinger: do democracies have different foreign policies from those of authoritarian states, and different problems in formulating them? Other dimensions examined are size, 'openness' or 'closedness', geopolitical complexion (islands, length of borders) and social composition. Correlations are sought with types of external behaviour, for example initiatory, dependent, oscillating, inflexible.

The behaviouralist approach has almost annexed the term 'comparative foreign policy', but this has not deterred others from considering the domestic sources of foreign policy in their own way. Thus there are now two fairly distinct camps within the field of foreign policy analysis. The first is analytical, often case-oriented, with links to history, political theory and the study of institutions. The second is formal, macro, and suffers from its inability to use the suggestive but 'non-scientific' work of Cohen [26], Almond [3] or Lukes [97], who have reflected on the *nature* of the political society lying behind any foreign policy system.

Whatever one's view of this particular methodological division, scholars of various persuasions have usefully grouped states into special classes such as less developed countries (LDCs) so as to theorize about their distinctive foreign policy problems or patterns of behaviour. Clapham has edited a useful series of introductory essays covering the various regions of the Third World [23], while Boyce [16] is short on theory and long on administrative and legal detail. Saxena [136] and A. Dawisha [29] provide interesting case studies. The debate about dependency has not yet focussed crisply on the specifically foreign policy aspects of 'neo-colonialism'. McGowan & Kegley [99] link national attribute theory modishly to the new interest in political economy, and Korany's article [88] puts the existing literature under the critical microscope.

Other groups of foreign policies are beginning to be compared systematically, for example Western Europe [65, 163] and socialist states [1, 158]. The latter comprise the other large group of states commonly singled out for special treatment.

Early studies on Soviet domestic and foreign policy were descriptive, but a change is epitomized by the title of Fainsod's classic *How Russia is Ruled*, transformed by Hough in the second edition to *How the Soviet Union is Governed* [74]. The unitary, totalitarian model of Soviet decision-making has been enlarged to admit some analysis of political processes. An implicit monolithic, rational-actor model can be detected in most descriptive works on Soviet foreign policy [168], and few decision-making studies had been published by 1975 [73]. Light [95] discusses the reasons for the lack of social science in Soviet studies and Hoffmann & Fleron [66] provide an excellent reader including a variety of approaches to Soviet foreign policy. Schwartz [137] and Bialer [13] consider the domestic context in which Soviet foreign policy is made.

Although much of the work on Soviet foreign policy is empirical, interesting research has built on Skilling's pioneering work on Soviet interest groups [144], for example [48, 83, 68, 118, 122, 39, 160]. The bureaucratic model has been tested on specific events in Paul [117], K. Dawisha [31], Valenta [159]. K. Dawisha [32] believes that ideology limits the applicability of the model, while Mitchell [108] examines how the ideology has changed. Gilbert [55], Schwartz [138] and Lenczowski [94] examine Soviet perceptions of the USA, while Cutler [28] combines organizational and cognitive perspectives to produce a model for Soviet foreign policy decision-making.

Theory is perhaps too grand a word to describe the considerable work that has been done on the instruments of foreign policy. Nevertheless, it has not been without conceptual content, and middle-range hypotheses are continually being generated. Diplomacy has usually been seen as an institution of international society as much as a national resource, but often the perspectives are combined, as in Watson [167]. Plischke provides a comprehensive single treatment of the nature and potential of diplomacy [119] and Feltham's handbook deals with the nuts and bolts [42]. Gradually the study of diplomacy has been widened to include the dynamics of negotiation and signalling which are dealt with in Chapter 9.

The grey area between diplomacy and military force, has been examined by George, Hall & Simons [53]. George & Craig [52] look rather generally at the interplay between force and negotiation through the whole modern period. Knorr [86] has shown that the successful exercise of military capability requires more than its mere possession, but Art & Waltz' well-known reader on the use of force [4] has more relevance to strategic studies.

The economic instruments of states point to the debate about imperialism (see Chapters 4 and 5). More prosaically, the main economic instruments used by states are trade, aid and sanctions but the literature is wanting with respect to the first two. Little of the writing on trade and aid focuses directly on the political costs and benefits accruing to states from preferential tariffs, or gifts of cash, food and military hardware, because in the liberal post-war era such agreements were often between groups of states. But there is still room for examination, say, of what the European Community actually gets from the Lomé Conventions, or the USSR out of its increasing military commitments. Holsti [69] and Spero [151] contain useful introductory material for this and White [169] has still to be superseded on aid. McGowan & Walker [101] survey different views on what the United States gets out of its foreign economic policy. Doxey [37] is the main specialist on economic sanctions, but Barber [8], Renwick [123] and Mayall [107] should also be consulted. R. Freedman has described the Soviet use of sanctions [47].

The remaining instruments of foreign policy fall into the loose category of propaganda, with 'cultural policy' exemplifying the softer side of such activity. Propaganda and persuasion assumes that a direct appeal to another state's population can constrain the actions of its government. Radio is now a major channel for such actions. Hale [57] is illuminating on its extent and potential influence. Browne [21] is more up to date and detailed. The printed media are still very important, of course, and demands for a 'new international information order' have been documented by Righter [125]. More elusive is the hidden persuasion of espionage and subversion. Andrew Scott pioneered serious writing about the relation of this to foreign policy proper and his remains the standard text [139].

The notion of crisis links foreign policy analysis and mainstream IR, since it is both a recurring phase of the system's evolution [11] and a special kind of decision-making. Lebow is useful on both dimensions [93]. Building on the definitional work of Hermann [62], Ole Holsti [71] and Paige [115], Brecher launched a massive co-ordinated study of behaviour in crisis conditions, by commissioning case-studies from a wide range of authors (e.g. A. Dawisha [30] and Shlaim [140]), and himself edited a collection of preliminary findings [20]. Stein & Tanter [154] is of more general interest than its title suggests. Williams' [172] survey includes decision-making, systemic effects and the practical problem of 'crisis management'.

This chapter has focussed on the domestic sources of foreign policy, and on the nature of decision-making as the central concerns of the evolving subject. But any study of a foreign policy issue which concentrated exclusively on such concerns would be both inadequate as an explanation and in danger of isolating foreign policy analysis from IR. Foreign policy, after all, is primarily to do with things foreign. It is, therefore, essential to consider the ways in which the external environment determines foreign policy, or at least conditions the possible choices. The external environment is intrinsically geopolitical in a world where states – the main actors – are shaped partly by natural frontiers, and take their strategic preoccupations from the interplay of technology, geography and political development. A good recent political geography text book has been produced by Short [141]. Ashley [5], basing his work on the concept of 'lateral expansion', makes an ambitious attempt to model the Sino-Soviet-American trilateral relationship. The norms of the external political environment are equally important, of course, and Henkin [61] has constructed a cogent argument for the influence of international law on national policy formulation. Wolfers [174] is a classic collection of essays on the relationship between foreign policy and international politics. The last decade has brought a considerable challenge (now perhaps fading) to the conceptual division between foreign and domestic policy, and the transnational literature is covered extensively elsewhere in this book. Despite this challenge foreign policy analysis seems certain to remain a viable and valuable level of analysis within IR.

Bibliography to Chapter 11

1. Adomeit, H. & Boardman, R. (eds), *Foreign Policy-Making in Communist Countries*. Farnborough, Hants., Saxon House and New York, Praeger, 1979.
2. Allison, G.T. *Essence of Decision*. Boston, Little, Brown, 1971.
3. Almond, G.A. *The American People and Foreign Policy*. Westport, CT and London, Greenwood Press, 1977.
4. Art, R.J. & Waltz, K.N. *The Use of Force: International Politics and Foreign Policy*. Lanham, MD, University Press of America, 1983.
5. Ashley, R.K. *The Political Economy of War and Peace: The Sino-Soviet-American Triangle and the Modern Security Problematique*. London,

Frances Pinter and New York, Nichols, 1980.
6. Axelrod, R. (ed.) *The Structure of Decision: The Cognitive Maps of Political Elites.* Princeton, NJ, Princeton University Press, 1976.
7. Bachrach, P. & Baratz, M.S. 'Decisions and Non-Decisions: An Analytic Framework'. *American Political Science Review*, vol. LVII, no. 3, 1963, pp. 632–42.
8. Barber, J. 'Economic Sanctions as a Policy Instrument'. *International Affairs*, vol. 55, no. 3, 1979, pp. 367–84.
9. _____ *Who Makes British Foreign Policy?* Milton Keynes, Open University Press and Philadelphia, PA, Taylor & Francis, 1976.
10. Barber, J. & Smith, M. (eds), *The Nature of Foreign Policy: A Reader.* Edinburgh, Holmes McDougall in association with the Open University Press, Milton Keynes, 1974.
11. Bell, C. *The Conventions of Crisis.* London, Oxford University Press for the Royal Institute of International Affairs, 1971.
12. Berman, M.R. & Johnson, J.E. (eds), *Unofficial Diplomats.* New York and Guildford, Columbia University Press, 1977.
13. Bialer, S. (ed.) *The Domestic Context of Soviet Foreign Policy.* London, Croom Helm and Boulder, CO, Westview, 1981.
14. Bloomfield, L.P. *The Foreign Policy Process: A Modern Primer.* Englewood Cliffs, NJ & London, Prentice Hall, 1982.
15. Boulding, K.E. *The Image: Knowledge in Life and Society.* London, Cresset Press and Ann Arbor, MI, University of Michigan Press, 1961.
16. Boyce, P.J. *Foreign Affairs for New States: Some Questions of Credentials.* St. Lucia, Australia, University of Queensland Press; Hemel Hempstead (distributed by Prentice Hall International), 1977 and New York, St. Martin's, 1978.
17. Braybrooke, D. & Lindblom, C.E. *The Strategy of Decision.* London, Collier-Macmillan and New York, Free Press, 1970.
18. Brecher, M. *Decisions in Crisis: Israel '67 and '73.* London & Berkeley, CA, University of California Press, 1980.
19. _____ *Decisions in Israel's Foreign Policy.* London, Oxford University Press, 1974 and New Haven, Yale University Press, 1975.
20. _____ (ed.) *Studies in Crisis Behaviour.* New Brunswick, NJ, Transaction Books, 1979.
21. Browne, D.R. *International Radio Broadcasting: The Limits of the Limitless Medium.* New York, Praeger, 1982.
22. Buzan, B. *People, States and Fear: The National Security Problem in International Relations.* Brighton, Wheatsheaf and Chapel Hill, NC, University of North Carolina Press, 1983.
23. Clapham, C. *Foreign Policy Making in Developing States.* Farnborough, Hants., Saxon House, 1977.
24. Clarke, M. 'Foreign Policy Implementation: problems and approaches'. *British Journal of International Studies*, vol. 5, no. 2, 1979, pp. 112–28.

25. Clarke, M. & White, B. *An Introduction to Foreign Policy Analysis: The Foreign Policy System*. Ormskirk and Northridge, G.W. & A. Hesketh, 1981.

26. Cohen, B.C. *The Public's Impact on Foreign Policy*. Lanham, MD, University Press of America, 1983.

27. Cottam, R.W. *Foreign Policy Motivation: A General Theory and a Case-Study*. London, Feffer & Simons and Pittsburgh, University of Pittsburgh Press, 1977.

28. Cutler, R.M. 'The formation of Soviet foreign policy: organizational and cognitive perspectives'. *World Politics*, vol. XXXIV, no. 3, 1982, pp. 418–36.

29. Dawisha, A. *Egypt and the Arab World: The Elements of Foreign Policy*. London, Macmillan and New York, Wiley, 1976.

30. _____ *Syria and the Lebanese Crisis*. London, Macmillan and New York, St. Martin's, 1980.

31. Dawisha K. *The Kremlin and the Prague Spring*. London and Berkeley, CA, University of California Press, 1985.

32. _____ 'The Limits of the Bureaucratic Politics Model: Observations on the Soviet Case'. *Studies in Comparative Communism*, vol. XIII, no. 4, 1980, pp. 300–26.

33. de Rivera, J. *The Psychological Dimension of Foreign Policy*. Columbus, OH, Charles E. Merrill, 1968.

34. Destler, I.M. *Presidents, Bureaucrats and Foreign Policy: The Politics of Organisational Reform*. Princeton, NJ, Princeton University Press, 1974.

35. Deutsch, K.W. *The Nerves of Government*. New York, Free Press. 1963.

36. Dixon, N.F. *On the Psychology of Military Incompetence*. London, Jonathan Cape, 1976 and Salem, NH, Merrimack, 1984.

37. Doxey, M.P. *Economic Sanctions and International Enforcement*. London, Macmillan for the Royal Institute of International Affairs, 1980.

38. East, M.A. *et al*, *Why Nations Act: Theoretical Perspectives for Comparative Foreign Policy Studies*. Beverly Hills, CA & London, Sage, 1978.

39. Eran, O. *The Mezhdunarodniki: An Assessment of Professional Expertise in the Making of Soviet Foreign Policy*. Ramat Gan, Israel, Turtledove Publishing, 1979.

40. Farrell, J.C. & Smith, A.P. (eds), *Image and Reality in World Politics*. New York, Columbia University Press, 1968.

41. Farrell, R.B. (ed.) *Approaches to Comparative and International Politics*. Evanston, IL, Northwestern University Press, 1966.

42. Feltham, R.G. *Diplomatic Handbook*. London and New York, Longman, 1983.

43. Frankel, J. *British Foreign Policy*. London, Oxford University Press for

the Royal Institute of International Affairs, 1975.

44. _____ *The Making of Foreign Policy.* London, Oxford University Press, 1963.

45. _____ *National Interest.* London, Pall Mall and New York, Praeger, 1970.

46. Freedman, L. 'Logic, Politics and Foreign Policy Processes: A Critique of the Bureaucratic Politics Model'. *International Affairs*, vol. 52, no. 3, 1976, pp. 434–49.

47. Freedman, R.O. *Economic Warfare in the Communist Bloc: A Study of Soviet Economic Pressure against Yugoslavia, Albania and Communist China.* New York, Praeger, 1970.

48. Gallagher, M.P. & Spielman, K.F. Jr. (eds), *Soviet Decision-Making for Defense: A Critique of US Perspectives on the Arms Race.* New York, Irvington, 1972.

49. Gallucci, R.L. *Neither Peace nor Honour: the politics of American military policy in Vietnam.* Baltimore & London, Johns Hopkins University Press, 1975.

50. George, A.L. *Presidential Decisionmaking in Foreign Policy: The Effective Use of Information and Advice.* Boulder, CO, Westview Press, 1980.

51. _____ *Propaganda Analysis.* London & Westport, CT, Greenwood Press, 1973.

52. George, A.L. & Craig, G.A. *Force and Statecraft: diplomatic problems of our times.* New York & Oxford, Oxford University Press, 1983.

53. George, A.L. *et al., The Limits of Coercive Diplomacy: Laos-Cuba-Vietnam.* Boston, Little, Brown, 1971.

54. George, A.L. & Smoke, R. *Deterrence in American Foreign Policy: Theory and Practice.* New York & London, Columbia University Press, 1974.

55. Gilbert, S.P. *Soviet Images of America.* London, Macdonald and Jane's, 1977.

56. Greenstein, F.I. *Personality and Politics.* New York & London, W.W. Norton, 1980.

57. Hale, J. *Radio Power: Propaganda and International Broadcasting.* London, Elek and Philadelphia, Temple University Press, 1975.

58. Halperin, M.H. *Bureaucratic Politics and Foreign Policy.* Washington, D.C., Brookings Institution, 1974.

59. Hanreider, W.F. *Comparative Foreign Policy: Theoretical Essays.* New York, McKay, 1971.

60. Hanrieder, W.F. & Auton, G.P. *The Foreign Policies of West Germany, France and Britain.* Englewood Cliffs, NJ & London, Prentice Hall International, 1980.

61. Henkin, L. *How Nations Behave.* New York, Columbia University Press, 1979.

62. Hermann, C.F. (ed.) *International Crises: Insights from Behavioural Research.* London, Collier-Macmillan and New York, Free Press, 1972.

63.   Hill, C. Implications of the World Society Perspective for National Foreign Policies. In *Conflict in World Society*, ed. M. Banks. Brighton, Wheatsheaf and New York, St. Martin's, 1984.

64.   _____ 'Public Opinion and British Foreign Policy'. *Millennium: Journal of International Studies*, vol. 10, no. 1, 1981, pp. 53–62.

65.   _____ (ed.) *National Foreign Policies and European Political Cooperation*. London & Edison, NJ, Allen & Unwin for the Royal Institute of International Affairs, 1983.

66.   Hoffmann, E.P. & Fleron, F.J. Jr. (eds), *The Conduct of Soviet Foreign Policy*. Chicago, Aldine-Atherton, 1981.

67.   Hoffmann, S. *Duties beyond Borders: On the Limits and Possibilities of Ethical International Politics*. Syracuse, NY, Syracuse University Press, 1981.

68.   Holloway, D. 'Technology and Political Decision in Soviet Armaments Policy'. *Journal of Peace Research*, vol. 11, no. 4, 1974, pp. 257–79.

69.   Holsti, K.J. *International Politics: A Framework for Analysis*. Englewood Cliffs, NJ & London, Prentice Hall International, 1983.

70.   _____ (ed.) *Why Nations Realign: Foreign Policy Restructuring in the Postwar World*. London & Edison, NJ, Allen & Unwin, 1982.

71.   Holsti, O.R. *Crisis, Escalation, War*. Montreal, McGill-Queen's University Press, 1972.

72.   Hopple, G.W. *Political Psychology and Biopolitics: Assessing and Predicting Elite Behavior in Foreign Policy Crises*. Boulder, CO, Westview, 1980.

73.   Horelick, A.L. *et al.*, *The Study of Soviet Foreign Policy: Decision-Theory-Related Approaches*. Beverly Hills, CA & London, Sage, 1975.

74.   Hough, J.F. & Fainsod, M. *How the Soviet Union is Governed*. Cambridge, MA & London, Harvard University Press, 1979.

75.   Hughes, B.B. *The Domestic Context of American Foreign Policy*. San Francisco & Oxford, W.H. Freeman, 1978.

76.   Janis, I.L. *Victims of Groupthink*. Boston, Houghton Mifflin, 1982.

77.   Janis, I.L. & Mann, L. *Decision-Making: A Psychological Analysis of Conflict, Choice and Commitment*. New York, Free Press, 1977 and London, Collier-Macmillan, 1979.

78.   Jensen, L. *Explaining Foreign Policy*. Englewood Cliffs, NJ & Hemel Hempstead, Prentice Hall, 1982.

79.   Jervis, R. *The Logic of Images in International Relations*. Princeton, NJ & Guildford, Princeton University Press, 1970.

80.   _____ *Perception and Misperception in International Politics*. Princeton, NJ & Guildford, Princeton University Press, 1976.

81.   Jones, R.E. *Analysing Foreign Policy: An Introduction to some Conceptual Problems*. London, Routledge & Kegan Paul, 1970.

82.   _____ *Principles of Foreign Policy: The Civil State in its World Setting*. Oxford, Martin Robertson and New York, St. Martin's, 1979.

83. Kass, I. *Soviet Involvement in the Middle East: Policy Formulation, 1966–1973*. Boulder, CO, Westview and Folkestone, Dawson, 1978.
84. Keohane, R.O. & Nye, J.S. *Power and Interdependence: World Politics in Transition*. Boston, Little, Brown, 1977.
85. Kinder, D.R. & Weiss, J.A. 'In lieu of rationality: psychological perspectives on foreign policy decisionmaking'. *Journal of Conflict Resolution*, vol. XXII, no. 4, 1978, pp. 707–35.
86. Knorr, K. *Military Power and Potential*. Lexington, MA & London, D.C. Heath, 1971.
87. _____ *The Power of Nations*. New York, Basic Books, 1975.
88. Korany, B. 'The Take-Off of Third World Studies? The Case of Foreign Policy'. *World Politics*, vol. XXXV, no. 3, 1983, pp. 465–87.
89. Krasner, S.D. 'Are Bureaucracies Important? (or Allison Wonderland)'. *Foreign Policy*, no. 7, summer 1972, pp. 159–79.
90. _____ *Defending the National Interest: Raw Materials Investments and US Foreign Policy*. Princeton, NJ & Guildford, Princeton University Press, 1978.
91. _____ (ed.) *International Regimes*. Ithaca, NY & London, Cornell University Press, 1983.
92. Lauren, P.G. (ed.) *Diplomacy: New Approaches in History, Theory and Policy*. London, Collier-Macmillan and New York, Free Press, 1979.
93. Lebow, R.N. *Between Peace and War: The Nature of International Crisis*. Baltimore & London, Johns Hopkins University Press, 1981.
94. Lenczowski, J. *Soviet Perceptions of US Foreign Policy: A Study of Ideology, Power and Consensus*. Ithaca, NY & London, Cornell University Press, 1982.
95. Light, M. 'Approaches to the Study of Soviet Foreign Policy'. *Review of International Studies*, vol. 7, no. 3, 1981, pp. 127–43.
96. Lindblom, C.E. *The Policy Making Process*. Englewood Cliffs, NJ & London, Prentice Hall, 1980.
97. Lukes, S. *Power: A Radical View*. London, Macmillan and Atlantic Highlands, NJ, Humanities Press, 1975.
98. McGowan, P.J. (ed.) *The Sage International Yearbook of Foreign Policy Studies, (vols. I–IV)*. Beverly Hills, CA, Sage, 1973–1976.
99. McGowan, P.J. & Kegley, C.W. (eds), *Foreign Policy of the Modern World System*. Beverly Hills, CA & London, Sage, 1983. (Sage International Yearbook of Foreign Policy Studies, vol. 8.)
100. McGowan, P.J. & Shapiro, H.B. *The Comparative Study of Foreign Policy: A Survey*. Beverly Hills, CA & London, Sage, 1973.
101. McGowan, P.J. & Walker, S.G. 'Radical and Conventional Models of U.S. Foreign Economic Policy Making'. *World Politics*, vol. XXXIII, no. 3, 1981, pp. 347–82.
102. McGrew, A.G. & Wilson, M.J. (eds), *Decision Making: Approaches and Analysis*. Manchester, Manchester University Press in association with the Open University, 1982.

103. McKenna, J.C. *Diplomatic Protest in Foreign Policy.* Chicago, Loyola University Press, 1962.

104. Macridis, R.C. (ed.) *Foreign Policy in World Politics.* Englewood Cliffs, NJ, Prentice Hall, 1985.

105. Maoz, Z. 'Crisis Initiation: A theoretical exploration of a neglected topic in international crisis theory'. *Review of International Studies,* vol. 8, no. 4, 1982, pp. 215–32.

106. May, E. *'Lessons' of the Past: The Use and Misuse of History in American Foreign Policy.* New York, Oxford University Press, 1973 and London, Oxford University Press, 1975.

107. Mayall, J. 'The Sanctions Problem in International Economic Relations: Reflections in the Light of Recent Experience'. *International Affairs,* vol. 60, no. 4, 1985, pp. 631–42.

108. Mitchell, R.J. *Ideology of a Superpower: Contemporary Soviet Doctrine on International Relations.* Stanford, CA, Hoover Institution Press, 1982.

109. Modelski, G.A. *A Theory of Foreign Policy.* London, Pall Mall and New York, Praeger, 1962.

110. Morgenthau, H.J. *Politics Among Nations: The Struggle for Power and Peace.* New York, Alfred Knopf, 1985.

111. Neustadt, R.E. *Alliance Politics.* New York & London, Columbia University Press, 1970.

112. Nicolson, H. *Diplomacy.* London & New York, Oxford University Press, 1963.

113. Northedge, F.S. The Nature of Foreign Policy. In *The Foreign Policies of the Powers,* ed. F.S. Northedge. London, Faber & Faber, 1974 and New York, Free Press, 1975.

114. The Open University, Social Sciences: A Second Level Course. *Decision Making in Britain.* Block VII: *The International Dimension.* Prepared on behalf of the Course Team by A.G. McGrew together with M. Smith and J. Vogler. Milton Keynes, The Open University Press, 1983.

115. Paige, G.D. *The Korean Decision, June 24–30, 1950.* New York, Free Press and London, Collier-Macmillan, 1968.

116. Parker, W.H. *Mackinder: Geography as an Aid to Statecraft.* Oxford & New York, Clarendon for the Oxford University Press, 1982.

117. Paul, D.W. 'Soviet Foreign Policy and the Invasion of Czechoslovakia: A Theory and a Case Study'. *International Studies Quarterly,* vol. 15, no. 2, pp. 159–202.

118. Payne, S.B. Jr. *The Soviet Union and SALT.* Cambridge, MA & London, MIT Press, 1981.

119. Plischke, E. (ed.) *Modern Diplomacy: The Art and the Artisans.* Washington, D.C. & Bromley, Kent, American Enterprise Institute, 1979.

120. Potter, W.C. 'Issue Area and Foreign Policy Analysis'. *International Organization,* vol. 34, no. 3, 1980, pp. 405–29.

121. Quandt, W.B. *Decade of Decisions: American Policy toward the Arab-Israeli Conflict, 1967–76.* Berkeley, CA & London, University of California Press, 1977.

122. Remnek, R.B. *Soviet Scholars and Soviet Foreign Policy: A Case Study in Soviet Policy towards India.* Durham, NC, Carolina Academic Press, 1975.

123. Renwick, R. *Economic Sanctions.* London, Croom Helm for the Harvard Center for International Affairs, 1982 and Lanham, MD, University Press of America, 1984.

124. Reynolds, P.A. *An Introduction to International Relations.* London & New York, Longmans, 1980.

125. Righter, R. *Whose News? Politics, the Press and the Third World.* London, Burnett Books in association with André Deutsch and New York, Times Books, 1978.

126. Rosati, J.A. 'Developing a Systematic Decision-making Framework: Bureaucratic Politics in Perspective'. *World Politics,* vol. XXXIII, no. 2, 1981, pp. 234–52.

127. Rosenau, J.N. *Domestic Sources of Foreign Policy.* New York, Free Press, 1967.

128. _____ *The Scientific Study of Foreign Policy.* London, Frances Pinter and New York, Nichols, 1980.

129. _____ *The Study of Political Adaptation.* London, Frances Pinter, 1980 and New York, Nichols, 1981.

130. _____ (ed.) *Comparing Foreign Policies: Theories, Findings and Methods.* New York & London, John Wiley, 1974. (Distributed by Halsted Press Division.)

131. _____ (ed.) *International Politics and Foreign Policy: A Reader in Research and Theory.* New York, Free Press, 1969.

132. _____ (ed.) *Linkage Politics: Essays on the Convergence of National and International Systems.* New York, Free Press, 1969.

133. _____ *et al., World Politics: An Introduction.* New York, Free Press and London, Collier-Macmillan, 1976.

134. Rothstein, R.L. *Planning Prediction and Policy Making in Foreign Affairs.* Boston, Little, Brown, 1972.

135. Rourke, F.E. *Bureaucracy and Foreign Policy.* Baltimore, Johns Hopkins University Press, 1972.

136. Saxena, S.C. *Foreign Policy of African States: Politics of Dependence and Confrontation.* New Delhi, Deep & Deep Publications, 1982.

137. Schwartz, M. *The Foreign Policy of the USSR: Domestic Factors.* Encino, CA, Dickenson, 1975.

138. _____ *Soviet Perceptions of the United States.* Berkeley, Los Angeles & London, University of California Press, 1980.

139. Scott, A.M. *The Revolution in Statecraft: Intervention in an Age of Interdependence.* Durham, NC, Duke University Press, 1982.

140. Shlaim, A. *The United States and the Berlin Blockade 1948–9: A Study in*

172   *Christopher Hill and Margot Light*

Crisis Decision-Making. Berkeley, CA & London, University of California Press, 1983.

141. Short, J.R. *An Introduction to Political Geography.* London & Boston, MA, Routledge & Kegan Paul, 1982.

142. Simon, H.A. *Administrative Behavior.* New York, Free Press, 1976.

143. Singer, M.R. *Weak States in a World of Powers: The Dynamics of International Relationships.* New York, Free Press & London, Collier-Macmillan, 1972.

144. Skilling, H.G. & Griffiths, F. (eds), *Interest Groups in Soviet Politics.* Princeton, NJ, Princeton University Press, 1971.

145. Smith, S.M. 'Allison and the Cuban Missile Crisis: A Review of the Bureaucratic Politics Model of Foreign Policy Decision-Making'. *Millennium: Journal of International Studies,* vol. 9, no. 1, 1980, pp. 21–40.

146. _____ *Foreign Policy Adaptation.* Aldershot, Hants., Gower and New York, Nichols, 1981.

147. Smith, S. & Clarke, M. (eds), *Foreign Policy Implementation.* London & Winchester, MA, Allen & Unwin, 1985.

148. Snyder, G.H. & Diesing, P. *Conflict among Nations.* Princeton, NJ & Guildford, Princeton University Press, 1977.

149. Snyder, R.C. *et al.*, *Foreign Policy Decision Making.* New York, Free Press, 1962.

150. Spanier, J. & Uslaner, E.M. *Foreign Policy and the Democratic Dilemmas.* New York, Holt, Rinehart & Winston (CBS College Publishing), 1982.

151. Spero, J.E. *The Politics of International Economic Relations.* London, Allen & Unwin, 1982 and New York, St. Martin's, 1985.

152. Spielmann, K.F. Jr. 'Defense Industrialists in the USSR'. *Problems of Communism,* vol. XXV, no. 5, 1976, pp. 52–69.

153. Sprout, H. & M. *The Ecological Perspective in Human Affairs.* London and Westport, CT, Greenwood Press, 1979.

154. Stein, J.G. & Tanter, R. *Rational Decision-Making: Israel's Security Choices 1967 & 1973.* Columbus, OH, Ohio State University Press, 1980.

155. Steinbruner, J.D. *The Cybernetic Theory of Decision.* Princeton, NJ & Guildford, Surrey, Princeton University Press, 1976.

156. Sullivan, M.P. *International Relations: Theories and Evidence.* Englewood Cliffs, NJ & Hemel Hempstead, Prentice Hall, 1976.

157. Tanter, R. & Ullman, R.H. *Theory and Policy in International Relations.* Princeton, NJ, Princeton University Press, 1971.

158. Triska, J.F. (ed.) *Communist Party-States: Comparative and International Studies.* New York, Bobbs-Merrill, 1969.

159. Valenta, J. *Soviet Intervention in Czechoslovakia, 1968: Anatomy of a Decision.* Baltimore & London, Johns Hopkins University Press, 1979.

160. Valenta, J. & Potter, W.C. (eds), *Soviet Decision-Making for National Security*. London, Boston & Sydney, Allen & Unwin, 1984.
161. Wallace, W. *Foreign Policy and the Political Process*. London, Macmillan, 1971.
162. _____ *The Foreign Policy Process in Britain*. London, Allen & Unwin for the Royal Institute of International Affairs, 1977.
163. Wallace, W. & Paterson, W.E. (eds), *Foreign Policy Making in Western Europe*. Farnborough, Hants., Saxon House and New York, Praeger, 1978.
164. Waltz, K.N. *Foreign Policy and Democratic Politics: The American and British Experience*. Boston, Little, Brown, 1967.
165. _____ *Theory of International Politics*. Reading, MA & London, Addison-Wesley, 1979.
166. Walzer, M. *Just and Unjust Wars: A Moral Argument with Historical Illustrations*. New York, Basic Books, 1977 and Harmondsworth, Middx., Penguin, 1980.
167. Watson, A. *Diplomacy: The Dialogue between States*. London, Eyre Methuen and Philadelphia, Institute for the Study of Human Issues, 1984.
168. Welch, W. & Triska, J.F. 'Soviet Foreign Policy Studies and Foreign Policy Models'. *World Politics*, vol. XXIII, no. 4, 1971, pp. 704–33.
169. White, J. *The Politics of Foreign Aid*. London, Bodley Head, 1974.
170. Whitson, J.B.K. & Larson, A. *Propaganda*. New York, Oceana Publications, 1964.
171. Wilkenfield, J. *et al.*, *Foreign Policy Behaviour*. Beverly Hills, CA & London, Sage, 1980.
172. Williams, P. *Crisis Management*. London, Martin Robertson and New York, Halsted Press, 1976.
173. Williams, P. & Smith, M. The Foreign Policies of Authoritarian and Democratic States. In *Year Book of World Affairs*, London, Methuen, 1976.
174. Wolfers, A. *Discord and Collaboration: Essays in International Politics*. Baltimore, Johns Hopkins University Press, 1966.

12 Integration and Disintegration

A.J.R. Groom
University of Kent at Canterbury and CAC
and
Alexis Heraclides
Mediterranean Studies Foundation, Athens

Integration and disintegration are age-old concerns of politics, political science, indeed, all social thought. Integration can be conceived in terms of a single dimension, such as the economy, groups of dimensions, or the totality of relationships. Moreover, it occurs at all levels of analysis from a family to world society. It can be seen as a state of affairs or as a process. As a state of affairs certain criteria must be met for integration to have occurred. Disintegration occurs when these criteria are no longer fulfilled. The criteria are usually specified by the observer or participant, since there is no generally accepted 'essentialist' definition of integration. When integration is conceived as a process, units are seen to move between conditions of complete isolation and complete integration. The focus is upon the process of moving towards one or other end of the spectrum rather than uniquely upon its integrative end. Thus integration involves movement towards (or disintegration away from) collective action based upon consensual values for the achievement of common goals in which the parties have long-term expectations of mutually compatible and acceptable behaviour. The process is self-maintaining. Coerced integration such as imperialism is not the concern of this chapter. Integration is ubiquitous in that no actor can exist in total isolation. Thus the process of integration and disintegration provides an organizing theme at all levels of society and between all 'disciplines' of the social sciences.

Integration, as a state of affairs, has traditionally not been seen as an important characteristic of world society. Inter-state relations are often described as anarchic – an anarchy consecrated in the doctrine of sovereignty. Indeed, this very anarchy, and especially the absence of a central world governing body with a monopoly of organized force ruling a constituency that has accepted a set of rights and duties in relation to that body, was used to justify the separation of international relations (IR) from political science. But the dichotomy is not that stark. Consensus is not always the dominant characteristic of relations within states. Nor is consensus entirely absent between states, as the work of many functional institutions attests, or within world society, where the growth of 'one world' problems, such as population or the environment, and their attempted solution by states and a variety of non-state actors is evident.

Integration is, however, not the dominant characteristic of either world society or of inter-state relations. Profusion is a better term – a profusion of systemic ties, whether power dominated or legitimized, extending over a variety of functional dimensions and involving a range of actors at and between various levels, which create world, regional, local and territorial ties. This profusion has been caused by a number of factors, of which the industrial and French revolutions are especially important. The industrial revolution brought about the makings of a world economy and led to a tremendous growth in transactions. The French Revolution was the harbinger of the nation-state which gradually imposed controls on these transactions, giving rise to a plethora of international institutions designed, for the most part, to facilitate the smooth flow of transactions across state boundaries; that is, to harmonize systemic demands with national and state affiliations and institutions. But a profusion of systemic ties and institutions does not make an integrated whole. There is no grand design. Perhaps this is no bad thing. Change within world society is rapid and great. The absence of an integrated whole increases the likelihood that the present repertoire will contain an appropriate response. Indeed, the extent to which integration should be encouraged is an open question. Although liberal Western democratic values assume that integration is a 'good thing' there are many examples in contemporary world society where 'independence', 'devolution', 'non-alignment', 'autonomy' and 'consociation' are prized values. Moreover, it is not a question of all or nothing, integration or isolation, but a question of how much integration in which sphere.

Studies of integration have been given a fillip in the post-war world by the example of the European Communities (EC) and decolonization. The EC attracted an inordinate amount of attention, particularly from US scholars, to the neglect of other, more important practical forms of integration, such as parallel national action in Scandinavia. This has now begun to correct itself. Decolonization has focussed attention on integration in two ways: there is the issue of integration and disintegration within states, such as Nigeria or Pakistan; and that of general or partial integration between states, as in the West Indies or West Africa. It is noteworthy that while federalism as a means of integration had a modicum of success in the earlier decolonization of the United States, Australia, Canada and South Africa, it has failed both within and between states in the post-war era in both the developed and developing worlds. Nevertheless, interest is provoked by failure as much as by success.

Insufficient attention has been focussed on disintegration in the contemporary world – movements away from unitary government or aspirations to autonomy, devolution, consociation and secession. This phenomenon is not restricted to the developing countries where there is little coterminality between colonially-derived boundaries and economic, social and cultural transaction systems. That the OAU decided to maintain colonial boundaries could turn out to be a costly short-term arrangement for a grievous problem that may trouble Africa for generations. But developed countries, too, are beginning to loosen their bonds: in Canada there is a call for 'sovereignty-association'; in Belgium a movement away from a unitary form of government; and Spain has recognized the autonomy of several regions. Britain has flirted with devolution and even in France, the epitome of centralized government, regionalism is in vogue. In Eastern Europe and the USSR the 'nationality' issue is smouldering.

A simultaneous process of both integration and disintegration is evident. Some states are coming together, for example in the framework of the European Communities. But the very same states are in a process of internal disintegration, leading to demands for an independent Scotland or Flanders in an integrating Europe. However, there has been a singular lack of imagination among both practitioners and academics in devising schemes to encompass and facilitate such diversity.

At the other end of the scale, the contemporary world is often described as 'one world' or a 'shrinking world'. This is not inaccurate: 'one world' problems abound such as population, food, environment, development, women ... The shrinking world is reflected in the prodigious movement and interdependence of goods, services, ideas and people. How can and should such developments be concep-tualized? The literature is heavily weighted in favour of certain integration theories – in particular neo-functionalism, regionalism and federalism – to the neglect of other approaches such as anarchism, co-operation or harmonization. Moreover, disintegration has only recently been taken seriously as something other than an anomaly or a pathological state. This introductory survey concludes with a brief comment on a wider range of modes of integration than is readily available in the literature, before broaching the notion of disintegration for which there is an emerging literature.

Co-operation is an attempt to adjust policies in a way that does not involve any immediate structural impact. The intention is to make agreements in specific areas for specific purposes without expecting or desiring task expansion or spillover. *Co-ordination* involves a continuous adjustment of government policies by a process of intensive consultation within an international institution to establish a programme designed to secure important goals that can only be achieved together. However, the structural impact of such arrangements is limited. *Harmonization,* on the other hand, involves institutionalized policy adjustment and alignment, often on the basis of some superordinate norm or standard. *Parallel national action* can lead to a surprising level of practical and effective integration through extensive routine policy adjustment. Compatible parallel legislation or practices are separately instituted by different actors in order to reduce the impact of boundaries. The scope can be considerable and although there is little formal institutionalization, there may be much informal contact and consultation. *Association,* on the other hand, has greater structural impact since it is embodied in a formal agreement. The agreements may be interim or link otherwise disparate actors who, nevertheless, have complementary interests in some areas. Paradoxically, association can enable both integration and separation to be pursued at the same time, promoting integration in certain domains, but restricting it in others, thereby denying the 'functional imperative' of task expansion and spillover. None of these modes of integration is likely to lead to an irrevocable derogation of sovereignty.

Regionalism, however, may stay within the existing state structure (its UN conception) or become the basis for state building. Region is a geographical concept and the doctrine of regionalism must be based on the assertion that geographical variables are a prime influence on behaviour. This is an empirical question and, although the notion of region may be helpful in individual dimensions, it does not appear to be the great organizing principle when considering multidimensional phenomena.

Neo-functionalism clearly does have implications for sovereignty, especially in the context of a regional or putative federal body coming to possess authority over national sub-systems, function by function. While such a body may aspire to wide scope and a high level of integration, it is firmly tied to a particular regional context. The end-goal of neo-functionalism is in fact a federation. *Federalism* stresses the importance of a constitutional instrument setting out the relationship and competences of the federal and local bodies within a defined territorial area. The scope and level of integration may be high. *Consociation* recognizes that units with great cleavages such as language, religion or ethnicity may nevertheless wish to establish or maintain an element of political unity. This can be achieved by establishing a 'grand coalition' of representatives of the segments, each of which maintains a veto, so as to encourage joint and consensual decision-making avoiding any possibility of the tyranny of the majority. These are state building theories, rather than state preserving or state by-passing modes of integration.

Informality, diversity and flexibility are the hallmarks of *networks* which are closely related to the *transactionalist approach*. Both are concerned with the waxing and waning of systems of transaction and the facilitation of intensely responsive institutional arrangements. *Regimes*, too, can have considerable flexibility involving both state and non-state actors in a situation of complex interdependence. *Anarchism* goes further in that its advocates propose mutual dependences without institutionalization of a formal kind, but it is relevant only at the micro-level. All of these modes of integration have implications for the centrality of the state system. Indeed, they tend to circumvent it and possibly to subvert it – but not by direct confrontation. Typical of this tendency is functionalism.

Functionalism has no fixed territorial base for organization. In advocating that form should follow function in an aterritorial manner, it is closely akin to networks and transactionalism. There is no end-state in functionalism, such as occurs in neo-functionalism, since the evolution of institutional forms is open-ended in response to changes in patterns of relationships, although the degree of integration may be very substantial in some systems. However, like neo-functionalists, functionalists stress the learning process whereby habits of co-operation in one area spill over into others as a result of the functional imperative. Whereas neo-functionalists stress that the learning process needs an act of political will, functionalists believe that the growth of cross-cutting ties leads fairly automatically to a working peace system. They differ, too, in that functionalists conceive of spillover systemically, whereas neo-functionalists see it as a means to inter-state integration in a new policy.

Perhaps the circle can be completed by returning to 'one world' problems. The notion of *collective goods*, borrowed from economics, is useful in analysing some aspects of these problems. 'One world' problems give rise to assets from which it is impossible to exclude 'free riders' or for which the consumption by one does not diminish availability to another. The theory of collective goods is apposite, particularly in the context of such approaches as regime building.

Disintegration is the antithesis of integration. It can be defined either as the final stage or a process whereby units of a whole assert themselves politically. It may involve the disintegration of multi-ethnic states, whereby regions seek territorial separatism ranging from autonomy to independence, or the disintegration of supra-national regional arrangements. The term disintegration tends to have a negative connotation, suggesting decomposition, the destruction of unity and integrity, the tearing apart of society's fabric or the shattering of the natural order of things. Furthermore, it tends to assume the pre-existence of integration. Now that the heroic years of integration theorizing are over, some theorists question integration and see it as a passing phase, incidental, something assumed but non-existent, since lack of overt conflict is an unreliable indicator of integration. Multi-ethnic states can function as fairly stable societies either based on a generally acceptable consociational framework or by way of coercive control. A more appropriate and non-commital term than disintegration is 'fission', or the more widely used 'separatism'. Disintegration could thus be used as a sub-category for the moving apart or final split of the constituent parts of a unitary state, federation, confederation or other supranational regional arrangement. Interestingly, any comprehensive study of disintegration is frequently seen as an affront, a retrogression, or an undue preoccupation with unfortunate events. But there is no inherent positive value in either integration or separation. It is a matter of choice: who wants what, where, when, and at whose expense. And like it or not, separatisms abound and are likely to multiply. No longer can we ignore this glaring anomaly in the integration paradigm.

Because disintegration is often seen as an undesirable and undesired crisis, disintegration theory is as yet unstructured and fairly novel. A theory of disintegration which would also be relevant to the study of international conflict should be able to provide answers to such questions as when and why separate groups persist and collective identities, in defiance of class or state, emerge, persist or resurge, becoming politically salient. What conditions facilitate a process of disintegration? When is secession most likely? What is the role of the international system in an emerging or continuing quest for various forms of territorial separatism and for secession?

In the last decade nascent direct or primary theories of disintegration have appeared, but previous approaches, concerned primarily with other issues, are also relevant. The latter can be divided into (a) negative theories of integration, (b) negative theories of cohesion, (c) indirect theories of disintegration or separatism. It is noteworthy that the most stimulating and productive area in integration theory of the last decade has, in fact, been concerned with the modalities of disintegration rather than with integration. But the literature reveals a failure in ingenuity and imagination which can ill be afforded if organizational structures are to be created which match the complexities and the necessities of the contemporary world and its most likely futures.

General Works

There are a number of general works on integration which cover several different approaches. Most of these are out of date. Taylor & Groom's [121] edited volume contains original contributions on most of the approaches mentioned in the preceding paragraphs. Designed as a textbook surveying different conceptual approaches to international organization and institutions, a fundamentally revised edition is now available [40]. Harrison [49] is essentially a theoretical work surveying the functionalist, neo-functionalist and federalist literature in the context of the European experience. Jacob & Toscano's volume [56] wears its years well and is noteworthy for also considering integration in cities and other fora.

Interstate Modes of Co-operation

There is surprisingly little theoretical literature about the ways in which governments come together to solve problems or to take advantage of opportunities by working together in concert without prejudicing their sovereignty. The chapters on co-operation, co-ordination, harmonization, parallel national action and association in [121, 40] and the more conceptual chapters of [39] offer an introduction and a guide to further reading.

Regionalism as a doctrine has been written into the security and economic provisions of the UN Charter. It had an ambivalent rationale. It was viewed as a half-way house between world government and the sovereign state, as a means whereby states with interests in common that were less than universal could work together and, finally, as a form of hegemonial control for great powers. Few, if any, of these hopes and fears have been realized. The literature is not recent, but Burton [8], Nye [90, 91], Cantori & Spiegel [10] and Russett [100] made a mark in their day. Thompson [122] is a useful review article, while Axline [2] is more recent.

State-building

Neo-functionalism is sometimes seen as federalism by instalments. The 'guru' of the neo-functionalists is undoubtedly Haas. Influenced by Mitrany, but aspiring to more rigorous methodology, he has pioneered the American study of European integration [46]. He has also applied the same approach to the ILO [43]. More recently he has expressed doubts about the whole neo-functionalist enterprise [44, 45], but, despite the current critical assessment of the neo-functionalist paradigm, the impetus given to the study of integration by Haas must be handsomely acknowledged, as should the work of Lindberg & Scheingold [72, 73, 74]. The neo-functionalists wrote prolifically and their articles have a prominent place in readers and anthologies. But their day is over. Too much of their theorizing was dependent on what turned out to be an unusual period in Western Europe and many of them have moved on to other fields. Taylor has made an excellent conceptual and empirical analysis of the present state of the EC [120]. Another work that grew out of Mitrany's initial impetus is by Sewell, who tested Mitrany's hypotheses in a study of the World Bank group [107].

Federation has been tried and failed since 1945, yet the doctrine is a very powerful one. There is a voluminous literature on federalism within states, fuelled not least by the doctrine being akin to holy writ in the United States. However, our emphasis is on federation as a means to integration or disintegration between states. Wheare, who helped to design several constitutions, has written the classic [128], while Birch has neatly summarized the different approaches to the subject [5].

Constitution-building has been most innovative of late in the domain of consocation. The leading theorist is Lijphardt [71], who deftly summarizes his thesis in later articles [31, 69, 70]. The theory is assessed by Cannon and Steiner [9, 116]. Earlier assessments were made by Lustick [77] and Nordlinger [89]. Like federalism, consociation enables groups to have their cake and eat it and it can be a stage in a process either of integration or disintegration. But the recent failures of federalism have created a growing interest in consocation. There is a felt need for flexible arrangements which can reflect diversity. Consocation and theories such as collective goods [99, 101, 92] offer the required flexibility.

Beyond the State System

As political science and IR became more rigorously empirical in their research methods, scholars began to examine more closely the flows and implications of all manner of transactions. Excellent pioneering and more recent work has been undertaken by Deutsch [21, 22, 23]. His lead was followed by an important edited volume by Keohane & Nye [62]. They, like Huntington, pointed to the significance of transgovernmental relations which led them towards the concept of regimes, albeit from a rather state-centric viewpoint [60, 61, 54]. Judge takes a different tack, relating transactionalism, transnationalism and networks [41, 57, 121]. He also acted as impresario for a thought-provoking symposium on the *Open Society of the Future* [93].

Regimes have captured the imagination of scholars in the USA. While acknowledging that the state-centric power political view of the world is only partial and that systemic, transactional approaches including non-state and state actors in a more legitimized framework are relevant, they do not yet have the courage of their convictions. This tension can be seen in Keohane & Nye's work [60], in a recent volume edited by Krasner [63] and in articles by Haas and Young [47, 130]. Yet the older functionalist approach still has potency.

While it is usually futile to attribute to any one writer the development of a seminal theory, the name of Mitrany does spring to mind in the case of functionalism. His classic essay, *A Working Peace*

System [86], the ideas of which were first published in the inter-war period, has had great influence. It is a cogent and powerful statement proposing an alternative to power politics in international relations. Mitrany died in 1975 aged 87, a few weeks after publishing some old and new essays [85] and some of his last contributions are amongst his best. A case in point is his 'The Prospect of Integration: Federal or Functional?' in Groom & Taylor [41], a collection of otherwise original essays on the theoretical aspects of functionalism, followed by case studies. The views expressed range from the committed to the opposed. There has been a revival of interest in functionalism in the last two decades. One of the earlier expressions was a Bellagio conference [42], while some have attempted to go *Beyond Functionalism* [96]. Most students of international organization are introduced to the theory of functionalism by Claude through his critique in [13]. Claude admits that functionalism is a very seductive approach to the problems of international organization. Nowhere can this be more clearly seen than in the neo-functionalist school which, despite denying the functionalist approach by being territorial, teleological and state-centric, nevertheless owes much to Mitrany's notion of a learning process giving rise to task expansion and spillover in order to create a working peace system [38].

Disintegration

The complexities of living in one world which is at the same time many worlds has given rise to conceptualizations not only of coming together, but also of coming apart. The last decade has seen the appearance of theories of disintegration *per se*, whereas previous theories were either negative theories of integration and cohesion or indirect theories of disintegration or separatism. Under negative theories of integration can be grouped the various explanations of nation-building and inter-state integration which attempt to explain the standstill or failure of integration. Deutsch, a pioneer in the analysis of 'nation-building', has suggested that integration is disrupted when mobilization outpaces assimilation [19, 20, 21]. A more refined and subtle approach to nation-building which attempts to retain the nation-building integration paradigm is that of Geertz [34] who points to 'primordialism', seen as a 'pathological situation' giving undue importance to ascriptive ties which thereby denies the secular essence of politics. The neo-functionalists have also suggested reasons for the reversal of integration, such as high politics, reversible elite interests, or, more generally, the unreliability of the economically based functional imperative. In addition, neo-functionalist or federal schemes of integration stumble when faced by the need to develop a social psychological community as Taylor [119] and Lodge [75] point out.

Among negative theories of cohesion can be grouped two theories, consociationalism and control, the tenets of which have been cogently summarized in an article by Lustick [77]. M.G. Smith [115 and in 66], Kuper [65, 66] and van den Berghe [124 and in 66] suggest that institutionalized control, although stable, is fraught with disintegrative propensities. In reply some Marxist writers – Edelstein [in 3] and Magubane [80] – see a similarity between M.G. Smith's model of the state as a plural society and the Marxist model of the bourgeois state. A collection of better known examples of these two approaches can be found in McRae [79] and the seminal Kuper & Smith volume [66]. Also useful is C. Young's blend of cultural anthropology and politics [129]. Indirect theories of disintegration point to revolution, inter-group conflict and even aggression, all of which present important cues for a theory of disintegration. These are discussed in the section on revolution in Chapter 9 and in Chapter 10.

Direct theories of disintegration have as their intellectual forebear the theory of nationalism and the notion of a nation-state. Important works include Deutsch [21], Emerson [27], A.D. Smith [110, 111], Kamenka [58] and Seton-Watson [105]. Because of the confusion engendered by the term nation, the concept of ethnic group and ethnicity has been used more recently, as well as novel compound terms such as ethnonationalism [16 and in 31], tribal nationalism [84], subnationalism [in 36], unsatisfied nationalism [106], resurgent nationalism [81], ethnic separatism [111], and others. There has been a great resurgence of interest in this area because the phenomenon of ethnic politics is growing everywhere – a phenomenon only recently recognized. It has considerable implications for conventional wisdom and it is likely to challenge powerful vested interests.

Two main approaches of the last decade can be considered as direct or primary theories of disintegration: internal colonialism and ethnicity (or the 'new ethnicist' position). In a very useful article Birch [6] summarizes both. Communalism, used in the study of intra-state communal conflict in developing countries, is a more general approach which acts as a useful bridge between these two opposed theories.

Internal colonialism was developed by Hechter [50] and corroborated by other Marxist and neo-Marxist social scientists such as Davis [18], Krippendorff [64] and Löwy [76] or proponents of the centre–periphery model such as Galtung [33]. According to this approach the very essence of politicized regional or ethnic assertiveness is a division between the political-economic-cultural centre and the periphery within a modern state. When ethnic differentiation is added to regional inequality, disintegration is almost unavoidable. This model is put to severe test by the disintegrative-separatist tendencies on the part of rich territories. While it can be claimed that separatism is due to an external sponsor, to past neglect or that its essence is simply economic, it remains doubtful whether the theory can predict and explain all or the majority of separatisms.

The proponents of ethnicity are a far larger and more disparate group. They include the early critics of the nation-building paradigm such as Connor and Enloe, theoreticians of nationalism such as A.D. Smith, the proponents of consociationalism and of control, Lijphardt, Kuper, van den Berghe and others. Schermerhorn [104], Isaacs [55] and more recently A.D. Smith [110] and Rothschild [98] are particularly noteworthy, and there are contributions in Kurokawa [67], Glazer & Moynihan [36], Cohen [14], Gelfand & Lee [35], Richmond [95], Bell & Freeman [3], A.D. Smith [114], Esman [31] and De Vos & Rommanucci-Ross [24].

The fundamental tenet of this approach is that ethnic identity (ethnicity) is the essential independent variable that leads to political assertiveness and militant separatism regardless of the existence of inequality or dominance. This approach has difficulty accounting for extended struggles on the part of groups that can hardly be characterized as ethnic groups. Clearly, many movements have been influenced in their separatism by extreme levels of inequality and discrimination. Thus internal colonialism and ethnicity can best be seen as the two polar models of disintegration between which separatism can oscillate.

The proponents of communalism, the third approach, focus mainly on modernization, the rise of aspirations, scarcity, the distribution of rewards, development, elite interests and the compartmentalization of institutions on communal grounds. Ethnicity is seen basically as a useful strategy. The main contributors in this area are Huntington [52, 53], Melson & Wolpe [83], Esman [30, 31] and Rabushka & Shepsle [94].

Other theories, models and hypotheses have also appeared in recent years which provide the fundamentals of models of the disintegration process. Wallerstein [126, 127], Bell & Freeman [3], Nafziger & Richter [88], and Wai [125] tend towards the internal colonialism premises. A.D. Smith [111], Rothschild [98] and Birch [6] fall under the ethnicity paradigm. C. Young [129], Duchasek [25, 26], Chong-Do Hah & Martin [12] and Mughan [87] are more middle of the road. Trent [123] provides the most detailed model of an etiology of territorial disintegration, akin to models of revolutionary violence, while the noted social psychologist Tajfel has presented a cogent image of the politicization of minorities [118].

IR has a traditional bias against non-state actors, and the issue of disintegration and non-state nationalist movements was taken up with some difficulty. Three useful introductory edited volumes comprising mainly case studies appeared almost simultaneously: Said & Simmons [102], Bertelsen [4] and Suhrke & Noble [117]. For the international legal aspects and the problem of secessionist self-determination Buchheit [7] is more eloquent than Ronen [97].

The rising trend of a literature of disintegration in political science and political sociology in the Anglo-Saxon scientific community is reflected in some fairly new journals such as *Ethnic and Racial Studies, Ethnicity, Research in Race and Ethnic Relations*, and the *Canadian Review of Studies in Nationalism*. Occasional articles on the subject also appear in *Comparative Politics, New Community*, as well as in IR journals such as *World Politics, Orbis* and *Millennium*.

Bibliography to Chapter 12

1.   Ake, C. *A Theory of Political Integration*. Homewood, IL, Dorsey Press, 1967.
2.   Axline, W.A. *Caribbean Integration: The Politics of Regionalism*. London, Frances Pinter and New York, Nichols, 1979.
3.   Bell, W. & Freeman, W.E. (eds), *Ethnicity and Nation-Building*. Beverly Hills, CA & London, Sage, 1974.
4.   Bertelsen, J.S. (ed.) *Nonstate Nations in International Politics*. New York & London, Praeger, 1977.
5.   Birch, A.H. 'Approaches to the Study of Federalism'. *Political Studies*, vol. XIV, no. 1, 1966, pp. 15–33.
6.   _____ 'Minority Nationalist Movements and Theories of

Political Integration'. *World Politics*, vol. XXX, no. 3, 1978, pp. 325–44.

7. Buchheit, L.C. *Secession: The Legitimacy of Self-Determination*. New Haven & London, Yale University Press, 1978.

8. Burton, J.W. Regionalism, Functionalism and the U.N. Regional Arrangements for Security. In *The United Nations*, ed. M. Waters. London, Collier-Macmillan and New York, Macmillan, 1967.

9. Cannon, G.E. 'Consociationism vs Control: Canada as a Case Study'. *Western Political Quarterly*, vol. XXXV, no. 1, 1982, pp. 50–64.

10. Cantori, L. & Spiegel, S.C. *The International Politics of Regions*. Englewood Cliffs, NJ & Hemel Hempstead, Prentice Hall, 1970.

11. Carter, A. *The Political Theory of Anarchism*. London, Routledge & Kegan Paul and New York, Harper & Row, 1971.

12. Chong-Do, H. & Martin, J. 'Towards a Synthesis of Conflict and Integration Theories of Nationalism'. *World Politics*, vol. XXVII, no. 3, 1975, pp. 361–86.

13. Claude, I.L. *Swords into Plowshares*. New York, Random House, 1971.

14. Cohen, A. (ed.) *Urban Ethnicity*. London, Tavistock Publications and New York, Methuen, 1974.

15. Connor, W. 'Nation-Building or Nation-Destroying?' *World Politics*, vol. XXIV, no. 3, 1972, pp. 319–55.

16. _____ 'A Nation is a Nation, is a State, is an Ethnic Group is a . . .'. *Ethnic and Racial Studies*, vol. 1, no. 4, 1978, pp. 377–400.

17. _____ 'The Politics of Ethnonationalism'. *Journal of International Affairs*, vol. 27, no. 1, 1973, pp. 1–21.

18. Davis, H.B. *Toward a Marxist Theory of Nationalism*. New York, Monthly Review Press, 1980.

19. Deutsch, K.W. *The Analysis of International Relations*. Englewood Cliffs, NJ, Prentice Hall, 1978.

20. _____ *Nationalism and its Alternatives*. New York, A. Knopf, 1969.

21. _____ *Nationalism and Social Communication: An Enquiry into the Foundations of Nationality*. Cambridge, MA & London, MIT Press, 1966.

22. _____ *Tides Among Nations*. London, Collier-Macmillan and New York, Free Press, 1979.

23. _____ *et al*, *Political Community and the North Atlantic Area*. London & Westport, CT, Greenwood Press and Princeton, NJ, Princeton University Press, 1957.

24. De Vos, G. & Romanucci-Ross, L. (eds), *Ethnic Identity: Cultural Continuities and Change*. Chicago, University of Chicago Press, 1983.

25. Duchasek, I.D. 'Antagonistic Cooperation: Territorial and Ethnic Communities'. *Publius*, vol. 7, no. 4, 1977, pp. 3–29.

26. _____ *Comparative Federalism: The Territorial Dimension of Politics.* New York & London, Holt, Rinehart & Winston, 1970.

27. Emerson, R. *From Empire to Nation: The Rise to Self-Assertion of Asian and African Peoples.* Cambridge, MA, Harvard University Press, 1960.

28. Enloe, C. *Ethnic Conflict and Political Development.* Boston, Little, Brown, 1973.

29. _____ 'Internal Colonialism, Federalism and Alternative State Development Strategies'. *Publius*, vol. 7, no. 4, 1977, pp. 145–60.

30. Esman, M.J. 'The Management of Communal Conflict'. *Public Policy*, vol. XXI, no. 1, 1973, pp. 49–78.

31. _____ (ed.) *Ethnic Conflict in the Western World.* Ithaca, NY, Cornell University Press, 1977.

32. Etzioni, A. *Political Unification.* New York, Krieger, 1974.

33. Galtung, J. The Territorial System. In *The True Worlds: A Transnational Perspective.* J. Galtung, New York, Free Press and London, Collier-Macmillan International, 1980. pp. 255–303.

34. Geertz, C. The Integrative Revolution: Primordial Sentiments and Civic Politics in the New States. In *Political Modernization*, ed. C.E. Welch, Jr. Belmont, CA, Wadsworth Publishing Co., 1971, pp. 167–88.

35. Gelfand, D.E. & Lee, R.D. (eds), *Ethnic Conflicts and Power: A Cross-National Perspective.* New York & Chichester, John Wiley and Sons, 1973.

36. Glazer, N. & Moynihan, D.P. (eds), *Ethnicity: Theory and Experience.* Cambridge, MA & London, Harvard University Press, 1976.

37. Groom, A.J.R. 'The Functionalist Approach and East/West Co-operation in Europe'. *Journal of Common Market Studies*, vol. XIII, nos 1 & 2, 1975, pp. 21–60.

38. _____ 'Neofunctionalism: A Case of Mistaken Identity'. *Political Science*, vol. 30, no. 1, 1978, pp. 15–28.

39. Groom, A.J.R. & Taylor, P. (eds), *The Commonwealth in the 1980s.* London, Macmillan and New York, Crane-Russak, 1984.

40. _____ (eds), *Frameworks for International Cooperation.* London, Frances Pinter, 1986.

41. _____ (eds), *Functionalism: Theory and Practice in International Relations.* London, University of London Press and New York, Crane-Russak, 1975.

42. _____ (rapporteurs), *Functionalism.* New York, Carnegie Endowment, 1969.

43. Haas, E.B. *Beyond the Nation State.* Stanford, CA, Stanford University Press, 1964.

44. _____ *The Obsolescence of Regional Integration Theory.* Berkeley, CA, University of California, Institute of International Studies, 1976.

45. _____ 'Turbulent Fields and the Theory of Regional Integration'.

International Organization, vol. XXX, no. 2, 1976, pp. 173–212.

46. _____ *The Uniting of Europe*. London, Stevens, 1958 and Stanford, CA, Stanford University Press, 1968.

47. _____ 'Why Collaborate? Issue Linkage and International Regimes'. *World Politics*, vol. XXXII, no. 3, 1980, pp. 357–405.

48. Haas, M. *International Organization: An Interdisciplinary Bibliography*. Stanford, CA, Hoover Institute, 1971.

49. Harrison, R.J. *Europe in Question*. London, Allen & Unwin and New York, New York University Press, 1974.

50. Hechter, M. *Internal Colonialism: The Celtic Fringe in the British National Government, 1536–1966*. London, Routledge & Kegan Paul, and Berkeley, CA, University of California Press, 1975.

51. Horowitz, D.L. 'Three Dimensions of Ethnic Politics'. *World Politics*, vol. XXIII, no. 2, 1971, pp. 232–44.

52. Huntington, S.P. 'Civil Violence and the Process of Development'. *Adelphi Papers*, no. 83, 1971, pp. 1–15.

53. _____ *Political Order in Changing Societies*. New Haven & London, Yale University Press, 1969.

54. _____ 'Transnational Organisations in World Politics'. *World Politics*, vol. XXV, no. 3, 1973, pp. 333–68.

55. Isaacs, H.R. *Idols of the Tribe: Group Identity and Political Change*. New York, Harper & Row, 1977.

56. Jacob, P.E. & Toscano, J.V. *Integration of Political Communities*. Philadelphia, J.B. Lippincott Co., 1964.

57. Judge, A.J.N. 'The World Network of Organizations'. *International Associations*, vol. 24, no. 1, 1972, pp. 18–24.

58. Kamenka, E. (ed.) *Nationalism, the Nature and Evolution of an Idea*. London, Edward Arnold and New York, St. Martin's, 1976.

59. Kasfir, N. 'Explaining Ethnic Political Participation'. *World Politics*, vol. XXXI, no. 3, 1979, pp. 365–88.

60. Keohane, R.O. & Nye, J.S. *Power and Interdependence: World Politics in Transition*. Boston, Little, Brown, 1977.

61. _____ 'Transgovernmental Relations and International Organizations'. *World Politics*, vol. XXVII, no. 1, 1974, pp. 39–62.

62. _____ (eds), *Transnational Relations and World Politics*. Cambridge, MA & London, Harvard University Press, 1973.

63. Krasner, S.D. (ed.) *International Regimes*. Ithaca, NY & London, Cornell University Press, 1983.

64. Krippendorff, E. 'Minorities, Violence and Peace Research'. *Journal of Peace Research*, vol. 16, no. 1, 1979, pp. 27–40.

65. Kuper, L. *Race, Class and Power*. London, Duckworth, 1977.

66. Kuper, L. & Smith, M.G. (eds), *Pluralism in Africa*. Berkeley, CA & London, California University Press, 1971.

67. Kurokawa, M. (ed.) *Minority Responses*. New York, Random House, 1970.

68. Levine, E.P. & Campbell, D.T. *Ethnocentrism: Theories of Conflict, Ethnic Attitudes and Group Behaviour.* New York, John Wiley and Sons, 1972.

69. Lijphardt, A. 'Consociational Democracy'. *World Politics*, vol. XXI, no. 2, 1969, pp. 207–25.

70. _____ 'Consociation and Federation: Conceptual and Empirical Links'. *Canadian Journal of Political Science*, vol. XXII, no. 3, 1979, pp. 499–515.

71. _____ *Democracy in Plural Societies.* New Haven & London, Yale University Press, 1980.

72. Lindberg, L. *The Political Dynamics of European Economic Integration.* Stanford, CA, Stanford University Press, 1963.

73. Lindberg, L. & Scheingold, S. *Europe's Would-Be Polity.* Englewood Cliffs, NJ & Hemel Hempstead, Prentice Hall, 1970.

74. _____ (eds), *Regional Integration.* Cambridge, MA & London (distributed by Oxford University Press), Harvard University Press, 1971.

75. Lodge, J. 'Loyalty and the EEC: The Limits of the Functional Approach'. *Political Studies*, vol. XXVI, no. 2, 1978, pp. 232–48.

76. Löwy, M. 'Marxists and the National Question'. *New Left Review*, no. 96, (March–April 1976), pp. 81–100.

77. Lustick, I. 'Stability in Deeply Divided Societies: Consociationalism versus Control'. *World Politics*, vol. XXXI, no. 3, 1979, pp. 325–44.

78. McKay, J. & Lewins, F. 'Ethnicity and the Ethnic Group: A Conceptual Analysis and Reformulation'. *Ethnic and Racial Studies*, vol. I, no. 4, 1978, pp. 412–27.

79. McRae, K. (ed.) *Consociational Democracy: Political Accommodation in Segmented Societies.* Toronto, McLelland & Stewart Ltd., 1974.

80. Magubane, B. 'Pluralism and Conflict Situations in Africa: A New Look'. *African Social Research*, no. 7, 1969, pp. 529–54.

81. Mayo, P.E. *The Roots of Identity: Three National Movements in Contemporary European Politics.* London, Allen Lane, 1974.

82. Mazrui, A.A. 'Africa: The Political Culture of Nationhood and the Political Economy of the State'. *Millennium: Journal of International Studies*, vol. 11, no. 3, 1983, pp. 201–10.

83. Melson, R. & Wolpe, H. (eds), *Nigeria: Modernization and the Politics of Communalism.* East Lansing, MI, Michigan State University Press, 1971.

84. Mercier, P. On the Meaning of "Tribalism" in Black Africa. In *Africa: Social Problems of Change and Conflict*, ed. P.L. van den Berghe. San Francisco, Chandler Publishing Co., 1965, pp. 483–501.

85. Mitrany, D. *The Functional Theory of Politics.* London, Martin Robertson, 1975 and New York, St. Martin's, 1976.

86. _____ *A Working Peace System.* Chicago, Quadrangle Books, 1966.

87. Mughan, A. 'Modernization, Deprivation and the Distribution of Power Resources: Towards a Theory of Ethnic Confict'. *New Community*, vol. 5, no. 4, 1977, pp. 360–70.
88. Nafziger, E.W. & Richter, W.L. 'Biafra and Bangladesh: The Political Economy of Secessionist Conflict'. *Journal of Peace Research*, vol. XIII, no. 2, 1976, pp. 91–109.
89. Nordlinger, E.A. *Conflict Regulation in Divided Societies*. Cambridge, MA, Harvard University, Center for International Studies, 1977.
90. Nye, J.S. *Peace in Parts: Integration and Conflict in Regional Organisations*. Boston, Little, Brown, 1971.
91. _____ (ed.) *International Regionalism*. Boston, Little, Brown, 1968.
92. Olson, M. *The Logic of Collective Action: Public Goods and the Theory of Groups*. Cambridge, MA & London, Harvard University Press, 1971.
93. *Open Society of the Future*. Brussels, Union of International Associations, 1973.
94. Rabushka, A. & Shepsle, K.A. *Politics in Plural Societies*. Columbus, OH, Merrill, 1972.
95. Richmond, A.H. (ed.) *Readings in Race and Ethnic Relations*. Oxford & Elmsford, NY, Pergamon Press, 1972.
96. Riggs, R.E. & Mykletun, I.J. *Beyond Functionalism*. Oslo, Universitets Forlaget and Minneapolis, University of Minnesota Press, 1979.
97. Ronen, D. *The Quest for Self-Determination*. New Haven & London, Yale University Press, 1982.
98. Rothschild, J. *Ethnopolitics*. New York, Columbia University Press, 1981.
99. Ruggie, J.G. 'Collective Goods and Future International Collaboration'. *American Political Science Review*, vol. LXVI, no. 3, 1972, pp. 874–93.
100. Russett, B.M. *International Regions and the International System*. London, Greenwood Press, 1976 and Westport, CT, Greenwood Press, 1975.
101. Russett, B.M. & Sullivan, J. 'Collective Goods and International Organization'. *International Organization*, vol. XXV, no. 4, pp. 845–65.
102. Said, A.A. & Simmons, L.R. (eds), *Ethnicity in an International Context*. New Brunswick, NJ, Transaction Books, 1976.
103. Sathyarmurthy, T.V. *Nationalism in the Contemporary World*. London, Frances Pinter and Totowa, NJ, Allanheld, 1983.
104. Schermerhorn, R.A. *Comparative Ethnic Relations*. Chicago and London, University of Chicago Press, 1979.
105. Seton-Watson, H. *Nations and States*. London, Methuen and Boulder, CO, Westview, 1977.
106. _____ 'Unsatisfied Nationalisms'. *Journal of Contemporary History*, vol. 6, no. 1, 1971, pp. 3–14.

107. Sewell, J.P. *Functionalism and World Politics*. Princeton, NJ, Princeton University Press, 1966.
108. Shibutani, T. & Kwan, K.M. *Ethnic Stratification: A Comparative Approach*. New York, Macmillan, 1965.
109. Smith, A.D. 'Ethnic Identity and World Order'. *Millennium: Journal of International Studies*, vol. 12, no. 2, 1983, pp. 149–61.
110. _____ *The Ethnic Revival in the Modern World*. Cambridge & New York, Cambridge University Press, 1981.
111. _____ *Nationalism in the Twentieth Century*. Oxford, Martin Robertson and New York, New York University Press, 1979.
112. _____ *State and Nation in the Third World*. Brighton, Wheatsheaf and New York, St. Martin's, 1983.
113. _____ 'Towards a Theory of Ethnic Separatism'. *Ethnic and Racial Studies*, vol. 2, no. 1, 1979, pp. 21–37.
114. _____ (ed.) *Nationalist Movements*. London, Macmillan, 1976 and New York, St. Martin's, 1977.
115. Smith, M.G. *Corporations and Society*. London, Duckworth, 1976.
116. Steiner, J. 'The Consociational Theory and Beyond'. *Comparative Politics*, vol. 13, no. 3, 1981, pp. 339–54.
117. Suhrke, A. & Noble, L.G. (eds), *Ethnic Conflicts in International Relations*. New York, Praeger, 1978 (Distributed in the UK by Holt-Saunders, Eastbourne).
118. Tajfel, H. *The Social Psychology of Minorities*. Minority Rights Group, Report no. 38, December 1978.
119. Taylor, P. 'The Concept of Community and the European Integration Process'. *Journal of Common Market Studies*, vol. VII, no. 2, 1968, pp. 83–101.
120. _____ *The Limits of European Integration*. London, Croom Helm and New York, Columbia University Press, 1983.
121. Taylor, P. & Groom, A.J.R. (eds), *International Organization: A Conceptual Approach*. London, Frances Pinter, 1978.
122. Thompson, W.C. 'The Regional Subsystem'. *International Studies Quarterly*, vol. 17, no. 1, 1973, pp. 89–117.
123. Trent, J. 'The Politics of Nationalist Movements – A Reconsideration'. *Canadian Review of Studies in Nationalism*, vol. 2, no. 1, 1974, pp. 157–71.
124. Van den Berghe, P.L. 'Pluralism and Conflict Situations in Africa: A Reply to B. Magubane'. *African Social Research*, no. 9, June 1970, pp. 681–9.
125. Wai, D.M. 'Sources of Communal Conflicts and Secessionist Politics in Africa'. *Ethnic and Racial Studies*, vol. I, no. 3, 1978, pp. 286–305.
126. Wallerstein, I. Ethnicity and National Integration in West Africa. In *Africa: Social Problems of Change and Conflict*, ed. P.L. van den Berghe. San Francisco, Chandler Publishing Co., 1965, pp. 472–82.
127. _____ The Two Modes of Ethnic Consciousness: Soviet Central

Asia in Transition. In *The Nationality Question in Soviet Central Asia*, ed. E. Allworth. New York & London, Praeger, 1973, pp. 168–75.

128. Wheare, K. *Federal Government*. London & Westport, CT, Greenwood Press, 1980.
129. Young, C. *The Politics of Cultural Pluralism*. Madison, University of Wisconsin Press, 1979.
130. Young, O.R. 'International Regimes: Problems of Concept Formation'. *World Politics*, vol. XXXII, no. 3, 1980, pp. 331–56.

13 Anthropological Aspects

A.V.S. de Reuck
University of Surrey and CAC

Since the 'behavioural revolution' of the 1960s, scholars of international relations (IR) have sought to enrich their field with insights borrowed from other disciplines: findings from organization theory or social psychology, for example, can often be applied directly to studies of governmental decision-making.

Anthropology is frequently concerned with societies that lack central authority or law-making institutions. International society shares these and other features with the traditional societies studied by anthropologists: for example, the problems engendered by norms of self-help in redressing grievances [17, 18]; the variety of institutionalized procedures for resolving conflicts [12, 14, 27, 36, 41, 44, 60]; overlapping group membership serving to reduce the level, if not the frequency, of disputes [12, 40, 79]; patterns of alliances and the use of brokers to mend or extend relationships [5, 6, 19].

The parallel between the present global system and some stateless societies is succinctly outlined by Masters in his classic paper on 'World Politics as a Primitive Political System' [58] and this is further developed in the context of rule enforcement without sanctions by Barkun [11] and others [24, 45].

The origins and conduct of tribal warfare may be approached through several useful symposia [18, 23, 39], while the vexed question of man's alleged inheritance of an aggressive instinct from his primate forbears is discussed at length by Ardrey [1, 2, 3, 4], Lorenz [56] and Montague [61, 62]. Of these, only the latter may be relied upon, at least so far as human beings are concerned.

A more significant and less hackneyed problem relates to the biological (evolutionary) basis for intraspecific co-operation (for example Wilson's work on sociobiology [82, 83] and [71, 29]), the nature of dominance [50] and its correlation with Chance and Larsen's important concept of attention structure [26] and the existence of alternative modes of interaction among primates, named

194

respectively 'agonistic' and 'hedonic' by Chance and Jolly [25].

Anthropology is no longer the study of non-literate peoples; its domain is essentially the diversity of human social structures and cultures. Human diversity is strangely neglected by international studies, which tends sometimes toward a blind ethnocentricity and suffers the more because this is largely unrecognized.

The work that might even begin to remedy this state of affairs has yet to be written, but those who wish to attain a glimmer of what it might be like to have their sight restored are recommended to read Benedict [15], Nakane [64] or Smith [75] on Japanese society, together with, say, Gorer [42] and Dumont [34] who discuss the American and the Indian people respectively. The structure and limitations of one's own language are apparent only to those who have learnt another language as well. A similar salutary shock may be had from comparing Turnbull's *The Mountain People* [78] with *The Forest People* [77] which describe a Hobbesian and a Lockean society respectively. Munch's *Crisis in Utopia* [63] affords a fine study of a small egalitarian society on Tristan da Cunha in both its domestic aspects and its external affairs (see also [85] and its bibliography).

Behavioural scholars who hope to borrow directly from anthropology or to have their theoretical foundations dug for them by labourers in other fields deserve to be disappointed, though Barth's famous *Models* [13, 66] and Park's *Structure* [67] are gifts to be prized, as is Mitchell's work on *Networks* [59].

Few scholars are proficient in both IR and anthropology, and cross-fertilization of these disciplines is rarely explicit. Two major works by Bozeman which attempt this task [21, 22] are, unfortunately, to be viewed with caution.

In development studies, on the other hand, there are a number of very important works, including those on the emergence of the nation and the state [43, 76] and the cultural concomitants of a progression from *Gemeinschaft* to *Gesellschaft* [70, 72, 52]. On millenarial reactions (cargo cults and the like) by tribal people to imperialist penetration there are [81, 86] and also [20]; and on the modernization process itself [16, 46, 47, 49, 52, 53, 54].

Political anthropology offers a number of elegant synoptic reviews [8, 10, 16, 38, 49, 69, 73]. For ethnic politics and inter-ethnic relations see [9, 35] and [37]. Slavery affords a great number of insights into exploitation, dominance, power and functionalism [28, 65, 68, 84].

What anthropology can do for IR is to raise new questions and so give rise to scholarly cognitive dissonance, the seed of all intellectual

196 *A.V.S. de Reuck*

growth. Familiar problems in unfamiliar contexts look different; unfamiliar problems in familiar contexts are disturbing. Even to surprise old theories coupling with exotic data may stir the loins of the imagination: only connect.

This therefore is a highly personal and idiosyncratic selection of works which make connections worthy of closer attention than they have hitherto received. There is no space here to develop these connections except to say that they relate as much to (a) conflict analysis, (b) inter-ethnic relations, or (c) modernization studies, as they do to foreign affairs. It should be added that there are doubtless many other works of equal or greater merit, for example, studies of the resurgence of Islam or the Iranian revolution [7] which are subject areas in themselves.

The sort of questions to which anthropologists draw our attention includes that of the relation between social structure and culture on the one hand and behaviour on the other [67], or how they change together but not quite synchronously [51]. The correlation between structure and culture has been the province of Douglas in a number of extraordinary books [30, 31, 33], of which the most recent [32] enquires why some people are more concerned than others about threats to the environment. Or even about a nuclear holocaust.

Bibliography to Chapter 13

1. Ardrey, R. *African Genesis*. London, Collins and New York, Atheneum, 1961.
2. _____ *The Hunting Hypothesis*. New York, Atheneum, 1976 and London, Fontana, 1977.
3. _____ *The Social Contract*. New York, Dell, 1971 and London, Fontana, 1977.
4. _____ *The Territorial Imperative*. New York, Bantam, 1978 and London, Fontana, 1977.
5. Bailey, F.G. *Stratagems and Spoils: A Social Anthropology of Politics*. Oxford, Basil Blackwell and New York, Schocken Books, 1973.
6. _____ (ed.) *Gifts and Poison: The Politics of Reputation*. Oxford, Basil Blackwell and New York, Schocken Books, 1971.
7. Bakhash, S. *The Reign of the Ayattolahs: Iran and the Islamic Revolution*. London, I.B. Tauris and New York, Basic Books, 1984.
8. Balandier, G. *Political Anthropology*. Harmondsworth, Penguin and New York, Vintage Books, 1972.
9. Banton, M. *Race Relations*. London & Toronto, Tavistock, 1967 & New York, Basic Books, 1968.

10. _____ (ed.) *The Social Anthropology of Complex Societies.* (ASA Monograph no. 4), London, Tavistock, 1966, and New York, Methuen, 1968.
11. Barkun, M. *Law Without Sanctions: Order in Primitive Societies and the World Community.* New Haven, CT, Yale University Press, 1968.
12. Barth, F. *Ethnic Groups and Boundaries.* London, Allen & Unwin and Boston, MA, Little, Brown, 1969.
13. _____ *Models of Social Organisation.* London, Royal Anthropological Institute, Occasional Paper no. 23, 1966.
14. _____ *Political Leadership among the Swat Pathans.* London, Athlone Press, 1965 and New York, Humanities Press, 1968.
15. Benedict, R. *The Chrysanthemum and the Sword: Patterns of Japanese Culture.* Cleveland, Meridian Books, 1967 and London, Routledge & Kegan Paul, 1977.
16. Binder, L. *et al., Crises and Sequences in Political Development.* Princeton, NJ & London, Princeton University Press, 1971.
17. Black-Michaud, J. *Cohesive Force: Feud in the Mediterranean and the Middle East.* Oxford, Basil Blackwell and New York, St. Martin's, 1975.
18. Bohannan, P. (ed.) *Law and Warfare: Studies in the Anthropology of Conflict.* Austin & London, University of Texas Press, 1977.
19. Boissevain, J.F. *Friends of Friends: Networks, Manipulators and Coalitions.* Oxford, Basil Blackwell and New York, St. Martin's, 1974.
20. _____ *Saints and Fireworks: Religion and Politics in Malta.* London, Athlone Press and New York, Humanities Press, 1969.
21. Bozeman, A.B. *Conflict in Africa: Concepts and Realities.* Princeton, NJ & Guildford, Princeton University Press, 1976.
22. _____ *Politics and Culture in International History.* Princeton, NJ, Princeton University Press, 1960.
23. Bramson, L. & Goethals, G.W. (eds), *War: Studies from Psychology, Sociology, Anthropology.* New York, Basic Books, 1968.
24. Burman, S.B. & Harrell-Bond, B.E. *The Imposition of Law.* London & New York, Academic Press, 1979.
25. Chance, M.R.A. & Jolly, C.J. *Social Groups of Monkeys, Apes and Men.* London, Jonathan Cape and New York, Dutton, 1970.
26. Chance, M.R.A. & Larsen, R.R. (eds), *The Social Structure of Attention.* New York & London, John Wiley, 1976.
27. Comaroff, J.L. & Roberts, S. *Rules and Processes: The Cultural Logic of Dispute in an African Context.* Chicago & London, University of Chicago Press, 1981.
28. Davis, D.B. *Slavery and Human Progress.* London & New York, Oxford University Press, 1985.
29. de Waal, F. *Chimpanzee Politics.* London, Jonathan Cape and New York, Harper & Row, 1983.
30. Douglas, M. *In the Active Voice.* London & Boston, MA, Routledge &

Kegan Paul, 1982.

31. _____ *Purity and Danger.* London & Boston, MA, Ark Paperbacks, 1984.

32. Douglas, M. & Wildavsky, A. *Risk and Culture: An Essay on the Selection of Technological and Environmental Dangers.* Berkeley & London, University of California Press, 1984.

33. Douglas, M. (ed.) *Essays in the Sociology of Perception.* London & Boston, MA, Routledge & Kegan Paul, 1982.

34. Dumont, L. *Homo Hierarchicus: Caste System and its Implications.* Chicago & London, University of Chicago Press, 1981.

35. Enloe, C. *Ethnic Conflict and Political Development.* Boston, Little, Brown, 1973.

36. Evans-Pritchard, E.E. *Nuer Religion.* London & New York, Oxford University Press, 1956.

37. Francis, E.K. *Interethnic Relations: An Essay in Sociological Theory.* Oxford, Elsevier and Westport, CT, Greenwood Press, 1976.

38. Fried, M. *The Evolution of Political Society.* New York, Random House, 1968.

39. _____ et al. (eds), *War: The Anthropology of Armed Conflict and Aggression.* New York, American Museum of Natural History, 1968.

40. Gluckman, M. *Custom and Conflict in Africa.* Oxford, Basil Blackwell, 1956 and Totowa, NJ, B & N Imports, 1969.

41. _____ *Order and Rebellion in Tribal Africa.* New York, Free Press, 1963.

42. Gorer, G. *The Americans: A Study in National Character.* London, Arrow Books, 1959 and New York, Norton, 1964.

43. Grillo, R.D. (ed.) *'Nation' and 'State' in Europe.* London & New York, Academic Press, 1980.

44. Gulliver, P.H. *Disputes and Negotiations: A Cross-Cultural Perspective.* London & New York, Academic Press, 1980.

45. Hamnett, I. (ed.) *Social Anthropology and Law.* (ASA Monograph no. 14), London & New York, Academic Press, 1977.

46. Heeger, G.A. *The Politics of Underdevelopment.* London, Macmillan and New York, St. Martin's, 1974.

47. Hoogvelt, A.M.M. *The Sociology of Developing Societies.* London, Macmillan, 1978.

48. Inglehart, R. *The Silent Revolution: Changing Values and Political Style Among Western Publics.* Princeton, NJ & Guildford, Princeton University Press, 1977.

49. Jaguaribe, H. *Political Development: A General Theory and a Latin American Case Study.* New York & London, Harper & Row, 1973.

50. Knipe, H. & Maclay, G. *The Dominant Man: The Pecking Order in Human Society.* New York, Delacorte Press, 1972 and London, Fontana/Collins, 1973.

51. Leach, E.R. *Political Systems of Highland Burma.* London, Athlone Press,

1970 and Dover, NH, Longwood Press, 1977.

52. Lerner, D. *The Passing of Traditional Society: Modernising in the Middle East*. New York, Free Press, 1975.

53. Lloyd, P.C. *Africa in Social Change*. Harmondsworth, Middx., Penguin Books, 1972.

54. _____ *Classes, Crises and Coups: Themes in the Sociology of Developing Countries*. London, Paladin, 1973.

55. Loizos, P. *The Heart Grown Bitter: A Chronicle of Cypriot War Refugees*. Cambridge, Cambridge University Press, 1981 and New York, Cambridge University Press, 1982.

56. Lorenz, Konrad *On Aggression*. London, Methuen, 1966 and New York, Harcourt Brace and Jovanovich, 1974.

57. Mair, L. *Primitive Government*. London, Scolar Press, 1977 and Indianapolis, Indiana University Press, 1978.

58. Masters, R.D. 'World Politics as a Primitive Political System'. *World Politics*, vol. XVI, no. 4, 1964, pp. 595–619.

59. Mitchell, J.C. (ed.) *Social Networks in Urban Situations*. Manchester, Manchester University Press and Atlantic Highlands, NJ, Humanities Press, 1969.

60. Mizruchi, E.H. *Regulating Society: Marginality and Social Control in Historical Perspective*. London, Collier-Macmillan and New York, Free Press, 1983.

61. Montagu, M.F.A. *The Nature of Human Aggression*. London & New York, Oxford University Press, 1979.

62. _____ (ed.) *Man and Aggression*. London & New York, Oxford University Press, 1973.

63. Munch, P.A. *Crisis in Utopia*. London, Longman and New York, Cromwell, 1971.

64. Nakane, C. *Japanese Society*. Harmondsworth, Middx., Penguin, 1973 and Berkeley, CA, University of California Press, 1970.

65. Nieboer, H.J. *Slavery as an Industrial System: Ethnological Researches*. The Hague, Martinus Nijhoff, 1900 and New York, B. Franklin, 1971.

66. Paine, R. *Second Thoughts About Barth's Models*. London, Royal Anthropological Institute Occasional Paper no. 32, 1974.

67. Park, G.K. *The Idea of Social Structure*. New York, Anchor Books, 1974.

68. Patterson, O. *Slavery and Social Death*. Cambridge, MA & London, Harvard University Press, 1982.

69. Pye, L.W. & Verba, S. *Political Culture and Political Development*. Princeton, NJ, Princeton University Press, 1965.

70. Redfield, R. *The Little Community* and *Peasant Society and Culture*. Chicago & London, University of Chicago Press, 1960.

71. Reynolds, P.C. *The Evolution of Human Behavior: The Argument from Animals to Man*. Berkeley, CA & London, University of California Press, 1981.

72. Riesman, D. *et al., The Lonely Crowd.* New Haven & London, Yale University Press, 1973.
73. Schapera, I. *Government and Politics in Tribal Societies.* London, Watts, 1956 and New York, Schocken, 1967.
74. Smith, A.D. *The Ethnic Revival in the Modern World.* Cambridge & New York, Cambridge University Press, 1981.
75. Smith, R.J. *Japanese Society.* Cambridge, Cambridge University Press, 1954.
76. Tivey, L. (ed.) *The Nation-State: The Formation of Modern Politics.* Oxford, Martin Robertson, 1982 and New York, St. Martin's, 1981.
77. Turnbull, C.M. *The Forest People.* London, Granada, 1984 and New York, Simon & Schuster, 1968.
78. _____ *The Mountain People.* London, Granada, 1984 and New York, Simon & Schuster, 1972.
79. Waterbury, J. *The Commmander of the Faithful: The Moroccan Political Elite – A Study in Segmented Politics.* London, Weidenfeld & Nicholson and New York, Columbia University Press, 1970.
80. Wiegele, T.C. *Biopolitics.* Boulder, CO, Westview, 1981.
81. Wilson, B. *Magic and the Millennium: Religious Movements of Protest among the Third World Peoples.* London, Paladin, 1975 and New York, Harper & Row, 1973.
82. Wilson, E.O. *On Human Nature.* Cambridge, MA & London, Harvard University Press, 1978.
83. _____ *Sociobiology: The New Synthesis.* Cambridge, MA & London, Harvard University Press, 1980.
84. Wittfogel, K.A. *Oriental Despotism.* New Haven, CT & London, Yale University Press, 1957 and New York, Random House, 1981.
85. Woodburn, J. 'Egalitarian Societies'. *Man* (N.S.), vol. 17, no. 3, 1982, pp. 431–51.
86. Worsley, P.C. *The Trumpet Shall Sound.* London, Paladin, 1970 and New York, Schocken, 1968.

14 Psychological Aspects

A.N. Oppenheim
London School of Economics and CAC

Introduction

Since international relations are concerned with what happens to large numbers of people, and carried out by people working in human organizations, psychological factors obviously enter willy-nilly into virtually every international process. They have been referred to throughout this book. Moreover, contributions by and borrowings from psychology are continuing and controversial, with changes following each new publication. Thus our references are perforce selective, focussing on a number of key areas.

The selection is not easy. The difficulty lies partly in greatly varying definitions of 'psychology', and the overlap with many other disciplines, e.g. sociology, administrative science, human biology. Another problem lies in the approach used, and the nature of evidence which is considered acceptable: international relations (IR) writers have sometimes rejected psychological contributions because 'they aren't IR', while psychological discussions by IR scholars have been repudiated by psychologists for being 'un-scientific'. Moreover, there are numerous aspects of IR which would repay psychological investigation, to which few psychologists have addressed themselves; in this sense, a good deal of research is still 'missing'. On the other hand, there are many broad findings and principles in psychology which could readily be applied to aspects of IR, e.g. social perception, group dynamics, stress research. Apart from these general findings, *some* psychologists (and others) have applied themselves directly to certain areas of IR, for example through simulation studies, research into conflict resolution, bargaining behaviour, and group decision-making. Both these aspects, the broader, and the more specific will be drawn upon.

Apart from books and the more specialized psychological literature, many psychological articles of relevance to IR appear regularly in the *Journal of Conflict Resolution* and the *Journal of Peace Research*. More recently, the International Society for Political Psychology has launched a valuable new journal, *Political Psychology*.

General Psychological Processes: Perception

Most of the broad determinants of human behaviour in *individuals* – such as thinking, remembering, the unconscious, learning, perceiving, becoming socialized, personality development, intelligence, attribution processes, attitudes and values – are of relevance to IR in trying to understand the behaviour of leaders and of decision-makers, in the selection and training of diplomats, or in the study of national stereotypes. However, in IR we are frequently concerned with the behaviour of people in groups or *organizations*, in institutions or bureaucracies or power hierarchies, and so we have to move from the individual to the collective level. One way of linking these two levels of analysis – of the individual on his own, and of the person as a role-player in a sub-system – is to consider them from the point of view of perceptual processes.

The process of perception is not a 'faithful recording of reality', like a film or tape recording. There is abundant evidence to show that perception is a *dynamic* process, not a passive one. It is not only determined by the outside world, but also by the perceiver's culture, attitudes, expectations, needs, experience and many other aspects. We are continuously engaged in selecting important from unimportant stimuli, in 'recognizing' people, things, or patterns of events, in 'interpreting' the behaviour of others or of groups, states or organizations. We make causal or probabilistic forecasts and 'explanations', and select from, define, and redefine the outside world in accordance with who we are and what we want to be, or do. In short, perception is subjective.

The processes of perception are connected with a range of other mental processes. The same 'subjectivity biases' which cause us to notice, to attend to, and to select, also cause us to retain (to store, to remember) and to recall selectively, to compare (to like/dislike/fear/ enjoy/etc.), to communicate, and to respond in much the same biased ways. These processes influence future perceptions, so that a closed circle is set up – vicious or adaptive, according to one's point of view. Most of the time, our habits-of-mind help to defend our ego and our opinions, to find consonance rather than dissonance and to give meaning and predictability to the world. Since virtually all stimuli are ambiguous, to some extent, they offer ample scope for such self-fulfilling dynamics. Divergent views or dissonant experiences can be ignored or internally overruled, so that only very occasionally do we have to revise the way our mind is made up.

We also perceive *ourselves*. Each of us has a 'self percept', a set of notions about who we are, what our roles are, what we are good or bad at, how we should dress, or speak, or behave. These ideas are strongly influenced by the evidence we receive of how others perceive us, though 'to see ourselves as others see us' is difficult. To understand a set of transactions or a relationship between two people, or two firms, or two states, we need to know how they see themselves as well as how they see each other. If these two sets of percepts are very different, they can be brought more into line with each other by an argument or a fight – or by trying to understand the dynamics which have led to the development of such divergent images. A considerable part of marriage guidance, for example, is concerned with such explorations, and the same processes have been tried in the field of conflict resolution between communities or between states (see Burton [9] and Hill [21]).

If communication between individuals is sometimes complicated because they do not 'see' things from the same point of view, then communication between groups is often more difficult still. If the groups belong to different countries or cultures – as they often do, in the field of foreign affairs – then they are further divided by language, values, images, history and other factors which influence their perceptions of each other and of the situation. Inevitably, such differences will also affect the decision-makers.

A useful basic textbook in social psychology which stresses various aspects of social cognition is Raven & Rubin [51]. Kelman's excellent reader [34] provided many links between social psychology and the international scene, and is still full of relevant insights. For a more detailed analysis of how perceptual processes affect decision-making in foreign affairs, see de Rivera [12], and some of the papers in Kriesberg [35] and Jervis [30]. North and colleagues have become well known for their content analysis of the documents produced by decision-makers, showing their perceptual and thought processes [46]. This area is ably reviewed by Hermann [18].

General Psychological Processes: Organizational Behaviour

Although analogies between individuals and organizations must obviously not be taken too far, several *structural* parallels suggest themselves when the level of analysis is shifted to organizations, especially decision-making bureaucracies, such as government departments. For example, embassies or foreign missions regarded as the 'eyes and ears' and sometimes as the 'mouth' of a foreign affairs ministry could be regarded in general terms, as sensors and communicators. The links between the missions and the policy-makers could be regarded as the nerve paths; the departmental archives and its library could be likened to the human memory; the human brain, which selects, compares and processes all this information has, as its organizational counterpart, the decision-making apparatus within the foreign affairs ministry.

It is also not difficult to find *functional* equivalents in the mind to the ways in which organizational decision-making works. The incremental, cumulative ways in which positions are taken, not necessarily on the widest consideration of the relevant evidence; the selective management of information; the playing down of some information sources in favour of others; the ways in which *recent* experience tends to be over-valued; the problems of overload and stress; the tendency to develop commitment; the problems of change and progression through time; the unwillingness to plan and look ahead, and the tendency to satisfice rather than to maximize; these are problems which are familiar from individual psychology, and which can readily be noted in the workings of organizations (see Janis [27], Deutsch [13]).

If this raises questions about the ways in which organizational procedures affect the ministry's perceptions, it must also make us wonder about the uses that are made of these perceptions when they enter the central decision-making process. Few studies (see Maoz [38]) have been made of the ways in which foreign affairs ministries arrive at their decisions and their policies, but from studies of similar organizations we can suggest some of the issues that should be raised. How, for example, does the 'organizational memory' operate? Can the files and the archives be used rapidly and effectively in the process of making decisions? Is the prevailing administrative style consensual, hierarchical or delegated? Does the organization try to create and maintain shared perceptual frameworks through departmentalization or by controlling selection, experience and careers? Remembering that 'knowledge is power', how is information distributed, summarized, selectively presented, checked, compared, and processed by the organization? Are the central decision-makers specially trained and experienced in their tasks, or are they diplomats on a temporary 'home posting'? How does the ministry perceive its 'attentive publics', and those whom it must 'take with it', or obtain clearance from? At what hierarchical level does most 'uncertainty absorption' take place, and with what effects? How serious is the tendency (which exists in most organizations) to give attention to the here-and-now at the expense of forward planning, in the field of foreign affairs? And how resilient is the organization under crisis conditions? These last two topics – anticipation of events, and crisis behaviour – are so important that we shall return to them presently.

Three further points should be stressed. First, that the issues we have raised have to do with the structures and the functioning of human organizations as 'bureaucratic machines', almost irrespective of the people who man them, the organization's tasks or objectives, or the country within which it operates. Second, in foreign affairs the problems of obtaining and using information, and of 'uncertainty-reduction' must be particularly difficult because of cultural and secrecy barriers between countries. Third, in addition to the usual interpersonal likes and dislikes, envy, clique formation, power exploitation and so on which can be found in any group of human beings, large decision-making organizations are subject to a phenomenon known as *bureaucratic politics*: career factors and personal motives tend to interact with the functioning of the organization. Officials will curry favour in order to get earlier promotion or a more pleasant posting, they will be tempted to produce 'sycophantic feedback' (telling their superiors what they want to hear), the old boy network will operate, and vested interests in sectors within the organization will fight each other. We should ask ourselves what *kinds* of bureaucracies are most likely to produce this type of behaviour, and what its effects may be on the long-term functioning of the organization.

There is considerable literature on the social functioning of organizations, in particular of industrial firms and commercial or governmental bureaucracies. March's handbook [39] is fundamental to anyone studying this area, and there are several classics in this field, such as March & Simon [40], Argyris [3], Katz & Kahn [32].

Likewise, there are numerous publications dealing with particular kinds of organizations (e.g. hospitals) or with particular types of problems (e.g. leadership, trade unions, information processing). Many of the more seminal contributions have first appeared in the pages of the *Administrative Science Quarterly*.

It is not easy to develop suitable methods and concepts for the study of complex organizations; Pugh *et al.* [50] have produced a survey of British research in organizational behaviour which amply illustrates these problems. Simulation methods have been widely used in the field and summaries are provided by Guetzkow *et al.* [17] and by Inbar & Stoll [26]. Simulation techniques can provide training and valuable insights, but they lack the precision (which is not without drawbacks) of the socio-psychological experiment. Hood & Dunsire [23] have provided a novel method for the study of bureaucratic processes.

The human process of drawing inferences from incomplete information has been studied by Inbar [25], Janis [27], and by Nisbett & Ross [45], and there are several chapters in Hopple [24] which bear on this.

The 'cognitive maps' approach, especially in the study of political leaders and their outlooks, is exemplified by studies such as those by Axelrod [4], and by Stuart & Starr [55].

Within this general area, there is a literature concerned with political decision-making (as distinct from industrial/commercial decision-making), and a smaller literature which has tried to link organizational research with foreign policy decision-making. The Open University reader [10] makes some useful psycho-sociological links between administrative science and political behaviour and there are several relevant chapters in Pruitt & Snyder's reader [49], and Pruitt is also the author of an early study of the functioning of the Department of State [48], a field to which Bacchus [5] and Argyris [3] have also contributed.

The internal workings of bureaucracies are well described by Downs [14] and by Hood *et al.* [23]. MacKenzie [37] gives an excellent and wide-ranging account of this whole area.

Psychological studies of peace-making and negotiation have recently come to the fore, and Dedring [11] offers an overview. Kelman [33] and Burton [9] have been very active in this area, and their approaches, together with that of Doob, have been compared and contrasted by Hill [21]. Deutsch [13] and Mitchell [42] have addressed themselves particularly to the peace-making process.

Specific Psychological Processes: Political Socialization

The term 'socialization' refers to the processes of social learning whereby an individual becomes a member of his culture and sub-culture. It covers a very wide field, including various aspects of childhood and adolescence as well as adult socialization (e.g. migration and social mobility), and complex problems of imitation, identification, introjection and conformity in the family, in peer groups, at school, and in mass media consumption.

The sub-area of *political* socialization is expanding rapidly, both in social psychology, and in political science and political sociology. These studies are relevant to such issues as the development of democracy, support for parties and regimes, and the perception by children of their national leaders, but few researchers have included items of specific relevance to IR. Fuller information on the development of children's stereotypes about other nations, their attitudes to war, to the UN, to various modes of conflict resolution, and their national and supranational loyalties would be interesting. Several of the works already mentioned have touched on one or other of these issues, but there is no effective cross-national summary of children's perceptions of international affairs.

The studies by Hess & Torney [20], and by Jennings & Niemi [29], of American youth, and Morrison & McIntyre of British children [44] have tried to assess the relative influence of home and school on political development. The ten-nation study by Torney, Oppenheim & Farnen [56] containing items dealing with the UN, with war and with conflict, represents both a considerable technical achievement and several theoretical advances.

Specific Psychological Processes: Aggression

The notion that war is due to man's 'animal nature' has long been part of the stock-in-trade of commentators on international affairs, and the study of 'aggression' has a long history in psychiatry and psycho-analysis. The subject has become more controversial because modern ecological studies have shown – *inter alia* – that animals rarely kill each other except for food, and have highly developed social and genetically based mechanisms for inhibiting aggression between members of the same species. Modern research by social psychologists studying aggression has cast further doubt on the extent to which aggression is 'built in', and has shown the importance of over-crowding and other social conditions.

This complex area is well summarized by Scherer *et al* [52] and by Montagu [43]. Lorenz' study [36] has become a classic of ecological research, though it has been sharply criticized for its conclusions. Ardrey [2] has done much to popularize this kind of topic. Berkowitz [6] illustrates work on human aggression in the socio-psychological laboratory and Blanchard [7] has shown how aggression can enter into policy-making.

Specific Psychological Processes: Decision-making under Stress

There have been several applications from the area of stress research to IR, in particular the stress experienced by foreign policy-makers under crisis conditions.

Crises can, of course, happen to individuals, but we are particularly concerned with what happens to a decision-making organization under stress. Typically, the organization will experience overloads: more information comes in, more decisions must be made, more rapidly, and more orders have to go out. Despite countermeasures, communication channels may get clogged, thus creating serious delays, and isolating the decision-makers more and more from events in the field. This, in turn, may cause them to 'go into crisis' and to engage in crisis behaviour: their perceptions become crudely polarized, they cannot think more than one or two moves ahead, they may become dominated by fear-motivated projections, they may tend to over-react and thus enter an escalation spiral. Janis [27] has coined the term 'group-think' for this kind of behaviour.

Hermann's book [18], Giffin [16], and Guetzkow *et al.* [17] summarize the findings obtained through simulation work. Milburn's paper, 'The Management of Crises' (in [18]), is a good example of the prescriptions and advice that have emerged from research in this field, while Lentner's chapter illustrates the measures that can be taken, for example to prevent communication overloads.

Steinbruner [54], Holsti [22], Janis [27] and others, have made detailed studies of real-life crises. Kahneman *et al* [31] have given us a much better understanding of the individual thought and decision-making processes under conditions of uncertainty, such as prevail in a crisis. Brecher [8] has shown in detail how the policy-making process is affected by a crisis and there are further insights in Frei [15]. Our existing knowledge in this field has been summarized by Oppenheim [47].

Specific Psychological Processes: Anticipation and Surprise

The risks and dangers associated with an international crisis are much increased if the decision-makers are caught by surprise. Typically, this may be attributed to a failure on the part of the intelligence services, but closer study may show that the information was, in fact, available at some levels within the organization, but was distrusted, or overlooked, or became swamped by other information, so that it never reached the top decision-makers. The decision-makers themselves may reject the information, if, for example, they have a strong expectation of some other more probable events, or when they distrust or fear the source of the information, which in turn will affect their perceptual processes. Some kinds of organization have a tendency to want to hear only 'good' news (sycophantic feedback), while in others the harbinger of 'bad' tidings may find his career blighted. In either case, the upper echelons will have deprived themselves of critical information. Thus we note once again the importance of subjective perceptual factors, both in individuals and in organizations.

Decision-makers may also be caught by surprise through lack of anticipation. As we have seen, perception is an active, dynamic process. Organizations should not merely wait passively for information to flow in, they must 'think ahead' and engage in 'information seeking'. This raises such issues as the relevant location and staffing of foreign missions, the value of political reporting, and the need for well-integrated planning departments within foreign affairs ministries. New methods for crisis forecasting are also being developed.

Janis [27] deals with a number of actual crises and, building on Wohlstetter's analysis of the Pearl Harbor attack [59], shows vividly how surprise factors operate. Another interesting case study (of Hitler's attack on the Soviet Union) is by Whaley [58], which extends

Wohlstetter's theoretical framework. The reasons for the Israelis' failure to anticipate the outbreak of the October 1973 war are analysed by Herzog [19].

Other Psychological Processes

Many of the more recent contributions to the field may be found in the pages of *Political Psychology*. Here, for example, we find the beginnings of Holocaust studies; work on terrorism, revolutionary wars and social change processes; research on psycho-history and the use of biographical materials in leadership studies; the findings of studies on operational codes and cognitive style. Some of this material is summarized in Hopple [24]. Political socialization research (e.g. Torney, Oppenheim & Farnen [56]) continues to expand, as does research on political participation and political protest [41]. These studies are becoming more cross-national and comparative.

A handbook must, of necessity, reflect the 'state of the art' at a given time. Important and useful socio-psychological work remains to be done (in ways that would make it relevant to IR) on psychological interaction between foreign policy and the mass media, including special pressure groups and 'attentive publics'. Outdated studies of national stereotypes need to be superseded by broader research on percepts and attitudes, both of members of the public, and of diplomats and decision-makers. The problems of communication and mis-communication between nations, so often highlighted in simulation studies, need to be explored in greater detail in real-life situations. Better studies are required on information management within organizations, including polarizing, stereotyping, sycophanting, risky shifts, exploitation, and other distortive processes. We are only just beginning to study at first hand the processes of bargaining and of negotiation. In this, as in other contexts, the personality, background, and attitudes of leaders, and the whole process of leadership, are of obvious importance. The rhetoric of conflict (see Oppenheim [47]), needs further exploration. Deterrence and the study of individual attitudes to power are other areas awaiting more psychological research.

In the long run, perhaps the most important psychological contributions will be those that are concerned with handling social change, conflict prevention, and conflict resolution.

Bibliography to Chapter 14

1. *American Behavioral Scientist*, vol. 20, no. 1, 1976 (special issue on political decision-making).
2. Ardrey, R. *The Territorial Imperative*. New York, Bantam, 1978 and London, Fontana, 1977.
3. Argyris, C. *Some Causes of Organisational Ineffectiveness Within the Department of State*. Washington, D.C., Government Printing Office, 1967.
4. Axelrod, R. (ed.) *The Structure of Decision: The Cognitive Maps of Political Elites*. Princeton, NJ, Princeton University Press, 1976.
5. Bacchus, W.I. *Foreign Policy and the Bureaucratic Process*. Princeton, NJ, Princeton University Press, 1974.
6. Berkowitz, L. *Aggression: A Social-Psychological Analysis*. New York & Maidenhead, McGraw Hill, 1962.
7. Blanchard, W.H. *Aggression American Style*. Santa Monica, CA, Goodyear and Glenview, IL, Scott, Foresman & Co, 1978.
8. Brecher, M. (ed.) *Studies in Crisis Behaviour*. New Brunswick, NJ, Transaction Books, 1979.
9. Burton, J.W. *Conflict and Communication*. London, Macmillan and New York, Free Press, 1969.
10. Castles, F.G. *et al.*, *Decisions, Organisations and Society*. Harmondsworth, Middx, Penguin Books in association with the Open University, 1976.
11. Dedring, J. *Recent Advances in Peace and Conflict Research*. Beverly Hills, CA & London, Sage, 1976.
12. de Rivera, J. *The Psychological Dimension of Foreign Policy*. Columbus, OH, Charles E. Merrill, 1968.
13. Deutsch, M. *The Resolution of Conflict*. New Haven, CT & London, Yale University Press, 1973.
14. Downs, A. *Inside Bureaucracy*. Boston, Little, Brown, 1967.
15. Frei, D. (ed.) *Managing International Crises*. Beverly Hills, CA & London, Sage, 1982.
16. Giffin, S.F. *The Crisis Game*. Garden City, NY, Doubleday, 1965.
17. Guetzkow, H. & Valadez, J.J. (eds), *Simulated International Processes: Theories and Research in Global Modelling*. Beverly Hills, CA & London, Sage, 1981.
18. Hermann, C.F. (ed.) *International Crises: Insights from Behavioural Research*. London, Collier-Macmillan and New York, Free Press, 1972.
19. Herzog, C. *The War of Atonement*. London, Weidenfeld & Nicholson and Boston, Little, Brown, 1975.
20. Hess, R.D. & Torney, J.V. *The Development of Political Attitudes in Children*. Chicago & London, Aldine, 1967.
21. Hill, B.J. 'An Analysis of Conflict Resolution Techniques'. *Journal of Conflict Resolution*, vol. 26, no. 1, 1982, pp. 109–38.

22. Holsti, O.R. *Crisis, Escalation, War.* Montreal, McGill-Queen's University Press, 1972.
23. Hood, C. & Dunsire, A. *Bureaumetrics.* Farnborough, Hants., Gower and University, ALA, University of Alabama Press, 1981.
24. Hopple, G.W. (ed.) *Biopolitics, Political Psychology and International Politics.* London, Frances Pinter and New York, St. Martin's, 1982.
25. Inbar, M. *Routine Decision-making.* Beverly Hills, CA & London, Sage, 1979.
26. Inbar, M. & Stoll, C.S. *Simulation and Gaming in Social Sciences.* New York, Free Press and London, Collier-Macmillan, 1972.
27. Janis, I.L. *Victims of Groupthink.* Boston, Houghton Mifflin, 1982.
28. Janis, I.L. & Mann, L. *Decision-Making: A Psychological Analysis of Conflict, Choice and Commitment.* London, Collier-Macmillan, 1979 and New York, Free Press, 1977.
29. Jennings, M.K. & Niemi, R.G. *The Political Character of Adolescence: The Influence of Families and Schools.* Princeton, NJ, Princeton University Press, 1974.
30. Jervis, R. *The Logic of Images in International Relations.* Princeton, NJ, & Guildford, Princeton University Press, 1970.
31. Kahneman, D. *et al.*, (eds), *Judgement under Uncertainty: Heuristics and Biases.* Cambridge & New York, Cambridge University Press, 1982.
32. Katz, D. & Kahn, R.L. *The Social Psychology of Organisations.* New York & Chichester, John Wiley, 1978.
33. Kelman, H.C. 'Creating Conditions for Israeli-Palestinian Negotiations'. *Journal of Conflict Resolution,* vol. 26, no. 1, 1982, pp. 39–75.
34. _____ (ed.) *International Behavior: A Social-Psychological Analysis.* New York, Holt, Rhinehart & Winston, 1965.
35. Kriesberg, L. (ed.) *Social Processes in International Relations.* New York, John Wiley, 1968.
36. Lorenz, K. *On Aggression.* London, Methuen, 1966 and New York, Harcourt Brace & Jonanovich, 1974.
37. MacKenzie, W.J.M. *Politics and Social Science.* Harmondsworth, Middx and New York, Pelican Books, 1967.
38. Maoz, Z. 'The Decision to Raid Entebbe'. *Journal of Conflict Resolution,* vol. 25, no. 4, 1981, pp. 677–707.
39. March, J.G. (ed.) *Handbook of Organizations.* Chicago, Rand-McNally, 1965.
40. March, J.G. & Simon, H.A. *Organizations.* New York & Chichester, John Wiley, 1958.
41. Marsh, A. *Protest and Political Consciousness.* Sage Library of Social Research, vol. 49, Beverly Hills, CA & London, Sage, 1977.
42. Mitchell, C.R. *Peacemaking and the Consultant's Role.* Farnborough, Hants, Gower and New York, Nichols, 1981.
43. Montagu, M.F.A. (ed.) *Man and Aggression.* London & New York, Oxford University Press, 1973.

44. Morrison, A. & McIntyre, D. *Schools and Socialisation*. Harmondsworth, Middx, Penguin, 1971.
45. Nisbett, R. & Ross, L. *Human Inference: Strategies and Shortcomings of Social Judgment*. Englewood Cliffs, NJ & Hemel Hempstead, Prentice Hall, 1980.
46. North, R.C. *et al.*, *Content Analysis: A Handbook with Applications for the Study of International Crises*. Evanston, IL, Northwestern University Press, 1963.
47. Oppenheim, A.N. Psychological Processes in World Society. In *Conflict in World Society*, ed. M. Banks. Brighton, Wheatsheaf and New York, St. Martin's, 1984.
48. Pruitt, D.G. *Problem Solving in the Department of State*. Monograph Series in World Affairs, vol. 2, 1964–1965 Ser., Book 2. Denver, CO, University of Denver Press, 1964.
49. Pruitt, D.G. & Snyder, R.C. (eds), *Theory and Research on the Causes of War*. Englewood Cliffs, NJ & London, Prentice Hall, 1969.
50. Pugh, D.S. *et al.*, *Research in Organizational Behavior*. London & New York, Heinemann Educational, 1975.
51. Raven, B.H. & Rubin, J.Z. *Social Psychology*. New York & Chichester, John Wiley, 1983.
52. Scherer, K.R. *et al.*, *Human Aggression and Conflict: Interdisciplinary Perspectives*. Englewood Cliffs, NJ & London, Prentice Hall, 1975.
53. Sherif, M. *Group Conflict and Co-operation*. London, Routledge & Kegan Paul, 1967.
54. Steinbruner, J.D. *The Cybernetic Theory of Decision*. Princeton, NJ & Guildford, Princeton University Press, 1976.
55. Stuart, D. & Starr, H. 'The "Inherent Bad Faith Model" Reconsidered: Dulles, Kennedy and Kissinger'. *Political Psychology*, vol. 3, no. 3/4, 1981/82, pp. 1–33.
56. Torney, J.V. *et al.*, *Civic Education in Ten Countries*. New York, Halsted Press, 1976.
57. Warr, P. *Psychology and Collective Bargaining*. London, Hutchinson, 1973.
58. Whaley, B. *Stratagem: Deception and Surprise in War*. New York, Praeger, 1973.
59. Wohlstetter, R. *Pearl Harbor: Warning and Decision*. Stanford, CA, Stanford University Press, 1962.

15 Textbooks

Dennis J.D. Sandole
George Mason University and CAC

Introduction

It is challenging, indeed daunting, to identify textbooks in a field which, according to Rosenau *et al*, who analysed 178 course syllabuses [84], is itself in need of definition. The works included in this report are in English – linguistic provincialism, as LaBarr & Singer called it [56] – and concerned with the field in a relatively broad sense, whether metaphysically, theoretically, substantively or methodologically, besides being still in print.

The works selected fall into the following categories: (1) studies of system and process: revealed paradigms; (2) surveys of approaches to the study of International Relations (IR); and (3) general introductions to IR.

Studies of System and Process: Revealed Paradigms

According to a comprehensive study by Vasquez [104], political realism has been, and still is the dominant paradigm in the study of IR. This is supported by Alker & Biersteker's finding [1] that, of the 792 relevant works listed in the 17 IR syllabuses they examined, 70 per cent were in the behavioural tradition, and most of those could be described as neo-realist. What introductory text best captures the essence of this tradition?

Rosenau and his co-researchers [84] found that Morgenthau's *Politics Among Nations* [67] was the most widely used course text both with regard to assigned and suggested readings. Also, it was among the most widely used general theoretical works in the syllabuses examined by Alker & Biersteker. But it is not the only statement of political realism. To obtain a full appreciation of views associated with the state-centric, power-based, primacy-of-politics image of a consistently anarchic world, IR students should also read Northedge [69] and Wight [107] and they should consult Bull [7], who argues that the present state system is *not* in decline and that order is achievable within it. The ever-present possibility of war whenever there are power shifts in the anarchic system is explored by Gilpin [32] and by Waltz in his classic multi-level analysis, *Man, the State and War: A Theoretical Analysis* [105]. Waltz later developed further his thesis that systemic factors (e.g. international anarchy) are more potent sources of influence on international behaviour than are 'reductionist' factors (e.g. the character of individuals or states) [106]. In Waltz' later work he also argues controversially that the notion of interdependence is a 'myth'. None of these works is as comprehensive as Morgenthau's classic text.

Aron's *Peace and War: A Theory of International Relations* [2] has Morgenthau's scope and, despite infelicities of translation, it should be on any general reading list. In addition to its theoretical, sociological, historical and praxeological aspects, it constitutes a critique of Morgenthau's version of American realism. His differences with Morgenthau notwithstanding, Aron shares with realists in general the sentiment that states co-exist in a Hobbesian state of nature. Nevertheless, some realists are rather critical about realist theory. Perhaps the classic 'self-analysis' among realists is Carr's *The Twenty Years Crisis, 1919–1939* [15]. Though he takes the political idealists to task, he does the same to realists, suggesting the need for both realism and idealism. Other examples of self-analysis among realists are Wolfers [109], who criticizes 'billiard-ball', state-centric notions of security and also Herz [36], who re-examines the applicability of traditional concepts of international politics in the light of changed conditions. Herz made explicit the idea of the security dilemma, i.e. the more that states attempt to seek power for reasons of insecurity, the less (and not more) secure they become.

Wolfers and Herz were followed by other self-analysts who argued in favour of what might be called the Carr model – i.e. some kind of integration between realism and idealism. For instance, Buzan [13] endeavours to reconceptualize security away from the extremes of both realism and idealism, and Hoffmann [38] argues that there are ways to reconcile the pursuit of power with the demands of morality. Cohen [19], on the other hand, argues that states are guided and constrained in their international politics by rules that are based on international law and organization as well as power considerations.

For further attempts to escape from the narrow confines of both realist and idealist conceptualizations, students should read Claude [18], who examines balance of power, collective security and world government in the context of the problem of the management of power in IR. In the selections edited by Buzan & Barry Jones [14] traditional notions of change are examined and the concept is redefined. Also relevant are M. Singer's attempt to reconceptualize power away from its traditional, narrow coercive meaning [91] and Beitz' development of an international normative political theory which is more satisfactory than both Hobbes and the natural law alternative [4]. Modelski [65] argues in favour of a 'geocentric' approach to the politics of world society in lieu of the prevailing ethnocentric tradition, thereby abandoning the nation-state as the sole model of political organization. Vasquez [104] has recently subjected political realism to a comprehensive assessment, determining not only its hold over the field, but also its lack of success in explaining international behaviour. Together with Mansbach [62], he argues that critics of political realism must make explicit a viable alternative theory as powerful, broad and as rich in policy implications as power politics. Mansbach & Vasquez have endeavoured to practise what they preach by describing and applying an 'issue paradigm' where issue has effectively replaced power as the central organizing device.

Most of the challenges and alternatives to realism specify the existence of actors other than states (international organizations, multinational corporations, terrorist groups), plus an increasing interdependence among actors at the global level. This applies to the selections in Keohane & Nye [48], including their concluding chapter where they suggest a 'world politics paradigm'. Mansbach, Ferguson & Lampert [61] pursue the theme of the growing irrelevance of the state-centric model and argue in favour of a new conceptualization of global politics. This is also the theme both of Rosenau's *The Study of Global Interdependence* [82] and Phillip Taylor's *Nonstate Actors in International Relations* [101].

Earlier mention was made of Waltz' views that the notion of interdependence is more myth than reality [106]. Various opinions can be found in an interesting collection of articles edited by Maghroori & Ramberg [60]. Scott [90] argues the case that a very complex world has emerged with new and unforeseen problems such as inflation, food and energy shortages and pollution, rendering us all mutually dependent. Interdependence in terms of ecological or 'ecopolitical' perspectives is analysed by the Sprouts [97] and by Pirages [75]. Their concerns with the pernicious consequences of economic, energy, ecological and environmental changes for world food supplies, social justice and human rights and the equitable and efficient distribution of world resources, are shared by scholars who subscribe to other paradigms, such as those associated with Marxism (see Chapters 1 and 4). Another dialectical, radical (but non-Marxist) approach may be found in the works of scholars associated with the World Order Models Project (WOMP), an organization committed to the realization of four values: (1) the minimization of war and its devastation; (2) the maximization of economic and social well-being; (3) the realization of basic personal freedom; and (4) the preservation of ecological balance [16]. Relevant works include those by Beres & Targ [5], Falk [27], Galtung [31] and Kim [49]. Kim effectively sums up this particular tradition as 'an alternative, non-Machiavellian, non-Marxist, non-violent, non-deterministic and non-apocalyptic approach to system transformation' [49, p. 12].

The work of Burton and his colleagues represents another paradigmatic response and alternative to political realism, which incorporates elements similar to those found in some of the other alternatives. Burton views world society as comprised of multiple actors at different levels, interacting in ways which transcend, if not violate, traditional state boundaries. His 'cobweb' model of IR contrasts with the 'billiard-ball' model associated with realism. Within this context, actors – be they state decision-makers, corporate executives, terrorists, or others – are influenced in their behaviour not only (if at all) by coercion, but by the value they attach to their relationships with others. They are also influenced by the extent to which certain basic needs are met. Burton's approach is unique not only because of its metaphysical and theoretical dimensions, but also because of its 'praxis' dimension – it is one of the few scholarly approaches which is accompanied by a methodology for third-party intervention into conflict situations. The approach is described in one of Burton's earliest works [10] and a compendious statement of his views can be found in [11] and, more recently, in [9]. Kent & Nielsson [46] have assembled articles by scholars who have used Burton's ideas as a 'teaching paradigm' with mid-career students from the international business, diplomatic and military communities in Britain and West Germany. The essays in Banks [3] examine and subject Burton's ideas to critical assessment.

Many of the works discussed in this section have looked at realism not so much as something to be replaced completely, but as something which should be included in a more comprehensive image of world affairs. Pettman [74] also argues that we must view 'global social structures' in terms of the combined images of pluralists and structuralists, and Kubálková & Cruickshank [53] suggest that world inequality should be examined in terms of the perspectives of the major approaches to inequality (liberal, socialist and conservative). Smith, Little & Shackleton [92] have put together a collection of articles on (1) power and security, (2) interdependence and transnational relations, and (3) dominance and dependence, to emphasize the point that 'these are not simply . . . different facets of an agreed "world" but rather . . . different versions of the "world" as a whole, which colour and at the same time reflect issues of method, values and action' [92, p. 13].

Surveys of Approaches to the Study of IR

Probably the pre-eminent general survey of approaches to the study of IR is by Dougherty and Pfaltzgraff [24]. This comprehensive book is for students who want to have in *one volume* some idea about theories and methodologies from a variety of disciplines which may offer insights into the dynamics of IR. A less dense overview of a somewhat reduced turf is provided by Morgan [66]. Frankel [29] is much briefer still, but covers a good deal of theoretical and methodological ground. This work is perhaps rendered unique by Frankel's interest in appealing to practitioners as well as to students of IR. Another brief study covering a good deal of ground is by Joynt & Corbett [42]. Their work may also be somewhat unique because of their chapters on the international impact of American theory and on ethics and IR. A weightier tome which approaches the status of a 'philosophy of science of IR' is by C. Reynolds [79]. This work examines critically the various kinds of explanation found in the social sciences and applies them to an interdisciplinary view of IR.

One of the finest collections of articles covering nearly the full range of theory and method in IR is still Rosenau's *International Politics and Foreign Policy* [86], while T. Taylor's very good collection of articles [102] summarizes the literature in selected categories of IR theory and method. A rather unique compilation of IR literature appears in Kornberg's *Political Science Reading Lists and Course Outlines* [52], a collection of syllabuses for IR courses taught at US and Canadian universities. Relevant to researchers as well as to teachers of IR, Kornberg's survey provided the bulk of the data-set used in the Alker & Biersteker study [1].

Implicit in most of these surveys is the 'Great Debate' between the two major competing approaches to the study of IR – the traditional or classical versus the behavioural or scientific approaches. Probably the single best collection of original articles on this issue is still that of Knorr & Rosenau [50]. Rosenau's *In Search of Global Patterns* [85] is a collection of articles by scholars who have been involved in the scientific 'search for global patterns', noting the origins and motivations of their studies, their achievements and failures and indicating the problems which must be resolved if patterns are to be discovered and knowledge cumulated. Kaplan, whose earlier work [43] effectively threw down the gauntlet for Bull [8], has endeavoured to discuss professional criticism, particularly as it applies to his earlier work, and to resolve any remaining misunderstandings [44]. He also examines systems analysis and international systems theory, and the distinction between political science and diplomatic history, concluding that diplomatic history is just as much in a 'pre-professional state' as is politics. The major research ventures in quantitative international politics (QIP) are summarized and discussed by Zinnes in [111]. Though this is a 'heavyweight' work, Zinnes assumes minimal methodological sophistication on the part of the reader and has added methodological explanations and an appendix to further her objective not just of summarizing and discussing, but also of suggesting a particular way of looking at the QIP literature. If C. Reynold's work [79] is the nearest to a philosophy of IR, then Zinnes' work is surely the research methods counter-part.

Sullivan's textbook [99] is clearly and, some might argue, excessively and narrowly in the behavioural tradition. He has, however, attempted what few have dared, namely to translate the welter of often conflicting and confusing results of empirical studies into something approaching coherence, and to encourage the view that IR research observations do, to an important extent, represent a cumulative body of knowledge. For anyone interested in a summation of the scientific approaches to IR, this book is required reading. For a brief overview of many IR-relevant studies, particularly relating to war, Newcombe's survey [68] may be, in the author's own words, 'superficial', but it is certainly comprehensive and that, plus its brevity, is its main value. Two readers in the behavioural tradition have been compiled by Rosenau, Davis & East [83] and Merritt & Russett [64].

Excellent examples of traditional scholarship, i.e. studies in the history of international political theory and philosophy and in the history of international relations are by Russell [87], Hinsley [37] and by Parkinson [71]. Two collections of articles based upon the use of such data-bases have been put together by the International Political Theory group in Britain and edited by Donelan [23] and Mayall [63]. Older works in this tradition are by Wight [108] and Butterfield & Wight [12]. The latter authors capture the essence of this orientation when they note in their introduction that their group has 'probably been more concerned with the historical than the contemporary, with the normative than the scientific, with the philosophical than the methodological, with principles rather than policy' [12, p. 12].

General Introductions to IR

Kuhn [55] tells us that following every 'scientific revolution', at least in the natural sciences, textbooks and the philosophical works and popularizations based on them are completely rewritten to reflect the ascendancy of the new paradigm. We have noticed that though political realism may be the dominant framework in IR, there is more than one interpretation of realism, plus other, more fundamental challenges and alternatives. The works discussed thus far have also revealed two fundamentally different approaches to the study of IR, behaviouralism and traditionalism. This diversity is also reflected in the general introductions to IR.

A very state-centric, power-oriented view of IR, expressed in the traditionalist mode, is by Hartmann [35]. Spanier [95] also writes in the realist tradition, though he is rather more interdisciplinary. Ziegler [110] covers the general turf of IR by using war as a central focus. Another, briefer realist work is by Stegenga & Axline [98]. Holsti [39] combines behavioural with traditional approaches. His book is ranked second in the study by Rosenau *et al.* [84]. W. Jones [41] uses perceptions as the central organizing device, while Deutsch [22] and Russett & Starr [88] emphasize methodological rigour in their tours of the IR horizon.

A growing number of works (Lerche and Said [57] among them) emphasize the changes that have been, and are taking place in the global system, changes that call into question the validity of political realism (or, for that matter, *any* particular framework), and stress the importance of examining these developments in terms of alternative frameworks. Frankel [30] provides a relatively brief but comprehensive examination of IR through the combined lenses of realism and idealism, using traditional and interdisciplinary approaches. Couloumbis & Wolfe [21] are more comprehensive, including syntheses between behaviouralism and traditionalism, and between realism and idealism, in the latter case arguing for 'prudent idealism'. For a somewhat similar view from India, students should look at Chandra's work [17].

Pearson & Rochester [72] draw upon behaviouralism and traditionalism, plus realism, idealism, Marxism and transnationalism. They use chapter summaries, tables, graphs, photographs and cartoons to enhance the quality of their exposition. Papp [70] is similarly eclectic, while Kegley & Wittkopf [45] attempt to reflect and respond to the intellectual challenges of competing paradigms. Chan [16] is concerned with alternative perspectives such as the pursuit of security, welfare and justice. These textbooks, all published since 1984, represent a new trend, bringing together the strongest explanatory points from the competing paradigms. One additional work deserves mention, although it is not a general introductory textbook in the normal sense – Plano & Olton's *The International Relations Dictionary* [76], which presents, under traditional chapter headings, definitions and statements of significance of concepts, theories, organizations and events that are basic to realist/idealist views of IR.

Conclusion

IR is a field in need of definition, a field in conceptual disarray and this survey has suggested some reasons for this. Political realism has occupied the paradigmatic throne for centuries, and even when it did not do so 'officially', it was always latent, awaiting some catastrophe, some holocaust to arouse it from its dormancy. The IR textbook literature suggests that realism now has serious competition. The self-analyses among realists, the attempts at reconceptualizations of basic terms, the attempts to marry realism and idealism, the alternatives to realism put forward by purveyors of transnational, interdependence, ecological, dialectical (Marxist, WOMP, world society) perspectives, all seem to suggest that IR is in the throes of what Kuhn [55] has termed a crisis. There are, as is indicated elsewhere, 'signs of discontent, debates over basic assumptions, and indications of a willingness to try something new [along with the preferred] alternatives to Political Realism' [89, p. 53].

Where is all this taking the field? Will it remain characterized, and perhaps paralyzed by multiple definitions of 'reality'? Will one of the candidates for the throne succeed either in replacing or co-opting realism? Perhaps the field is moving further in the direction of Easton's 'Postbehavioural relevance' [26], towards Alker & Biersteker's 'more theoretically cosmopolitan approach, one which gives *serious* consideration to each of the major competing traditions' in a 'global interdiscipline of International Relations', characterized by a 'broader and deeper kind of political and epistemological self-consciousness' [1, pp. 132, 138]. Some exciting developments may be awaiting us!

Bibliography to Chapter 15

1. Alker, H.R. Jr. & Biersteker, T.J. 'The Dialectics of World Order: Notes for a Future Archeologist of International Savoir Faire'. *International Studies Quarterly*, vol. 28, no. 2, 1984, pp. 121–42.
2. Aron, R. *Peace and War: A Theory of International Relations*. London, Weidenfeld and Nicholson, 1967 and Melbourne, FL, Krieger, 1981.
3. Banks, M. (ed.) *Conflict in World Society: A New Perspective on International Relations*. Brighton, Wheatsheaf and New York, St. Martin's, 1984.
4. Beitz, C.R. *Political Theory and International Relations*. Princeton, NJ & Guildford, Princeton University Press, 1979.
5. Beres, L.R. & Targ, H.R. *Constructing Alternative World Futures: Reordering the Planet*. Cambridge, MA, Schenkman, 1977.
6. Brucan, S. *The Dialectic of World Politics*. New York, Free Press and London, Collier-Macmillan, 1978.
7. Bull, H.N. *The Anarchical Society: A Study of World Order*. London, Macmillan and New York, Columbia University Press, 1977.
8. _____ 'International Theory: The Case for the Classical Approach'. *World Politics*, vol. XVIII, no. 3, 1966, pp. 361–77.
9. Burton, J.W. *Global Conflict: The Domestic Sources of International Crisis*. Brighton, Wheatsheaf and College Park, MD, Center for International Development, University of Maryland, 1984.

10. _____ *Systems, States, Diplomacy and Rules*. Cambridge, Cambridge University Press, 1968.

11. _____ *World Society*. London & New York, Cambridge University Press, 1972.

12. Butterfield, H. & Wight, M. (eds), *Diplomatic Investigations: Essays in the Theory of International Politics*. London, Allen & Unwin and Cambridge, MA, Harvard University Press, 1966.

13. Buzan, B. *People, States and Fear: The National Security Problem in International Relations*. Brighton, Wheatsheaf and Chapel Hill, NC, The University of North Carolina Press, 1983.

14. Buzan, B. & Barry Jones, R.J. (eds), *Change and the Study of International Relations: The Evaded Dimension*. London, Frances Pinter and New York, St. Martin's, 1981.

15. Carr, E.H. *The Twenty Years Crisis, 1919–1939*. London, Macmillan, 1981 and New York, Harper & Row, 1964.

16. Chan, S. *International Relations in Perspective: The Pursuit of Security, Welfare and Justice*. London, Collier-Macmillan and New York, Macmillan, 1984.

17. Chandra, P. *International Relations*. New Delhi, Vikas Publishing House, 1979 (distributed in the US by Advent Books, New York).

18. Claude, I.L. *Power and International Relations*. New York, Random House, 1962.

19. Cohen, R. *International Politics: The Rules of the Game*. London & New York, Longman, 1981.

20. Coplin, W.D. *Introduction to International Politics*. London & Englewood Cliffs, NJ, Prentice Hall, 1980.

21. Couloumbis, T.A. & Wolfe, J.H. *Introduction to International Relations: Power and Justice*. London & Englewood Cliffs, NJ, Prentice Hall, 1982.

22. Deutsch, K.W. *The Analysis of International Relations*. Englewood Cliffs, NJ, Prentice Hall, 1978.

23. Donelan, M.D. (ed.) *The Reason of States: A Study in International Political Theory*. London & Winchester, MA, Allen & Unwin, 1978.

24. Dougherty, J.E. & Pfaltzgraff, R.L. Jr. *Contending Theories of International Relations: A Comprehensive Survey*. New York & London, Harper & Row, 1981.

25. Duchasek, I.D. *Nations and Men: An Introduction to International Politics*. Lanham, MD & London, University Press of America, 1983.

26. Easton, D. 'The New Revolution in Political Science', *American Political Science Review*, vol. LXIII, no. 4, 1969, pp. 1051–61.

27. Falk, R.A. *A Study of Future Worlds*. New York, Free Press and London, Collier-Macmillan, 1975.

28. Forsyth, M.G. *et al.* (eds), *Selected Texts from Gentili to Treitschke*. London, Allen & Unwin, 1970.

29. Frankel, J. *Contemporary International Theory and the Behaviour of*

States. Oxford & New York, Oxford University Press, 1973.

30. _____ *International Relations in a Changing World.* Oxford & New York, Oxford University Press, 1979.

31. Galtung, J. *The True Worlds: A Transnational Perspective.* New York, Free Press and London, Collier-Macmillan International, 1980.

32. Gilpin, R. *War and Change in World Politics.* Cambridge & New York, Cambridge University Press, 1984.

33. Groom, A.J.R. & Mitchell, C.R. (eds), *International Relations Theory: A Bibliography.* London, Frances Pinter and New York, Nichols, 1978.

34. Haas, E.B. & Whiting, A.S. *Dynamics of International Relations.* London & Westport, CT. Greenwood Press, 1975.

35. Hartmann, F.H. *The Relations of Nations.* London, Collier-Macmillan and New York, Macmillan, 1983.

36. Herz, J.H. *International Politics in the Atomic Age.* New York, Columbia University Press, 1962.

37. Hinsley, F.H. *Power and the Pursuit of Peace: Theory and Practice in the History of Relations between States.* London & New York, Cambridge University Press, 1963.

38. Hoffmann, S. *Duties beyond Borders: On the Limits and Possibilities of Ethical International Politics.* Syracuse, N.Y., Syracuse University Press, 1981.

39. Holsti, K.J. *International Politics: A Framework for Analysis.* Englewood Cliffs, NJ & London, Prentice Hall International, 1983.

40. Isaak, R. *Individuals and Worlds Politics.* Monterey, CA, Duxbury Press, 1981.

41. Jones, W.S. & Rosen, S.J. *The Logic of International Relations.* Boston, Little, Brown, 1985.

42. Joynt, C.B. & Corbett, P.E. *Theory and Reality in World Politics.* London, Macmillan and Pittsburgh, University of Pittsburgh Press, 1978.

43. Kaplan, M.A. *System and Process in International Politics.* New York, Krieger, 1975.

44. _____ *Towards Professionalism in International Theory: Macrosystem Analysis.* London, Collier-Macmillan and New York, Free Press, 1979.

45. Kegley, C.W. Jr. & Wittkopf, E.R. *World Politics: Trend and Transformation.* New York, St. Martin's, 1985.

46. Kent, R.C. & Nielsson, G.P. (eds), *The Study and Teaching of International Relations: A Perspective on Mid-Career Education.* London, Frances Pinter and New York, Nichols, 1980.

47. Keohane, R.O. & Nye, J.S. *Power and Interdependence: World Politics in Transition.* Boston, Little, Brown, 1977.

48. _____ (eds), *Transnational Relations and World Politics.* Cambridge, MA, & London, Harvard University Press, 1973.

49. Kim, S.S. *The Quest for a Just World Order.* Boulder, CO, Westview, 1984.

50. Knorr, K. & Rosenau, J.N. (eds), *Contending Approaches to International Politics*. Princeton, NJ & Guildford, Princeton University Press, 1969.
51. Knorr, K. & Verba, S. (eds), *The International System: Theoretical Essays*. London & Westport, CT, Greenwood Press, 1982.
52. Kornberg, A. (ed.) *Theories of International Relations*. Political Science Reading Lists and Course Outlines, vol. 5, Durham, NC, Eno River Press, 1981.
53. Kubalkova, V. & Cruickshank, A.A. *International Inequality*. Beckenham, Croom Helm and New York, St. Martin's, 1981.
54. _____ *Marxism-Leninism and the Theory of International Relations*. London & Boston, Routledge & Kegan Paul, 1980.
55. Kuhn, T.S. *The Structure of Scientific Revolutions*. (International Encyclopaedia of Unified Science), Chicago & London, University of Chicago Press, 1970.
56. LaBarr, D.F. & Singer, J.D. *The Study of International Politics: A Guide to the Sources for the Student, Teacher, and Researcher*. Santa Barbara, CA & Oxford, CLIO Books, 1976.
57. Lerche, C.O. Jr. and Said, A.A. *Concepts of International Politics in Global Perspective*. London & Englewood Cliffs, NJ, Prentice Hall, 1979.
58. Levi, W. *International Politics: Foundations of the System*. Minneapolis, University of Minnesota Press, 1974.
59. Lieber, R.J. *Theory and World Politics*. Boston, Little, Brown, 1977.
60. Maghroori, R. & Ramberg, B. (eds), *Globalism Versus Realism: International Relations' Third Debate*. Boulder, CO, Westview, 1982.
61. Mansbach, R.W. *et al.*, *The Web of World Politics: Non State Actors in the Global System*. Englewood Cliffs, NJ, Prentice Hall and London, Prentice Hall International, 1976.
62. Mansbach, R.W. & Vasquez, J.A. *In Search of Theory: A New Paradigm for Global Politics*. New York & Guildford, Columbia University Press, 1981.
63. Mayall, J. (ed.) *The Community of States: A Study in International Political Theory*. London & Winchester, MA, Allen & Unwin, 1983.
64. Merritt, R.L. & Russett, B.M. (eds), *From National Development to Global Community: Essays in Honor of Karl W. Deutsch*. London & Boston, MA, Allen & Unwin, 1981.
65. Modelski, G.A. *Principles of World Politics*. London, Collier-Macmillan and New York, Free Press, 1972.
66. Morgan, P.M. *Theories and Approaches to International Politics: What Are We To Think?* New Brunswick, NJ & London, Transaction Books, 1981.
67. Morgenthau, H.J. *Politics Among Nations: The Struggle for Power and Peace*. New York, Alfred Knopf, 1985.
68. Newcombe, H. 'Survey of Peace Research', *Peace Research Reviews*, vol.

IX, no. 6, 1984, pp. 3–95.

69. Northedge, F.S. *The International Political System*. London, Faber & Faber, 1976.
70. Papp, D.S. *Contemporary International Relations: Frameworks for Understanding*. London, Collier-Macmillan and New York, Macmillan, 1984.
71. Parkinson, F. *The Philosophy of International Relations: A Study in the History of Thought*. Beverly Hills, CA & London, Sage, 1977.
72. Pearson, F.S. & Rochester, J.M. *International Relations: The Global Condition in the Late Twentieth Century*. London & Reading, MA, Addison-Wesley, 1984.
73. Pettman, R. *Human Behavior and World Politics*. New York, St. Martin's, 1975.
74. _____ *State and Class: A Sociology of International Affairs*. London, Croom Helm and New York, St. Martin's, 1979.
75. Pirages, D. *The New Context for International Relations: Global Ecopolitics*. North Scituate, MA, Duxbury Press, 1978.
76. Plano, J.C. & Olton, R. *The International Relations Dictionary*. Oxford & Santa Barbara, CA, ABC-CLIO, 1982.
77. Quester, G.H. 'Teaching International Relations to American Students', *News for Teachers of Political Science*, 40, Winter 1984, pp. 13–17.
78. Ray, J.L. *Global Politics*. London & Boston, MA, Houghton Mifflin, 1982.
79. Reynolds, C. *Theory and Explanation in International Politics*. London, Martin Robertson, 1975.
80. Reynolds, P.A. *An Introduction to International Relations*. London & New York, Longman, 1980.
81. Rosecrance, R.N. *Action and Reaction in World Politics*. Westport, CT, Greenwood Press, 1977.
82. Rosenau, J.N. *The Study of Global Interdependence: Essays on the Transnationalization of World Affairs*. London, Frances Pinter and New York, Nichols, 1980.
83. Rosenau, J.N. *et al.*, *The Analysis of International Politics: Essays in Honor of Harold and Margaret Sprout*. London, Collier-Macmillan and New York, Free Press, 1972.
84. _____ 'Of Syllabi, Texts, Students, and Scholarship in International Relations: Some Data and Interpretations on the State of a Burgeoning Field'. *World Politics*, vol. XXIX, no. 2, 1977, pp. 263–341.
85. Rosenau, J.N. (ed.) *In Search of Global Patterns*. London, Collier-Macmillan International and New York, Free Press, 1976.
86. _____ *International Politics and Foreign Policy: A Reader in Research and Theory*. New York, Free Press, 1969.
87. Russell, F.M. *Theories of International Relations*. New York, Ayer, 1972.

88. Russett, B. & Starr, H. *World Politics: The Menu for Choice.* San Francisco & Oxford, W.H. Freeman, 1985.

89. Sandole, D.J.D. The Subjectivity of Theories and Actions in World Society. In *Conflict in World Society,* ed. M. Banks. Brighton, Wheatsheaf and New York, St. Martin's, 1984.

90. Scott, A.M. *The Dynamics of Interdependence.* Chapel Hill, NC, University of North Carolina Press, 1982.

91. Singer, M.R. *Weak States in a World of Powers: The Dynamics of International Relationships.* London, Collier-Macmillan and New York, Free Press, 1972.

92. Smith, M. *et al.* (eds), *Perspectives on World Politics.* London, Croom Helm for the Open University Press, 1981.

93. Smith, S. 'Foreign Policy Analysis: British and American Orientations and Methodologies'. Paper presented at the 23rd Annual Convention of the International Studies Association, Cincinnati, 24 March, 1982.

94. _____ 'The Study of International Relations: Geographical and Methodological Divisions'. *International Studies Notes,* vol. 10, no. 3, 1983, pp. 8–10.

95. Spanier, J. *Games Nations Play.* London & New York, Holt, Rinehart and Winston, 1984.

96. Spiegel, S.L. *Dominance and Diversity: The International Hierarchy.* Lanham, MD, University Press of America, 1983.

97. Sprout, H. & M. *Toward a Politics of the Planet Earth.* London & New York, Van Nostrand Reinhold, 1971.

98. Stegenga, J.A. & Axline, W.A. *The Global Community: A Brief Introduction to International Relations.* London & New York, Harper & Row, 1982.

99. Sullivan, M.P. *International Relations: Theories and Evidence.* Hemel Hempstead & Englewood Cliffs, NJ, Prentice Hall, 1976.

100. Targ, H.R. *International Relations in a World of Imperialism and Class Struggle: An Essay on the History of Ideas.* Cambridge, MA, Schenkman, 1983.

101. Taylor, P. *Nonstate Actors in International Politics: From Transregional to Substate Organizations.* London & Boulder, CO, Westview, 1984.

102. Taylor, T. (ed.) *Approaches and Theory in International Relations.* London & New York, Longman, 1978.

103. Thompson, K.W. *Understanding World Politics.* Notre Dame, IN & London, University of Notre Dame Press, 1975.

104. Vasquez, J.A. *The Power of Power Politics: A Critique.* London, Frances Pinter and New Brunswick, NJ, Rutgers University Press, 1983.

105. Waltz, K.N. *Man, the State and War.* New York, Columbia University Press, 1959.

106. _____ *Theory of International Politics.* Reading, MA & London, Addison-Wesley, 1979.

107.   Wight, M. *Power Politics*. Leicester, Leicester University Press and New York, Holmes & Meier, 1978.

108.   _____ (ed. H.N. Bull), *Systems of States*. Leicester, Leicester University Press and Atlantic Highlands, NJ, Humanities Press, 1978.

109.   Wolfers, A. *Discord and Collaboration: Essays in International Politics*. Baltimore, Johns Hopkins University Press, 1966.

110.   Ziegler, D.W. *War, Peace and International Politics*. Boston, Little, Brown, 1984.

111.   Zinnes, D.A. *Contemporary Research in International Relations: A Perspective and a Critical Appraisal*. London, Collier-Macmillan and New York, Free Press, 1976.

Notes on Contributors

Michael Banks is a Lecturer in International Relations at LSE, and has served as Visiting Professor at Dartmouth College, the University of Southern California and in diplomatic training programmes in Nairobi and Lusaka. A founding member of CAC, he has also served on the Councils of the International Peace Research Association and the Conflict Research Society. He has written on systems analysis, simulation, conflict theory, peace education, diplomacy, British and United States foreign policy, African politics and several aspects of the general theory of IR. He edited *Conflict in World Society* in 1984.

Chris Brown graduated from LSE in 1968 and has been Lecturer in Politics and Government at the University of Kent at Canterbury since 1970. He taught at the University of Massachusetts (Amherst) in 1981–2 and has published a number of articles on aspects of the theory of IR.

John Burton was educated at Sydney University (B.A.) and London University (Ph.D. and D.Sc.). He was Permanent Head of the Australian Department of External Affairs 1945–50. His academic appointments have included the Australian National University, University College London and the University of Kent. He is the founder of CAC, and is currently associated with the Center for International Development, University of Maryland. His books include: *The Alternative*, 1954; *Peace Theory*, 1962; *International Relations: A General Theory*, 1965; *Systems, States, Diplomacy and Rules*, 1968; *Conflict and Communication*, 1969; *World Society*, 1972; *Deviance, Terrorism and War*, 1979; *Dear Survivors*, 1982; *Global Conflict: The Domestic Sources of International Crises*, 1984.

229

Anthony de Reuck is Head of International Relations at the University of Surrey. As a physicist he worked at Imperial College, as an editor of *Nature* and on the International Relations staff of the Royal Society. He later edited 30 books including *Conflict in Society* (1966), *Caste and Race* (1967), and *Communication in Science* (1968) for the Ciba Foundation. He joined CAC in 1969 and graduated again from University College London in IR. He has held office in the Conflict Research Society and the Royal Anthropological Institute. He was a founder member of the International Science Policy Foundation, London, and of the Foundation of International Conciliation, Geneva. Current research includes the group dynamics of conflict resolution (*Man, Environment, Space and Time*, 3 (1) Spring 1983, pp. 53–69) and the transactional theory of IR.

A.J.R. Groom is Professor in International Relations at the University of Kent at Canterbury and Co-Director of CAC. Prior to teaching at the University of Kent, he was for thirteen years a lecturer at University College London. He received his doctorate from the University of Geneva, and his higher education was previously in the United States and at University College London. Prof. Groom has authored, co-authored or edited nine books and published over 40 articles. His most recent publications are *The Commonwealth in the 1980s*, edited with Paul Taylor, (Macmillan, 1984) and *Britain between East and West: a Concerned Independence*, co-authored with J.W. Burton, Margot Light, C.R. Mitchell and D.J.D. Sandole (Gower, 1984). He is currently completing a volume on Strategy and Conflict Research.

Alexis Heraclides studied Political Science in the Panteios School of Political Science, Athens, and IR at University College London (M.Sc.) and the University of Kent at Canterbury (Ph.D.). He is currently attached to the Ministry for Foreign Affairs of Greece as an expert on Human Rights and Minorities and is a research assistant in the Mediterranean Studies Foundation, Athens. His special interests are separatism and conflict resolution.

Christopher Hill has been a Lecturer in International Relations at LSE since 1974, apart from a year spent on leave at the Royal Institute of International Affairs, and two months at the Woodrow Wilson International Center for Scholars, Washington, DC. He is the editor of *National Foreign Policies and European Political Cooperation* (1983) and has contributed to many other books and scholarly journals. His main interests are in foreign policy analysis, British foreign policy, and European Political Cooperation.

Mark Hoffman is a Temporary Lecturer in International Relations at the University of Keele. He did his undergraduate work at the University of Massachusetts and the University of Kent and received his Master's degree from the London School of Economics in 1981. He is currently working on a critical study of the interrelationship between strategic studies, conflict research and peace research. He was Editor of *Millennium: Journal of International Studies* in 1981 and has been Associate Editor since 1982.

Margot Light is a Lecturer in International Relations and Soviet Studies at the University of Surrey. She is a member of CAC and a founder member of the Soviet and East European Resource Group. Her current research interests include IR theory and Soviet foreign policy. She has published articles on both subjects and is co-author (with J.W. Burton, A.J.R. Groom, C.R. Mitchell and D.J.D. Sandole) of *Britain between East and West: a Concerned Independence* (Gower, 1984).

Richard Little is Senior Lecturer in the Department of Politics at the University of Lancaster. He was previously a lecturer at the Open University where he helped to prepare a course on Perspectives on World Politics. He is the author of *Intervention: External Involvement in Civil Wars* (Martin Robertson, 1975) which uses a series of case studies to explore the factors which influence the decision to intervene into domestic conflict. More recently he has collaborated on a project which examined foreign aid allocation and written a number of articles on the theory of IR.

Chris Mitchell is Senior Lecturer in International Relations and Co-ordinator of the Conflict Management Research Group at The City University, London. He has published two books on varied aspects of international conflict, *The Structure of International Conflict* (Macmillan, 1981) and *Peacemaking and the Consultant's Role* (Gower, 1981), as well as numerous articles in the field. At present, he is working on a book examining the ending of conflicts, looked at from a decision-making perspective and as a problem in successful de-escalation. He is also involved in the practicalities of applying scholarly findings regarding successful mediation to the establishment of dispute settlement services within conflict-prone local communities.

Michael Nicholson was educated at Trinity College, Cambridge where he read economics and later took a Ph.D. in the same discipline. He subsequently held faculty positions in various universities in Britain and North America. From 1970–82 he was Director of the Richardson Institute for Conflict and Peace Research, first when it was an independent Institute in London, and subsequently when it became a part of Lancaster University. He is currently Hallsworth Fellow in the Department of Decision Theory in Manchester University, having recently been a Fellow of the Netherlands Institute for Advanced Study. His most recent book is *The Scientific Analysis of Social Behaviour: A Defence of Empiricism in Social Science* (Frances Pinter, 1983).

Bram Oppenheim has been the Reader in Social Psychology at LSE for over twenty years. He has long been interested in conflict studies and peace research, and teaches a Master's course in the Social Psychology of Conflict. He has done much research in Political Socialization and in the work of foreign affairs ministries and is the past director of the Conflict Research Unit at LSE. Author or co-author of half-a-dozen books and over 30 articles and monographs, he has been a consultant and has carried out field research in many countries. He is a founder member of the European Society for Experimental Social Psychology, of CAC, and of the International Society for Political Psychology. In his few spare moments he collects mixed metaphors. His religion is the practice of disappointment.

Dennis Sandole is Associate Professor of Government and Politics at George Mason University, where he is also an Associate with the Center for Conflict Resolution. He has a Ph.D. from Strathclyde University, and has taught at University College London, University of Southern California (German and British Graduate Programs in IR), Kingston Polytechnic, and The City University. His teaching and research interests include IR theory and methodology, conflict analysis and management, attitude change and paradigm shifts.

Author Index

233

Cantori, L., 181, 187
Cardoso, F.H., 64, 71
Carr, E.H., 10, 14, 17, 22, 27, 28, 32, 39, 215, 223
Carter, A., 187
Castles, F.G., 211
Chamberlain, N.W., 130, 134
Chan, S., 221, 223
Chance, M.R.A., 101, 108, 194, 195, 197
Chandra, P., 221, 223
Charlesworth, J.C., 95
Chase-Dunn, C., 123, 135
Chen, L.C., 30
Chong-Do, H., 186, 187
Choucri, N., 127, 135
Clapham, C., 161, 165
Clark, I., 15, 22, 28, 39, 145, 151
Clarke, M., 157, 165–6, 172
Clarke, S., 75, 86
Clarkson, G.P.E., 95
Claude, I.L., 15, 22, 113, 119, 183, 187, 216, 223
Clausewitz, C. Von, 143, 151
Coates, C.H., 150, 151
Cockcroft, J., 71
Cohan, A.S., 151, 153
Cohen, A., 147, 185, 187
Cohen, B.C., 158, 161, 166
Cohen, B.J., 14, 22, 83, 86
Cohen, M., 34, 39
Cohen, R., 215, 223
Cohen, S.P., 133, 137
Cohen, S.T., 144, 155
Coleman, J.S., 70
Comaroff, J.L., 197
Connor, W., 185, 187
Coplin, W.D., 223
Corbett, P.E., 29, 39, 218, 224
Coser, L.A., 124, 135
Cottam, R.W., 159, 160, 166
Couloumbis, T.A., 221, 223
Cox, R.W., 19, 22
Craig, G.A., 162, 167
Cruickshank, A.A., 19, 23, 218, 225

Curle, A., 132, 135
Curry, R.L., 108
Cutler, R.M., 162, 166
Cyert, R.M., 95

Dahl, R.A., 115, 119
Dahrendorf, R., 123, 135
Danielson, P., 35, 39
Davies, J.C., 54, 58, 135, 147, 151
Davis, D.B., 197
Davis, H.B., 185, 187
Davis, V., 220
Dawisha, A., 161, 163, 166
Dawisha, K., 162, 166
Dean, P.D., 86
Debnam, G., 119
Debray, R., 147, 151
Dedring, J., 122, 135, 206, 211
de Kadt, E., 71
d'Entreves, A.P., 33, 39
de Reuck, A.V.S., 133, 135
de Rivera, J., 158, 166, 203, 211
Destler, I.M., 166
Deutsch, K.W., 16, 86, 95, 109, 115–16, 117–18, 119, 159, 166, 182, 183, 184, 187, 220, 223
Deutsch, M., 124, 135, 204, 206, 211
Deutscher, I., 19
De Vos, G., 185, 187
de Waal, F., 197
Diesing, P., 172
Dixon, N.F., 158, 166
Dockrill, M., 34, 43, 98
Dollard, J., 123, 135
Donelan, M.D., 10, 22, 34, 39, 220, 223
Doob, L.W., 206
Doppelt, G., 36, 39
dos Santos, T., 64
Dougherty, J.E., 11, 22, 218, 223
Douglas, M., 196, 197–8
Downs, A., 206, 211
Doxey, M.P., 163, 166
Dray, W.H., 93, 95